CHRISTMAS IN YIDDISH TRADITION

Christmas in Yiddish Tradition

The Untold Story

Jordan Chad

NEW YORK UNIVERSITY PRESS

New York

NEW YORK UNIVERSITY PRESS
New York
www.nyupress.org

Library of Congress Cataloging-in-Publication Data
Names: Chad, Jordan, author.
Title: Christmas in Yiddish tradition : the untold story / Jordan Chad.
Description: New York, N.Y. : New York University Press, 2025. |
Includes bibliographical references and index.
Identifiers: LCCN 2025004477 (print) | LCCN 2025004478 (ebook) |
ISBN 9781479840786 (hardback) | ISBN 9781479840793 (ebook) |
ISBN 9781479840809 (ebook other)
Subjects: LCSH: Christmas. | Jews—Europe, Eastern—Social life and customs. |
Christmas in literature. | Yiddish literature—History and criticism.
Classification: LCC GT4985 .C375 2025 (print) | LCC GT4985 (ebook) |
DDC 394.2663089/924047—dc23/eng/20250210
LC record available at https://lccn.loc.gov/2025004477
LC ebook record available at https://lccn.loc.gov/2025004478

This book is printed on acid-free paper, and its binding materials are chosen for strength and durability. We strive to use environmentally responsible suppliers and materials to the greatest extent possible in publishing our books.

The cover image is adapted from a front page drawing in the Christmas 1897 edition of the Yiddish daily *Forverts*.

The manufacturer's authorized representative in the EU for product safety is Mare Nostrum Group B.V., Mauritskade 21D, 1091 GC Amsterdam, The Netherlands. Email: gpsr@mare-nostrum.co.uk.

Manufactured in the United States of America

10 9 8 7 6 5 4 3 2 1

Also available as an ebook

CONTENTS

Jews never celebrated the birth of Jesus. Christmas can therefore be a complicated time for Jews. Larry David, for example, claims to "detest" the holiday, yet he describes eating Chinese food on Christmas as "a cherished yearly ritual."[1] How far back in history does the complex Jewish relationship with Christmas go? Many people assume that Jewish engagement with Christmas first arose in the twentieth century, when Jews began to assimilate into the New World. This book uncovers a very different story. It demonstrates that the situation posed by twentieth-century assimilation did not cause Jews to *start* engaging with Christmas. Rather, in what many readers are likely to find surprising, assimilation led most Jews to *stop* enjoying Christmas traditions and expressing their joy in the Yiddish language.

This book thus offers a new interpretation of the Jewish relationship with Christmas. It challenges the narrative that Christmas was historically uneasy or dangerous for European Jews. And it makes the case that the behavior that European Jewish communities exhibited on Christmas Eve, far from being an oppositional response to a Christian holiday (as many scholars have taken it to be), was actually what it looked like: *Jews celebrating Christmas.*

Through examination of diverse historical texts about Christmas, this book uncovers the historical role that Christmas played in Yiddish discourse and popular Jewish practice. Typical Christmas Eve activities for Eastern European Jews ranged from social deviance with excess drinking and gambling to telling unhinged stories about Jesus defecating into holy Judaica. The book demonstrates that such behavior should not be understood as Jews responding to a Christian holiday, but rather, that Christmas did not actually become the strictly Christian holiday that it is today until the very period when Jews began to assimilate into the New World. This period was a time when both Christians and Jews were reinventing their cultural identities for modernity, and doing away with their shared history of crass interreligious polemics on Christmas Eve and through the year.

This book traces the earliest roots of midwinter folk traditions among Jews and gentiles before any of these traditions came to be associated with the birth of Jesus. It tracks the parallel evolution of these traditions among Jews and Christians, with Christians introducing a celebration of "Christ's Mass" as a component of a midwinter culture that was otherwise largely alike between the two groups. And it traces how Jews and Christians came to reevaluate their traditional midwinter celebrations in modern times, at which point they both came to regard the entire midwinter festival, "Christmas," as a Christian holiday that is antithetical to Judaism. The Christmas traditions historically transmitted in Yiddish hence did not develop in opposition to a Christian holiday. They rather developed as variants of similar Christmas traditions that were widespread across European communities, albeit with any anti-Jewish embellishments inverted as anti-Christ.

A few clarifications are required at the outset.

First, what is Christmas? The Collins dictionary defines it as "the annual festival of the Christian church commemorating the birth of Jesus."[2] Yet in a non-Christian context, the definition of Christmas must be broadened. When one walks into a shopping mall in early December to find sparkling ornaments, sentimental melodies, and children sitting on Santa's lap, one is bombarded with thoughts of "Christmas," but not necessarily of baby Jesus. In this book, I define Christmas as the popular festive season associated with December 25, not restricted to church observance. This working definition makes it possible to describe people as "celebrating Christmas" without them necessarily celebrating the Nativity of Christ.

The definition of Yiddish is also murky. According to the Collins dictionary, Yiddish is "a language derived from Middle High German, spoken by E[astern] European Jews and their descendants in other countries."[3] Based on this definition, the Germanic language that Eastern European Jews spoke in the decades prior to the Holocaust can be clearly identified as Yiddish. But what about the Germanic language that Jews spoke in high medieval Germany—was this already "Yiddish," or simply a dialect of German? Linguists have not reached a consensus.[4] In this book, I use the term Yiddish in the broadest sense: the Germanic

Jewish vernacular from high medieval Germany to modern Eastern Europe. This definition aptly distinguishes vernacular culture from sacred Jewish tradition transmitted in Hebrew and Aramaic, as well as from non-Germanic Jewish vernaculars such as Ladino and Judeo-Arabic that are not the subject of the current study.

A few technical points are also in order.

I transliterate Yiddish words using the Romanized orthographic convention of the YIVO Institute for Jewish Research, which can be reviewed at www.yivo.org/Yiddish-Alphabet. This convention is based on phonology in Standard Yiddish rather than any specific regional or temporal dialect. Hebrew words follow this same convention, and thus differ from their phonology in Modern (Israeli) Hebrew. Exceptions to the YIVO convention are made for Hebrew and Yiddish words that are widely used in English, such as Torah (instead of *toyre*) and Hanukkah (instead of *khanike*). The Hebrew and Yiddish scripts of Romanized words are listed in the glossary at the back of the book.

All translations from non-English sources are my own, except in a few instances noted in the endnotes. I opted for literal translations in most cases, but I took liberties with certain passages to make minor clarifications and retain the original flavor.

The idea that Christmas was, in the Old World, not (yet) a strictly Christian holiday, and that Jews embraced and celebrated it, is obviously counterintuitive. Understanding this history casts new light on the challenges that contemporary Jews face during what can be seen as anything from the most detestable to the most wonderful time of the year.

Introduction

Jews and Christmas

On a cold, snowy evening in December 2016, I walked into Toronto's Jazz Bistro to check out the annual show *A Jewish Boy's Christmas*. It was the fifth consecutive year that local jazz singer Sam Broverman was celebrating being a "Jewish boy" at Christmastime. His setlist included many of the great American Christmas songs—"White Christmas," "The Christmas Song," "Rudolph the Red-Nosed Rein-deer," "Silver Bells," "Santa Baby," "It's the Most Wonderful Time of the Year," "Rockin' Around the Christmas Tree," "Christmas (Baby Please Come Home)," "A Holly Jolly Christmas," among others—all written by Jews. I took my seat as Broverman walked on stage. Following an opening performance of his own original song "What's a Jew to Do on Christmas?," Broverman explained that the purpose of his show was to offer his fellow Jews a way of curbing their feelings of exclusion from the Christian holiday by reclaiming it as their own—as a holiday in which Jews played an important historical role by creating its secular song culture.[1]

When it came time for Broverman to sing "Let It Snow," he did something entirely unexpected. He sang it in Yiddish. I watched with fascination as the audience erupted into laughter. Why does singing a Christmas song in Yiddish evoke such a reaction? I turned to a neigh-boring audience member after the show to ask what he found comical about a Christmas song being performed in Yiddish. Yiddish, he an-swered, is the one language in which nobody would ever expect to hear about Christmas. It's the language that Jews spoke back in the days when they were culturally segregated from Christian society, before they had any reason to be occupied with Christmas. On this premise, Broverman's pairing of Christmas and Yiddish is innovative, providing a new avenue for Jews to connect with Christmas.

A Jewish Boy's Christmas is one of countless contemporary Jewish responses to Christmas. In the 2012 book *A Kosher Christmas*, Joshua Eli Plaut describes how American Jews employ strategies to conquer the feelings of exclusion and isolation that Christmas elicits in them.[2] He argues that the challenges of Christmas are a consequence of twentieth-century assimilation. Back in the Old World, Plaut writes, "very few Jews had embraced Christmas customs," as most Jews "avoided all contact with their Christian neighbors during Christmas."[3] Arriving in the New World, however, many Jews turned the page on their former Yiddish-speaking lives of segregated Torah adherence. The prospect of assimilation posed a dilemma about what it means to be a Jew, with the ultimate question pertaining to Christmas: Is it possible for Jews to reconcile the joy of Christmas with Jewish identity, or is Christmas a distinctly Christian holiday that Jews should continue to avoid? As Plaut notes, some Jews chose to embrace a de-Christianized Christmas, decorating Christmas trees and composing Christmas songs without regard to the birth of Christ. Other Jews viewed any celebration of Christmas as a rejection of Judaism and instead promoted the coinciding minor Jewish holiday of Hanukkah. Still other Jews found ways to adapt certain aspects of Christmas into Jewish culture. For instance, they devised the hybrid "Chrismukkah," or participated in a custom of eating Chinese food on Christmas. Overall, as Plaut puts it, Jews "transformed a once-silent night into a holiday season characterized by a flurry of activity."[4]

Plaut's account is consistent with the view that Christmas and Yiddish have little in common. A main message of his book is that the story of "Jews and Christmas" begins where the story of "Jews and Yiddish" ends. Plaut does remark that the topic of Christmas was not completely absent from Old World Yiddish discourse. He writes that Eastern European Jews called Christmas Eve *nitl-nakht*, a Yiddish term that roughly translates to "nothing night," in line with their aversion to Christmas. Jews "lived in fear" on *nitl-nakht*, writes Plaut, although he does not go into the specifics of the source of this fear. He instead uses his brief discussion of *nitl-nakht* to reinforce the argument that Yiddish-speaking Jews were disconnected from Christmas, and that Jewish engagement with Christmas did not begin until Jews assimilated and abandoned Yiddish. In this view, any Christmas discourse conducted in Yiddish was insignificant, as it was merely based on contemporaneous Jewish antipathy toward a foreign Christian holiday.[5]

This view comes into question, however, when we consider the many Christmas stories that twentieth-century Jewish immigrants wrote in Yiddish. Plaut does not mention these Yiddish stories, as he presents a discontinuity between the joyful Christmas songs that American Jews wrote in English and the trivial *nitl-nakht* of their Yiddish past. The Christmas stories that American Jews wrote in Yiddish, conversely, include vivid descriptions of the old, fearful *nitl-nakht*. Evidently, then, the apparent historical fear of Christmas played a more significant role in Yiddish culture than Plaut suggests. The fear was associated with a broader Yiddish folklore, invoked by Yiddish authors across North and South America. Take, for example, the following excerpt from a Yiddish Christmas story by a Jewish immigrant in Argentina, Jaime Goldzac (1910–1977), depicting Christmas Eve in the Old World:

> All Jews lock their doors and windows. The white and cold world stares out with a frosty breath. An unfamiliar fear sweeps everything and everybody. [. . .] Jews are startled by any sudden noise, whether it be the shattering of a window or a Jew shrieking "he-e-e-e-lp!"[6]

Where does this "unfamiliar fear" come from? Plaut is quiet on the details of a Yiddish Christmas folklore, but Jeffrey Shandler discusses such a folklore in his 2009 study of American Jewish responses to Christmas.[7] Shandler writes that before coming to the New World, Yiddish-speaking Jews "engaged Christmas at some remove" through a "pattern of simultaneously expressing and flouting fear."[8] The source of this fear, according to Shandler, is a Yiddish folk belief that a sinister revenant Jesus returns on Christmas Eve to haunt and torment the Jews. This belief is recounted in a Yiddish Christmas story by a Jewish immigrant in America, Joseph Opatoshu (1886–1954):

> My parents bolted the door and shutters on Christmas Eve. We placed pieces of iron atop all barrels and buckets of water so that *Yosl Pandrek* ["Joe Mr. Shit," i.e. Jesus] does not commit any sorcery and poison the water. And any passerby who knocked on our door on Christmas Eve would freeze to death before being let in.[9]

We will set aside the details of Jesus's behavior for now and instead turn our attention to the more general question: Why did Yiddish have a frightful Christmas folklore? If Yiddish-speaking Jews were disconnected from the Christian holiday, why should they have occupied themselves with an elaborate folklore about Christmas at all?

The simplest explanation is that the frightful Yiddish Christmas folklore arose because Christmas was a perilous time for Jews in the Old World. Plaut comments that Christians had incited violence against Jews during the Christmas season since the Middle Ages up until the outbreak of World War II.[10] And there is no shortage of Yiddish essays by Jewish immigrants recalling the dangerous Christmas of the Old World. In a Yiddish essay entitled "Christmas," for example, immigrant Abraham Goldberg (1883–1942) contrasts young American Jews participating in Christmas festivities with the Christmas back in Eastern Europe. He explains that in Europe, drunk Christians would rage with religious zeal and beat Jews on Christmas Eve, and that it was safer for Jews to hide at home that evening.[11] It therefore seems sensible to deduce that Jews historically locked their doors and windows on Christmas Eve out of fear of physical danger, and they later developed folklore that personified this Christian danger as a menacing Jesus.

The available documentation on Christian violence toward Jews, however, does not suggest that the danger to Jews on Christmas was exceptional. It is rather the holiest day in Christianity, Easter, and the days leading up to it, that is well-documented to have been an exceptionally violent period of stoning and rioting against Jews across Christian Europe since antiquity and through World War II. Easter violence toward Jews served as a ritual form of Christian "revenge" for the Passion and crucifixion of Jesus commemorated on Good Friday.[12] Christmas—a more minor religious event in Christianity than Easter, and one that took place when the weather was freezing—is not known to have evoked comparable anti-Jewish violence among European Christians.[13] The idea that the fear depicted in Yiddish Christmas folklore reflects an exceptional physical danger on Christmas is therefore not supported by historical fact.

If Old World Jews were not disproportionately assaulted on Christmas Eve, how did they spend the evening? A search for references to Christmas in Yiddish memoirs of Old World Jewish life reveals insights that appear to contradict the notion that Christmas was an unsettling time for Jews. Eastern European Jews apparently celebrated Christmas. They did not, of course, celebrate the birth of Jesus—they rather told chilling stories about a menacing Jesus—but, even so, Jewish men who grew up in Eastern Europe consistently described the Christmas of their youth as an eagerly awaited vacation from rigorous Torah study, full of games and merriment. To put this in context, Yiddish memoirs typically describe Jewish boys spending long hours studying Torah in a cramped room (the "*kheyder*"). There was limited allotment for leisure in this lifestyle, as Jewish tradition maintained that any free time must be used for Torah study (the concept of "*bitl-toyre*"). Yet the jolly holiday of Christmas was the exception. One such memory comes from a Jewish immigrant in Canada, Shmuel-Mortkhe Zeltshen (1885–1960):

> Since the earliest years of childhood, we engraved in memory the only Jewish holiday that does not fall in the Jewish calendar. We were free from *kheyder* that evening [Christmas Eve], and that, of course, was no small feat. And moreover, as soon as the lamp in the house was lit, we immediately rushed to the prohibited cards and played the games "sixty-six" and "fool"—activities which on an ordinary day would earn us ardent slaps from "the higher authorities"—and today nobody says anything to us![14]

Joyful Christmas memories like this are widespread in Yiddish memoirs of Eastern Europe. While scholars have long been aware that Yiddish-speaking Jews took a break from studying Torah to play games on Christmas Eve,[15] none of these scholars has come up with a plausible explanation for why they did so. In the most recent article on the topic, Rebecca Scharbach writes that all existing attempts to explain this "bizarre" Jewish Christmas behavior "possess so little explanatory power that they have been summarily dismissed as 'unsatisfactory' by most researchers."[16] Studies of Jews and Christmas rarely broach the topic of the historical Christmas vacation from Torah study, since they usually describe Jewish Christmas merriment as a product of New World assimilation. In the one Yiddish-language study of Jews and Christmas, however, Isaac Rivkind (1895–1968) argues that Christmas has always been just as merry a holiday for Jews as it was for Christians.[17] Rivkind points to the following stanza of a Yiddish Christmas poem by a Jewish immigrant in America, Naftoli Gross (1896–1956), as illustrative of Old World Jewish sentiments toward Christmas:

> A wonderful white Christmas Eve!
> A stillness lingers in all corners;
> The fire flickers and the windowpanes sparkle,
> My father plays cards instead of studying;
> The evening buzzes with children and with games,
> With gruesome stories about *Yoyzl* ["Joey," i.e. Jesus] of Nazareth.[18]

The word "gruesome" is significant, as it reveals the major difference between what Jews and Christians did on Christmas Eve. The more striking message of this poem, however, is that Jews of the Old World seem to have celebrated Christmas somewhat akin to Christians, with the Christological aspect of Christmas inverted among Jews based on an anti-Christian perspective. It is conceivable why Jews would have inverted the Christological aspect, but it is not immediately clear why Jews would have been interested in Christmas to begin with, as opposed to other major Christian holidays like Easter. The violence that Christians exhibited on Easter had direct implications on Jewish life, and Christian authorities historically advised (or physically forced) Jews to remain in their homes on Easter,[19] yet Easter was not associated with elaborate Yiddish traditions. Even the Yiddish name *nitl-nakht* is perplexing. Its apparent meaning "nothing night" seems to imply an inversion of the Christian significance of Christmas, but, as Rivkind notes, German-speaking Christians referred to Christmas Eve by a very similar name, *Nidelnacht*.[20]

How can we make sense of all this? From the perspective of the notion that Jews were historically disconnected from Christmas, and that the development of frightful Yiddish Christmas folklore was no more than an aversive reaction to a foreign Christian holiday, the described Jewish Christmas traditions are certainly strange. In Old World Jewish life, Torah study was usually paramount and cardplaying was usually prohibited—and the one time of year when Jews would communally break from studying Torah to play cards and games was Christmas? And if this behavior is not puzzling enough, why did Jewish immigrants often claim that Jews celebrating Christmas is a strictly New World phenomenon, contrasting it with the "dangerous" Christmas of the Old World? It is astounding that despite all the contemporary interest in devising strategies for Jews to connect with Christmas, there is so little understanding of how Jews connected with Christmas in the past. The present-day feelings of isolation that Christmas elicits among many Jews are based on the idea that Jews have no ethnic connection to Christmas. Perhaps this idea only exists because the story of Christmas in Yiddish tradition has yet to be told.

This book aims to uncover this story by seeking answers to seven key questions:

1. How did the topic of Christmas arise in Yiddish?
2. Why does Yiddish folklore portray Jesus as a menacing Christmas demon?
3. Is the Yiddish *nitl-nakht* related to the German *Nidelnacht*?
4. Did Eastern European Jews really celebrate Christmas?
5. How did Jews come to regard Christmas as historically dangerous?
6. Did "Christmas spirit" exist in Yiddish?
7. Why were Yiddish Christmas stories prevalent in the New World?

The conventional starting point for answering these questions would be to assume that Yiddish is the language of a people who were excluded from mainstream Christian celebrations of Christmas. In recent decades, however, scholarship has suggested that this assumption may not be reasonable. As Israel Yuval points out, "The widespread image, in research and among the general public, of Ashkenazic [Yiddish-speaking] Jewry as being cut off from the Christian milieu, reflects [. . .] very modern points of view."[21] It is becoming increasingly recognized that Jews and Christians formed a more cohesive and symbiotic European society than commonly appreciated, with relatively minor demarcations in their folk culture based on differing religious traditions and social-structural positions.[22] In turn, it is becoming increasingly recognized that Christmas played a fundamental role in secular European society and was not as "Christological" or antithetical to Judaism as is often assumed. Most Christmas traditions did not pertain to celebrating the birth of Jesus, but were rather based on popular beliefs in supernatural winter spirits that had nothing to do with Christianity.[23] It is hence no longer reasonable to assume that Jews who spoke Yiddish were inherently disconnected from Christmas, or that mainstream Christmas folklore was necessarily less compatible with Yiddish than it was with the languages in which Jews and Christians intermingled.

This book casts doubt on the assumption that Christmas always belonged within the strict cultural realm of Christians, and that Jews only engaged it at a remove. This is not to say that Jews celebrated "Christ's Mass," but that Christ and Mass were not the focus of Christmas in European popular culture. As Judith Flanders notes in her history of Christmas, "That Christmas was once religious [. . .] is such a common idea that it comes as a surprise when the actual make-up of the day is examined."[24] The idea that European Jews were somehow removed from the main secular aspects of Europe's most pervasive holiday is implausible. Scholars have previously interpreted any Christmas traditions that were transmitted in Yiddish to be reactions to an external Christian holiday, but as this book will demonstrate, Christmas was just as internal to Yiddish as it was to other European languages. The differences between the Christmas traditions transmitted in Yiddish and Christian languages were not based on fundamental ideological differences, but rather based on mundane differences in the religious and social circumstances of Christians and Jews. Since these circumstances evolved over time, so too did the Yiddish conception of Christmas Eve, *nitl-nakht*. For this reason I do not attempt to devise a single explanation of *nitl-nakht* as if it were a static artifact of history. Instead, I chronicle a dynamic story of how the relationship between Jews and Christmas unfolded as the social situations of Christians and Jews evolved—culminating with the modern Christian reclamation of Christmas, and the concomitant erasure of Christmas from Jewish culture.

Ultimately, this book's goal is to contribute to the ongoing conversation about how contemporary Jews can respond to the challenges of Christmas by shedding light on how these challenges originally came about. In order for Jews to find meaning at Christmastime and balance Christmas with their Jewish tradition, they need to appreciate the role that Christmas historically played *within* their Jewish tradition.

1

Ghosts of Christmas Past

We begin by seeking an answer to our first question: How did the topic of Christmas arise in Yiddish? This question has intrigued historians, folklorists, and rabbinic scholars over the past century, but little progress has been made on reaching an answer. The only consensus is that Yiddish Christmas folklore presumably originated as an antagonistic response to the Christian holiday, with the grim aspects of the folklore reflecting an anti-Christian perspective.[1] Jeffrey Shandler sums up this view as that Yiddish Christmas folklore was a "counterculture" that Jews developed to subvert the Christian holiday "through lore and practices of their own making."[2] Unfortunately, this hypothesis does not explain why Yiddish-speaking Jews chose to enjoy Christmas Eve with games and leisure. Nor does it explain the specific details that scholars have recorded about Yiddish Christmas folklore. The folklore maintains, for example, that the way to protect oneself from the evil revenant Jesus who returns on Christmas Eve is to refrain from both Torah study and sex. The rationale for refraining from study, according to Yiddish folklore, is that studying Torah in the presence of revenant Jesus would relieve the anguish inflicted upon him in the afterlife and thereby aid his wicked endeavors. The rationale for abstaining from sex is that if a child is conceived in the presence of revenant Jesus, the child will be corrupted by Jesus to become an apostate and convert to Christianity.[3] Why these very specific details would have originated as part of an antagonistic response to Christmas is unclear. And there is a feature of Yiddish Christmas folklore that is apparently inconsistent with the notion that it arose to subvert a Christian holiday. The folklore pertains only to the hours before the Christological celebration of Christmas begins at midnight.[4] If Yiddish Christmas folklore originated as an anti-Christian subversion of Christmas, one would think that the danger of an evil Jesus should pertain to the time when Christians are celebrating Jesus's birth. Yet, according to the Yiddish tradition, as soon as Christians begin to celebrate the first Eucharist of the Feast of the Nativity, the danger of evil Jesus suddenly disappears. Evidently, there is more to the origin story for Yiddish Christmas folklore than that it originated as an anti-Christian response to Christmas.

In 2013, Rebecca Scharbach published the sole detailed origin theory for Yiddish Christmas folklore.[5] She focused her theory on the unusual depiction of Jesus in this folklore, attempting to explain why the folklore "portrays the Christian savior as a foul revenant condemned to walk the earth and molest its inhabitants."[6] The source of this portrayal of Jesus is, according to Scharbach, the Christmas folklore of Christians. She points to the early modern German tradition of the *Christkindl* [Little Christ Child], a mummer of baby Jesus who traveled house-to-house to deliver gifts before Midnight Mass. In the hours prior to midnight, she describes, Christians regarded Christmas Eve as a frightful time "when the unrepentant dead returned to earth to harass the living,"[7] and the mummed Christlike figure who visited Christian households "occasionally took on some of the grotesque characteristics of his [evil revenant] companions."[8] Scharbach proposed that, in the context of a major Christian holiday being a presumably unsettling time for the per-secuted Jewish minority, "this accidental mélange of images and tales resonated strongly with contemporary Jewish anxieties,"[9] so Jews began spreading their own folklore about an evil revenant Jesus who visits be-fore midnight on Christmas Eve.

Scharbach's origin theory is compelling, but it has a major problem. The Yiddish folklore about a Christmas Eve visit from Jesus predates the *Christkindl* by at least a century. The German *Christkindl* tradition has a well-documented origin. It began with Martin Luther (1483–1546) telling his children that they will receive gifts from the *Heiliger Christ* [Holy Christ] on Christmas Eve, rather than from the traditional *Hei-liger Nikolaus* [St. Nicholas] on St. Nicholas Eve (December 5). Luther was attempting to shift the emphasis of the Christmas season away from Catholic saints and toward the solemnity of Jesus. This Luther family tradition is first documented in 1531, when Luther's oldest child was age five.[10] The Lutheran Church subsequently promoted the practice of a mummed baby Jesus delivering gifts on Christmas Eve, which became conflated with demonic revenant mumming among the German masses by the mid-to-late seventeenth century.[11] Yet, the notorious Jewish-born apostate and anti-Jewish preacher Johannes Pfefferkorn (1469–1523), who sought to expose the anti-Christian "blasphemy" embedded in Jewish culture, wrote as early as 1511 about a profane Yiddish legend that he learned in his youth: Jesus, who is "punished by God to wander" after death for "his apostasy and false teaching," returns to provoke "fear and worry" among Jews on Christmas Eve.[12] Numerous independent accounts of this same Yiddish legend were reported in exposés by more Jewish apostates over the ensuing century, before we find any records of demonic *Christkindl* mumming in the mid-seventeenth century.[13] It is therefore not possible that Jews adapted their Yiddish Christmas folklore from a German folklore about the *Christkindl*, as the Yiddish folklore originated before the *Christkindl* had been invented.

Scharbach's theory is, nevertheless, very helpful in the quest to uncover the origin of Yiddish Christmas folklore. Scharbach astutely points out that the frightful nature of Christmas folklore was not unique to Jews. This observation—the commonality of frightful Christmas folklore among Christians and Jews—is analogous to Isaac Rivkind's observation of the commonality of Christmas merriment among Christians and Jews, as described earlier. In combination, Rivkind's and Scharbach's observations beg the question of why Christmas was historically so similar between Jews and Christians. Why was Christmas a merry time for Jews if Jews were not supposed to be celebrating Christmas? And why was Christmas a frightful time for Christians if Christians *were* supposed to be celebrating Christmas?

This chapter combines and builds upon these two observations by proposing that Jews and Christians historically observed Christmas in similar ways. It argues that Yiddish Christmas folklore did not originate as an anti-Christian response to Christmas. The folklore rather began as a variant of an extrinsic European Christmas folklore that had nothing to do with Jesus. The following pages will take us on a journey through a supernatural world of demons, ghosts, and revenants that formed the basis of the old forgotten Christmas. The shortcomings of previous scholarly attempts to decipher Yiddish Christmas folklore stem from overestimating the historical pertinence of Christmas's Christological aspect. Jews lived in a society where Christians were always celebrating Jesus for one reason or another, and the fact that Christians incidentally celebrated Jesus's birth on Christmas turns out to be largely irrelevant for understanding how the topic of Christmas arose in Yiddish. Once we rethink our understanding of Christmas in a non-Christological manner that is generalizable to Jews, it will become clear how Yiddish Christmas folklore originated.

The Fright Before Christmas

Let us start by recalling that Christmas originated as an observance of the winter solstice, dated December 25 in the ancient Julian calendar.[14] In the Middle Ages, the winter solstice was one of the four quarterly periods that Europeans (both Christians and Jews) believed to be exceptionally ominous times, when demons were unabated and free to pollute the earth.[15] According to medieval Jewish sources, a unique guardian angel presides over each of the four seasons, and angelic protection is relaxed when the angels change guard during the solstices and equinoxes.[16] Christians marked the coming of each quarterly period with a set of fast days known as Quatember or Ember days (from the Latin *quatuor tempora*, four times) that they believed to coincide with sinister supernatural phenomena.[17] Among Jews, each quarterly period was known as a *tkufe* (from the Hebrew for "cycle"), marked by sealing vessels of water to protect against demonic pollution.[18] The winter solstice was the darkest and coldest of these quarterly periods and therefore instilled the most fear out of all of them. We can imagine people cuddling around a fire to share spooky stories about the demonic forces that rule the long night. Despite the calendar date of the winter solstice shifting over time, beliefs about demonic midwinter forces remained attached to the eve of December 25 in most European cultures up to the modern era. Accordingly, to quote Christmas folklorist Al Ridenour, there was "a deep-rooted European understanding of Christmas as a time of supernatural mayhem."[19] Traditional Christmas folklore was characteristically spooky and dark, and Yiddish was far from the only language to depict a frightful Christmas Eve.

What varied between languages was the exact identity of the demonic forces that reigned on Christmas Eve. The specific Christmas demons that a given community feared were whichever frightening creatures happened to exist in its folklore throughout the year. Thus, among the folks in early modern northeastern Europe who were besotted with werewolves, Christmas Eve was believed to be a dangerous night of werewolf transformations.[20] Olaus Magnus (1490–1557) describes the situation in Prussia, Livonia, and Lithuania:

> On the feast of the Nativity of Christ, at night, such a multitude of wolves transformed from men gather together in a certain spot, arranged among themselves, and then spread to rage with wondrous ferocity against human beings [. . .] for when a human habitation has been detected by them isolated in the woods, they besiege it with atrocity.[21]

In southeastern Europe, where early modern folks were more concerned about vampires than werewolves, Christmas Eve was believed to be a perilous night of vampire risings.[22] These vampire figures took the form of goblin-like Callicantzari in the Balkans, as John Cuthbert Lawson (1874–1935) recounts:

> The rest of the year they live in the lower world, and [. . .] each Christmas [. . .] the time comes for their appearance in the upper world. [. . .] Foremost among Christian precautions is the custom of marking a cross in black upon the house-door on Christmas Eve; and the same emblem is sometimes painted upon the various jars and vessels in which food is kept to ensure them against befouling by the Callicantzari.[23]

We will turn our attention further west, however, since the earliest Yiddish-speaking Jews lived in the so-called Ashkenaz region of Central Europe, and this is the region where Jewish apostates first exposed Yiddish Christmas folklore. Rather than werewolves and vampires, the notorious demons in early modern Central Europe were ghosts and revenants. Johann Geiler von Kaysersberg (1445–1510) of Strasbourg describes the nature of these restless dead beings:

> The common people say that those who die before the time that God has set for them, and those who run into combat and get stabbed, hanged or drowned, must wander for a long time after their death [. . .] and are usually seen on the Ember Days, especially the Ember Days before Christmas.[24]

This belief is worthy of our close attention, as it bears similarity to the Yiddish belief that Jesus must wander after his death and is seen on the night before Christmas. Midwinter sightings of the restless dead date back to Germanic paganism,[25] but the idea that the dead are serving a sentence of wandering is of Christian provenance. The belief emanated out of growing speculation about the fate of the dead that took place in the high medieval period between England and Austria. Christians were becoming increasingly uneasy over the idea that anybody who sins goes straight to hell upon death. Another idea was then popularized, namely, that the sinful dead first wander in purgatory: Following a period of restless wandering as penance, the dead can be purged of their sins to be made fit for heaven and thereby attain respite.[26] This concept resulted in a plethora of popular stories about people being doomed to suffer in restless wandering or laboring upon death, and that their period of suffering can only be shortened if living people provide them with suffrage.[27] The frightful night of Christmas Eve became known as a night when the wandering dead return to earth and beseech relief from the living.[28] Orderic Vitalis (1075–c. 1142) provides a legendary account of a priest being petrified by this phenomenon following Christmas 1090:

> The priest, frozen with terror, stood motionless, leaning on his staff. [. . .] All [the wandering revenants] were making great lamentations and urging one another to hasten their steps. Among them the priest recognized a number of his neighbours who had lately died, and heard them bewailing the excruciating sufferings with which they were tormented for their evil deeds.[29]

Were Jews likewise terrorized by the wandering dead's bewailing? In the 2020 book *Final Judgement and the Dead in Medieval Jewish Thought*, Susan Weissman argues that the changing high medieval ideas about death were not restricted to Christians.[30] Jews, like Christians, began to tell stories about sinful dead people being doomed to wander until they receive sufficient suffrage. Weissman notes that medieval Jews frequently reported seeing processions of wandering revenants demanding relief—reports that were remarkably similar to those that Christians reported on Christmas Eve.[31] A Hebrew report circa 1200, for example, describes a living man who sees a horde of revenants tirelessly pulling wagons. The revenants lament to the man that they are doing penance for having courted young women when they were alive.[32] Such reports generally do not indicate the season of the event, so Weissman does not consider that Jews perceived the processions of wandering revenants on the specific night of Christmas Eve. She instead remarks that, according to the Hebrew rabbinic literature, Jews believed that the dead return to seek rest on the weekly Sabbath (the day of rest for everybody, including the wandering dead).[33]

Nevertheless, it is perfectly reasonable to consider that Jews also shared their neighbors' belief that the wandering dead return to seek rest on Christmas Eve, as Jews were not segregated from the popular Christmas culture. Medieval Jews did business with Christians on the day of Christmas Eve,[34] and Jews and Christians regularly exchanged stories that were not recorded in the Hebrew literature. Surviving medieval Yiddish manuscripts demonstrate that the stories that circulated among Jews were often variants of the same stories that circulated among Christians, such as stories about King Arthur's court.[35] Given that Christmas Eve coincided with the perceived night of the winter solstice in the Jewish calendar (the *tkufe*), Jews already believed demons to roam free on this long night.[36] This was not a time for Jews to dismiss alarming stories about respite-seeking revenants.

To glean more specific details of these stories, we can consult Ronald Hutton's 2014 analysis of the recorded Christian testimonies of the returning wandering dead. Hutton notes that these stories are consistent in describing processions of revenants soliciting relief, but "different storytellers perceived different figures in these processions."[37] Storytellers described perceiving whichever wandering dead penitents happened to exist in the folklore of their community. Walter Map (1130–c. 1210), for example, describes the revenants as late combatants from the Welsh Marches during the reign of King Henry II.[38] Otloh of St. Emmeram (c. 1010–1070), for another example, tells of a man who claims to identify his own late father among the penitential revenants, crying out to his son "Why don't you help me? [. . .] On this night [of Christmas Eve], when souls deserve to find rest."[39] Which specific wandering revenants might medieval Jews have perceived in the legendary Christmas Eve processions? The Yiddish Christmas folklore documented in modern times tells of all sorts of demons and evil spirits that rule Christmas

Eve,[40] but there is no Christmas folklore recorded in the medieval Jewish literature.

There is, however, a Sabbath legend about the wandering dead that is recorded repeatedly in the high medieval rabbinic literature. The identity of the dead person in this legend—who is doomed to wander without rest until the living provide sufficient suffrage—is Jesus.[41] In the legend, dead Jesus calls on a living rabbi to find a way to alleviate his suffering, begging him:

> Please do not delay me, lest those presiding over me will get angry. [. . . I am] dead, and every day they send me to chop wood [. . .]. Please do not delay me, lest those in charge of my suffering will get angry, for there is no relief [for me].[42]

We will return later to why Jews told stories about a penitential dead Jesus. What we note for now is that the specific revenants whom a given European community feared on Christmas Eve were whichever wandering dead penitents happened to be familiar in the folklore throughout the year. Since Jewish communities were familiar with Jesus as a wandering dead penitent in the rabbinic literature, it fits that Jewish apostates named Jesus as a revenant whom they grew up fearing on Christmas Eve. Jewish-born apostate Ernst Ferdinand Hess, for instance, reported in 1598 that Jews "instill great fear and fright" in their Christmas Eve tales of revenant Jesus being restlessly "forced to travel,"[43] and fellow apostate Johann Adrian reported in 1609 that the frightening revenant Jesus "has no rest" because he is doing "penance."[44] The fear conveyed in this Yiddish Christmas folklore did not originate out of some uniquely Jewish fear of a Christian holiday, as Christians expressed the very same fear of rest-seeking revenants on Christmas Eve. The fact that Jews believed Jesus to be among these revenants is merely a technical detail of the Yiddish version of this folklore.

An indicator that this Yiddish folklore is a variant of an extrinsic European folklore is that it is consistent with a European folk belief not rooted in Judaic thought: Children born or conceived when ominous forces reign become corrupted by the forces.[45] Those born on Christmas Eve in ghost-wandering northwestern and Central Europe, for example, were said to be cursed to become "ghost-sighted" and be able to see ghosts.[46] In northeastern Europe, those born on Christmas Eve were feared to become werewolves,[47] while in Balkan lands, those born on Christmas Eve were fated to become vampiric Callicantzari.[48] Leo Allatius (1586–1669) describes how Greek folks defended themselves against children born on Christmas:

> To prevent encounters with Callicantzari, folks drag those children born on Christmas by their feet to a bonfire in the marketplace [. . .] for they think that their nails will be cut off and burned by the heat of the fire; and once the nails are gone, the Callicantzari will not be immune to weapons.[49]

Folklore about those conceived on Christmas Eve is less documented, since Christian couples traditionally abstained from sex during the time leading up to the Feast of the Nativity.[50] Nevertheless, in Romanian villages, Harry Senn (1939–2017) recorded as recently as the 1970s that those conceived on Christmas Eve would be corrupted by werewolves to develop features such as wolf ears and harelips.[51] Yiddish-speaking communities shared this same fear about the vulnerability of infants born or conceived on Christmas Eve. One modern Yiddish Christmas story tells of the birth of a girl on Christmas Eve who is corrupted by the demonic forces that rule the night.[52] More notably, a well-documented Yiddish folk belief is that Jews conceived on Christmas Eve are corrupted by the sinful Wandering Jesus in the same way that Jesus's followers were corrupted: They will abandon Judaism for Christianity. Just as Romanians restricted sexual relations on Christmas Eve to avoid the conception of wolflike children, Jews did the same to avoid the conception of apostate children. Rabbi Haim Palache (1788–1868) of Turkey describes the Jewish tradition in Eastern Europe:

> It is warned against having sexual intercourse with one's wife on [Christmas Eve . . .] because on this night he will father a dissenting son. [. . .] All of the apostates in the world were conceived on this night.[53]

We therefore find that the Christmas folklore transmitted in Yiddish was a mere variant of the same Christmas folklore transmitted in other European languages. The topic of Christmas arose in Yiddish not because of a distinctly Jewish fear of a Christian holiday, but rather because of a common fear of the darkest time of the year.

Joy to the World

The main coping mechanism for overcoming the darkest time of year has always been lively entertainment. Christmas historian Bruce Forbes sums up the concept of the ancient midwinter festival as "a festival of lights, with candles, and burning logs, and anything else to push back the darkness," with festivities such as "feasts, and drinking, and dancing."[54] Each European culture had its own local festival according to its geographic circumstances and cultural heritage. The midwinter festival in harshly cold Scandinavia was Yule, which boasted feasting and heavy drinking to chase away midwinter revenants.[55] The midwinter festival in the less cold Roman Empire, Saturnalia, commemorated the dedication of the Temple of Saturn on December 19, 497 BCE. As far back as 217 BCE, the merriment of Saturnalia lasted for five days.[56] Saturnalia was marked by a mock king presiding over a topsy-turvy world with the roles of slaves and masters inverted, alongside the lighting of candles and exchange of candles as gifts.[57] A week after December 25, once the days appeared to lengthen again, the merriment in the Roman Empire resumed as Romans held a "birthday party" for the sun on the Kalends (first of the month) of January, that is, New Year's Day.[58] The midwinter festival in the Roman province of Judea was a Jewish analog of Saturnalia called Hanukkah, a festival of lights that commemorated the dedication of the Temple of Jerusalem instead of the Temple of Saturn.[59]

Forbes argues that Christmas inherited the midwinter merriment of pre-Christian cultures to become the Christian midwinter festival. Hanukkah, meanwhile, was retained as the Jewish midwinter festival, despite Hanukkah often falling weeks before midwinter (the Jewish calendar is not fully solar). On this premise, scholars have ruled out the possibility of a common source for the Christian and Jewish merriment on the night of the Christian festival—Christmas Eve was a night for Christians to celebrate, not Jews. Marc Shapiro, in attempting to comprehend why Jews replaced Torah study with fun and games on Christmas Eve, writes that "it is difficult if not impossible to imagine that the study of Torah would be suspended so that Jews, including Torah scholars, could participate in Gentile amusements."[60] I contend, however, that it is not appropriate to interpret Christmas Eve amusements as having been any more "Gentile" than they were "Jewish." Paul Frodsham, an archaeologist of pre-Christian midwinter festivities, writes that the ability for Christmas to alleviate midwinter gloom "transcends Christianity and relates to the very nature of human existence."[61] Frodsham does not mention Jews per se, but Jews were just as afraid of midwinter as Christians, and they would have shared the same drive to alleviate this fear. I therefore propose discarding the conventional interpretation of any Christmas merriment as belonging to the Christian side of a Christian–Jewish dichotomy. Instead, I argue that Jews and Christians both reacted to the longest of nights in the same way—by replacing tranquil religious activity with lively entertainment.[62]

While we do not have enough sources to confirm an unbroken chain of continuous practice since antiquity, Jewish and Christian merriment on Christmas can both be effectively traced back to pre-Christian merriment related to the midwinter "rebirth" of the sun. A fourth-century Roman preacher described how "the common people call [December 25] 'a new sun,' and confirm it with so great an authority of theirs that Jews and Gentiles concur in this mode of speech."[63] There is evidence that rabbis attempted to recontextualize why Jews in the Roman Empire were participating in pagan midwinter festivities. According to a rabbinic explanation recorded in the Talmud, primordial Adam was afraid of the long nights, so he instituted Saturnalia and the Kalends of January before and after the *tkufe* "for the sake of heaven." Only later were these festivals corrupted by gentiles "for the sake of idol worship," say the rabbis, asserting that the Jewish celebration of midwinter predates paganization.[64] Similarly, upon the fourth-century Christianization of Rome, Christian leaders attempted to recontextualize why Christians were participating in these pagan midwinter festivities. December 25 marked the rebirth of light, and Christianity identified Jesus as the "Light of the World" (John 8:12), so Roman Christian leaders insisted that December 25 was not *natalis solis invicti* [birthday of the invincible sun] but rather *natalis domini corporalis* [birthday of the physical Lord].[65] By the medieval period, the Church had Christianized the fearful weeks leading up to midwinter with liturgy to prepare for the Advent of Christ. This Advent season began with the chant of the poem "*Dies irae*" that emphasized fear of Final Judgment amid Christ's Second Coming, and concluded with a commemoration of Christ's First Coming alongside the recitation of the herald angel's proclamation of "Fear Not!" (Luke 2:10).[66] It thus became Church dogma that Jesus was born at midnight on the eve of December 25, concluding the fearful Advent season and initiating a twelve-day feasting season celebrating the Nativity of Christ.[67]

Yet this Christianization did little to change the folk culture of midwinter. Ronald Hutton explains that while Christian churches instituted the Feast of the Nativity to coincide with the midwinter festivities, "they encountered the problem of ensuring that the veneration of Christ would remain predominant in it."[68] Instead of becoming a pious occasion, midwinter remained the one time of year when pagan Saturnalian inversions continued to prevail, as the masses temporarily surrendered their solemn religion in favor of rowdy exuberance. In the 1935 book *The Fool*, Enid Welsford (1892–1981) summarizes how ecclesiastical sources across medieval Western Europe denounced Christians parodying Advent church services.[69] "Solemn Mass was punctuated with brays and howls," Welsford describes, and "censing was done with pudding and sausages."[70] Such behavior is illustrated in an account of a Mass celebration in Beauvais (northern France) on December 18, 1697:

> They chose a beautiful young girl, put a child in her hands, and mounted her on an ass which they led in procession from the Cathedral Church to the Church of St Stephen. Placing the ass and his lovely burden in the Sanctuary there on the Gospel side, they sang [. . .] *he haw*.[71]

This spectacle is certainly not the somber Mass that one would expect to honor the Advent of Christ. According to nineteenth-century German and Austrian folklorists, some people even avoided all Christian prayer and entering any church during the four weeks of Advent, in hopes that they would receive a reward from the Devil who presides over midwinter.[72] The evasion of solemn religion also extended into the east. The medieval Orthodox Church named the twelve days of the festival as the "holy days" (*svyatki*), but folks widely refrained from holy religious rites on these days. Gail Lenhoff notes that as early as the twelfth century, the Orthodox Church understood the *svyatki* as "a period of open blasphemy, brazen lies, night dances, demonic songs, masks, fortune telling, and other carnival behavior."[73] In Bulgaria, some people knew the "holy days" as the "pagan days" (*pogani dni*). They avoided all Christian religious rites during the twelve days to prevent the spiritual energy of Christianity from strengthening Callicantzari (the sinister midwinter forces in Bulgaria), which could only be weakened by pagan-like behavior.[74]

It is hence not out of keeping that midwinter religious rites were shunned in the setting where Yiddish was first spoken. People in high medieval northwestern and Central Europe maintained that the wandering dead seek relief from their torments by feeding off the living's religious sparks. According to Christian testimonies, the dead commonly pleaded with the living to offer them Masses as suffrage.[75] An 1135 account by Hugues de Mans, for example, describes a revenant begging for a Mass celebration to release him from his anguished retinue:

> Since coming from remote lands and through many perils, I have suffered
> from storms, snow and cold. [. . .] A wicked throng that is eager to work
> evil has come in with me and will retreat with me when I leave. So that
> I may leave the pernicious road they travel and fully enjoy eternal rest,
> please celebrate a Mass for me.[76]

Unfortunately for this revenant, the living knew better than to let any of the wandering dead enjoy rest on the eve of midwinter. Wolfgang Heider (1558–1626) explains that midwinter is given over to the Devil, and that the sinful wandering dead work under the Devil at midwinter as they coax people on earth into relieving them.[77] As such, while Christians celebrated Masses to alleviate the repentant dead's suffering in purgatory throughout the year, they did not celebrate a Vigil Mass for the Nativity, according to medieval church liturgy.[78] Instead, medieval churches traditionally hosted an evening Matins service with an irreverent Nativity play that mirrored the evening's diabolical nature, typically following the Devil plotting against the birth of Jesus.[79]

And at the same time that Christians withheld solemn Mass celebrations, Jews desisted from their religious study, maintaining that the holy sparks of Torah would relieve the diabolical midwinter revenants. The source of this latter belief is found in the Sabbath legend mentioned earlier that is recorded throughout the high medieval Jewish literature, in which studying Torah relieves the wandering dead Jesus:

[A living person] studied Torah, and the Shema prayer, and the Grace after Meals. And he stood in front of the congregation and said "*borkhu*," and the congregation answered "*borukh adenoy ha'mevoyrokh*" [the Jewish call to prayer and Torah reading]. At that moment, [dead Jesus] was relieved of his suffering.[80]

Torah study thus functioned as a parallel practice to Mass celebrations in terms of being able to relieve the wandering dead. These parallel practices were central to medieval European life year-round apart from midwinter, as Europeans sought to free the suffering of their wandering dead loved ones when it was safe to do so. To put this in chronological context, Jews had looked down upon studying religious texts before coming to Europe (at any time of the year), since rabbis conventionally insisted that the Torah be learned orally.[81] In high medieval Ashkenaz, however, Jews adopted a routine of studying written transcripts and commentaries of their Torah and rabbinic tradition.[82] This new routine provided a means for Jews, a people who did not celebrate Mass, to alleviate the repentant dead's suffering in the afterlife throughout the year.[83] Jews only omitted the year's longest night from this routine, the night when the suffering dead returned to harass those on earth. As Jewish apostate Johann Adrian reported in 1609, Jews "do not study" on this one occasion because sinful Jesus "must do penance" and "has no rest except for when he hears [Jews] studying."[84]

There remains the question of why Jews chose to resume their study at midnight. As one modern Yiddish text describes, "The Jews go off to their study halls at midnight, just as the gentiles go celebrate their holy night."[85] The answer to this question lies in the New Testament passage "the reason the Son of God appeared was to destroy the Devil's work" (1 John 3:8). According to folkloric sources (collected since the Romantic era), Christians popularly believed that the Devil dies at midnight, when Jesus is born.[86] Thus, as many folklorists have recorded, Christians believed that the diabolic behavior of the dead ceased at midnight as animals miraculously spoke and water turned to wine, at which point the unrepentant dead returned to the flames of purgatory while the gates to heaven opened for the repentant dead to find prolonged rest.[87] Consistent with this belief, Catholic priests since at least Peter the Venerable (c. 1090–1156) have practiced a tradition of saying three Masses on December 25 after the Devil dies at midnight, allowing Christians to pro-vide prolonged rest to the repentant dead once the danger has passed.[88] Midnight Mass, as we know, became a central event of the Christian midwinter festival. The midnight ringing of church bells marked both the birth of Jesus and the death of the Devil, with this ringing known in English folklore as the "Devil's Knell."[89] High medieval English ecclesi-astical sources hence began to refer to the freshly Christianized midwin-ter festival as "Christmas" [Christ's Mass], and high medieval German ecclesiastical sources began to refer to the night of the festival as *Christ-nacht* [Christ Night] and *Weihnacht* [Holy Night].[90]

Before midnight, however, people fought their fear with rowdy activi-ties that would ward off rather than provide rest to the wandering dead, or to any other demons serving the Devil. Remnants of this behavior are recorded in nineteenth-century collections of Christian folklore. Her-mann Kletke (1813–1886) writes that "when everybody makes merry on Christmas Eve, the Devil and all things devilish have no rest."[91] Johann Krainz (1847–1907) likewise writes that the purpose of making merry on Christmas Eve is for "the Devil and his comrades to have no rest."[92] The Jewish apostates who exposed Yiddish Christmas folklore provide strik-ingly similar testimonies. Samuel Friedrich Brenz reported in 1614 that Jews replace religious piety with "making merry and eating and drinking to excess" on Christmas Eve because they believe "a house full of read-ing and praying provides [Wandering Jesus] with better rest and allows him to crawl into the corners of the house."[93] Dietrich Schwab likewise reported in 1616 that Jews refrain from their usual religious activities on Christmas Eve to ensure that the Wandering Jesus "has no rest or re-spite."[94] While these apostates focus their reports on exposing the pro-fane depiction of Jesus in Yiddish folklore (they omit mentioning any other demons that Jews feared on Christmas Eve), we should not let the apostates' agenda distract us from the overarching similarities between the Christmas folklore of Jews and Christians. It is evident that all folks, Jewish and Christian, had some ideology that licensed them to overcome their fear of midwinter by reverting to topsy-turvy Saturnalian behavior.

It follows that Christmas was a singular time when both Christian and Jewish authorities permitted people to play dice, spinning tops, and cards in early modern Europe.[95] In a 1644 sermon condemning the "su-perstition and profanation" of Christmas, Presbyterian leader Edmund

Calamy (1600–1666) complained that some Christians "did not play at cards all the year long, yet they must play at Christmas."[96] Isaac Rivkind analogously notes that some Jews "would never otherwise touch a card in their entire lives," yet they would play cards on Christmas Eve.[97] It was only after midnight that folks returned to their social mores as they believed the danger to subside, when Christians celebrated Midnight Mass and Jews celebrated their holy books—and both Christian and Jewish couples could go back to having sex.[98] Overall, then, the folkloric traditions associated with Christmas differed between Christians and Jews only in their technical details, which becomes apparent once we rethink our understanding of Christmas beyond its Christological component.

Conclusion

The origin of Yiddish Christmas folklore has long posed a mystery to scholars. This mystery is only difficult to solve, however, under the assumption that Jews were originally responding to a Christian holiday from the perspective of an outsider community. If we consider that Jews and Christians both historically viewed Christmas as the marking of midwinter, rather than as a purely Christian religious festival, it becomes clear that the Christmas folklore transmitted in Yiddish was a mere cultural variant of a more general European Christmas folklore. The pairing of spooky midwinter tales with games and merriment transcended any Christian–Jewish dichotomy. The belief that protection from harm can be achieved by refraining from religious activity and sex makes little sense within the realm of Jewish thought, but it is completely consistent with the broader European phenomenon. And the fact that the Yiddish variant of this folklore concerns only the hours before Christmas's Christological component begins—a detail that is difficult to comprehend if this folklore originated as a polemic against a Christian holiday—is precisely what would be expected from a community to whom the Christological component is irrelevant. In sum, the Christian Feast of the Nativity was not the motivation for the development of a Yiddish Christmas folklore. The reason that Christmas evoked such a tremendous folkloric response across languages is because of its perception as the darkest time of the year, not because it commemorates the birth of Jesus. Yiddish is no exception.

2

Christ in Yiddish Tradition

Our second question—why does Yiddish folklore portray Jesus as a menacing Christmas demon?—has been the focus of previous scholarship on Yiddish Christmas folklore. Scholars concordantly assume that the presence of Jesus in this folklore originated out of an anti-Christian reaction to Christians celebrating Jesus on Christmas. Rebecca Scharbach describes her theory of the origin of Yiddish Christmas folklore, summarized earlier, as resting upon the notion that "Christmas was a time when Jesus was uniquely present in community affairs" and that Christian celebrations of Jesus "were often unsettling times for the minority [Jewish] community."[1] Shai Alleson-Gerberg describes Yiddish Christmas folklore as "ritually inverting Christmas," arguing that "Jews responded to the celebration of Jesus' birth by creating a cynical version of Christmas Eve lampooning him."[2] Daniel Barbu shares the interpretation of the Jews' demonic Jesus folklore as "the Jews' inverted Christmas,"[3] and Maria Diemling likewise interprets the Jews' "engagement with [. . .] the figure of Jesus" as a strategy of "resistance" to the celebration of Jesus's birth that Jews "were not part of."[4] Taken together, our question already has an established scholarly answer: Yiddish folklore portrays Jesus as a menacing Christmas demon because Jews responded to Christians celebrating his birth from the perspective of an anti-Christian minority, inverting the figure of Jesus from the Christian emblem of light into an emblem of midwinter darkness.

It is thus broadly accepted that the historical Jewish engagement with Jesus on Christmas was directly related to Christians celebrating Jesus on Christmas. I contend that this intuitive notion might not be true. As we saw, Yiddish Christmas folklore did not originate out of Jews inverting a Christian holiday, but rather out of Christmas being a holiday that transcended Christianity—Yiddish Christmas folklore began as a variant of a folklore that Christians and Jews shared. In the local regions where the Yiddish variant originated, people believed that wandering dead penitents return to harass the living on Christmas Eve. A well-known wandering dead penitent in Jewish lore throughout the year happened to be Jesus. From this perspective, the origin of Jesus's presence in Yiddish Christmas folklore might not have anything at all to do with Christians celebrating Jesus on Christmas.

This perspective does not, of course, rule out the possibility that Jesus's presence was also motivated by the night's Christian celebration. If his presence was indeed motivated by what Christians were doing on Christmas Eve, however, it would have been motivated by what they were doing before midnight, at the same time that Jews were telling stories about a menacing Jesus. And as we will see, Christians spent this time telling stories about the menacing Jewish demons in their own Christian folklore. It is hence plausible that the primary motivation for Jews to proclaim Jesus as a menacing Christmas demon was not in fact an ambition to attack the midnight Christian celebration of Jesus. Instead, Jews may have been implicitly participating in a mutually antagonistic dialogue with Christians prior to the midnight celebration, on this bleak midwinter night when each group's archenemies were most acutely feared.

This chapter continues to tease out a revised understanding of Christmas in a non-Christological manner—as a holiday that Jews and Christians historically observed in similar rather than detached ways. It argues against the notion that Jews told stories about a menacing Jesus on Christmas because Christians celebrated Jesus on Christmas. The notion ignores the fact that Jews told stories about a menacing Jesus beyond Christmas. This chapter therefore begins by reviewing the role that menacing Jesus played in Jewish folklore irrespective of his theological significance on Christmas. It then traces the origin of how Jesus came to assume the role of the most well-known wandering dead penitent in medieval Jewish folklore, whose restlessness can be relieved by Torah study. Finally, the chapter establishes that the most well-known wandering penitent in medieval Christian folklore was a wandering anti-Jesus Jew. These medieval Jewish and Christian folklores culminated in what I interpret as a covert debate between early modern Jews and Christians as to whether the most frightening wandering penitent who returns on Christmas Eve is a Wandering Jesus or a Wandering

Jew. Ultimately, this chapter demonstrates that even if Christians did not celebrate Jesus's birth on Christmas, Jews would have still nevertheless been haunted by Jesus on Christmas Eve.

Jesus in Jewish Folklore

The presence of Jesus in Jewish folklore, including Yiddish folklore, is well established by scholars.[5] It is beyond the scope of this book to undertake a comprehensive analysis of the folklore and delineate its regional and temporal heterogeneity. Instead, I will briefly review some recorded details that were relatively consistent across time and space, as we will be regularly referring back to them through the remainder of the book. The reader should bear in mind that Jesus was a topic of strife within both Christianity and Judaism, so my descriptions of aggregate "Jewish" and "Christian" beliefs about Jesus will be based on generalizations.

Jesus emerged as a figure in Jewish folklore as soon as Christianity emerged as a sect of Judaism in the first-century Roman province of Judea. The historical Jesus was, apparently, a controversial Jew who was subject to crucifixion under the order of the province's governor.[6] This crucifixion took place at a time of great political unrest in Judea following the death of King Herod and full annexation by Rome. The Jews who became Christians believed Jesus to be the Messiah, resulting in them abandoning their Torah adherence for a new covenant with God. The Jews who did not become Christians, henceforth "Jews," reacted to their peers' threatening veneration of Jesus by developing their own subversive counterfolklore. Whereas Christians believed Jesus to be a miracle worker who truly turned water to wine, Jews believed Jesus to be a charlatan. Rabbinic tradition maintained that the ruthless gentiles of the Roman Empire chained the real Messiah to the gates of Rome while Jesus deceived the masses into believing that he is their savior.[7] Among Jews, Jesus's Hebrew name *Yishue*, which translates to "salvation," was shortened into *Yishu*, effectively denying Jesus's association with salvation.[8] Jews later deemed the name *Yishu* to be an acronym for *Yi'makh sh'moy v'zikhroy*, "May his name and memory be forgotten," a curse reserved for the Jews' gravest enemies.[9] This name alone illustrates the historical Jewish antipathy toward Jesus.

Some of the earliest divergences between Christian and Jewish lore about Jesus concerned his heritage, via a dispute that is recorded as early as the second century.[10] Christians believed that Jesus was the son of God and that his mother Mary was a virgin. According to Jews, Mary was no virgin and Jesus did have a mortal father, a soldier named Panthera. Jews presumably understood the Latin name "Panthera" as satire: It not only implies that Jesus's father was a Roman pagan, thereby mocking the purported Davidic lineage of Mary's husband Joseph, but it is also an anagram of a corrupted Greek word for virgin, *parthena*.[11] As Roman hegemony eventually faded into history, Jews instead came to regard Jesus's father as an ignoramus Jew named Joseph Pandera. Medieval Jews believed Jesus to be a bastard and his mother an adulteress who had an affair with Joseph Pandera. This belief is recorded in the Talmud, which mentions that Jesus was the son of Pandera and Sotada. "Sotada" is explained as an epithet for Mary derived from the Hebrew word for adulteress, *sota*.[12] By the early modern period, most Jewish sources posited that Jesus's mother was not an adulteress but rather a pious Jewish woman whom Joseph Pandera raped while she was menstruating. Jesus was thus not only a bastard but a bastard son of a menstruant, rendering him "double" impure.[13] In modern Yiddish, Pandera, pronounced *Pandre*, was better known as *Pandrek*, which literally means "Mr. Shit," although less profane variants of the name included *Pandrik*, *Pondrik*, and *Pondrak*. Jesus ultimately became known under diminutives of Joseph Pandera: His modern Yiddish nicknames included *Yoyzl* [Joey], *Yoshke Pandre* [Jojo Pandre], and *Yosl Pandrek* [Joe Mr. Shit].

Jews disputed the Christian testimonies of *Yosl Pandrek*'s miracles. The New Testament recounts that King Herod was resentful upon learning of Jesus's birth because people believed Jesus to be "King of the Jews," a title that belonged to tyrannical Herod. To escape Herod's vengeance, baby Jesus and family temporarily fled to Egypt—which happened to be the world center for magic and sorcery. According to second-century attestation, Jews maintained that Jesus learned magic in Egypt and used it to deceive his disciples into believing that he is the son of God.[14] By the medieval period, Jewish sources instead explained Jesus's miracles as that he broke into the Jerusalem Temple and learned the inscribed name of God, of which only the consonants YHWH were publicly known. Jews believed that those who pronounced this ineffable name aloud were able to carry out divine, supernatural phenomena.[15] Jews further believed that two of Jesus's disciples were undercover heroes who did not truly fall for Jesus's deception. One such disciple was Judas Iscariot, whom the New Testament describes as having delivered Jesus to his arresting officers in exchange for money, directly leading to Jesus's execution. According to Christian lore, Judas was a villain who only later realized his sin and ultimately hanged himself. According to Jewish lore, Judas was a hero who likewise learned to pronounce God's ineffable name and used its powers to defeat Jesus.[16] The other heroic disciple according to Jewish lore was Simon Peter, whom the New Testament describes as selfishly dissociating himself from Jesus following Jesus's arrest. According to Christian lore, Simon Peter atoned for this sin and ultimately became the first Pope, helping separate Christianity from Judaism by shifting the center of Christianity from Judea to Rome. According to Jewish lore, Simon Peter separated Christianity from Judaism as part of an undercover plot to save the Jews from conflict with Jesus's followers, the latter of whom got naively manipulated into founding a hoax religion.[17]

Jewish and Christian lore about Jesus further diverged in their respective accounts of his execution. Jews and Christians agreed that Jesus suffered brutal torture immediately prior to his execution, and that his persecutors placed a woven crown of thorns on his head to mock his reputed title of "King of the Jews." Jews and Christians did not agree on the manner by which he was subsequently executed. Christians accurately described Jesus's execution as a Roman crucifixion, although Christian tradition focused on Jewish responsibility for the crucifixion. The New Testament repeatedly claims that "the Jews" (Greek: *Ioudaioi*, "Judeans") were responsible for sentencing Jesus to death, and that the execution was a Roman-style crucifixion only because the Jewish court happened to be subject to Roman rule. And yet, despite Christians regularly using this claim to justify their attacks on Jews, the Jews' own folklore amplified the claim further. According to the Talmud, Jesus was not crucified by the Romans but rather hanged by the Jews.[18] Jews evidently felt that if Jesus was such a troublemaker, they should have been astute enough to take care of him themselves, in a manner that their own tradition dictated for dealing with criminals. Religion scholar Peter Schäfer interprets the legend of the Jewish "hanging" of Jesus as symbolic of Jews proudly proclaiming responsibility for Jesus's execution.[19] Jews came to derogatorily refer to Jesus as the *Tole*, "Hanged One," and they often dubbed their version of Jesus's life story as the *Mayse Tole*, "Story of the Hanged One."

Needless to say, the most significant divergence between Jewish and Christian lore about Jesus concerned what happened following his execution. Christians maintained that Jesus was resurrected on the Sunday after his crucifixion and ascended to heaven forty days later. They memorialized his Eternal Life by routinely celebrating the Eucharist (Mass), reenacting the sacrifice of his body and blood with an offering of consecrated bread and wine to his Father. Christians traditionally viewed the consecrated bread, the Eucharistic hosts, as heavenly food that would allow them like Jesus to live forever. And they repeatedly chastised Jews for desecrating these hosts by throwing them into privies filled with feces.[20] Jewish sources widely associate Jesus's "Eternal Life" with excrement. Rather than ascending to heaven, the Jesus in the Talmud is eternally condemned to boil in excrement in *gehenem*, a Jewish version of hell or purgatory that is only eternal for those whose sins are completely irredeemable.[21] Christians, according to Jewish folklore, were simply unaware that Judas transferred Jesus's dead body to another burial site, misinterpreting this transfer as Jesus having miraculously escaped his grave. Early modern descriptions of the *Mayse Tole* magnify the association of Jesus's death with excrement even further. In one description, Jesus falls into a privy of excrement upon his defeat by Judas.[22] In another, the local Jews drag Jesus's dead body through privies.[23] And yet another version has Judas burying Jesus's body in a cellar full of chamber pots.[24] Jesus therefore came by his epithet "Mr. Shit" honestly. Peter Schäfer interprets the Jewish association of Jesus with excrement as Jews inverting heavenly food into bodily food, satirically depicting Jesus as "punished by forever sitting in hell in the excrement of his followers, who believe that through eating his flesh and drinking his blood, they will live forever."[25]

Whereas the basis of Christianity rests upon the mythology of Jesus being resurrected and ascending to heaven, the basis of Yiddish folklore about Christianity rested upon Jesus having remained dead. This Yiddish folklore on the eternal death of Jesus remained pervasive up to modern times. The main Eastern European Yiddish expression for rejecting something as an utter falsehood was "*nisht geshtoygn, nisht gefloygn*" [he didn't rise up and didn't fly], and among the most popular Yiddish nursery rhymes was *"Yoshke Pandre ligt in dr'erd / oysgepeygert vi a ferd"* [*Yoshke Pandre* lies dead in muck / died like a horse, he's dead as fuck].[26]

The Origin of the Wandering Jesus

It is now fairly clear why Jews believed Jesus to be a dead sinner who is doomed to suffer in excrement. It is less clear why, according to the lore we saw earlier, they believed him to be doomed to a liminal state of *wandering* in the excrement, such that he can be relieved of his restless suffering if Jews study Torah on Christmas Eve. All of the other details about Jesus in Jewish folklore that we saw are clearly polemical, having evidently originated to counter the Christian claims that conflicted with an enduring Judaism. The belief that Jesus can be purged of his sins if a living Jew studies Torah is not consistent with the anti-Christian polemic that Jesus's sins are irredeemable. Surviving manuscripts of the *Mayse Tole* end with Jesus condemned to boil in excrement eternally. The paradoxical detail that Jesus is able to be relieved of this punishment on Christmas Eve was restricted to oral Yiddish tradition, until the apostates recorded it in their exposés.

Did the Yiddish stories about a wandering, redeemable Jesus originate as an anti-Christian polemic? History suggests that these stories can be better understood as part of a secular folk culture than as a polemical response to Christianity. As scholars have shown, the details in Yiddish stories about Jesus were not always polemical.[27] One nonpolemical detail is that the events of the *Mayse Tole* were often set one hundred years before the time of the New Testament, a detail so puzzling that it spawned G. R. S. Mead's 1903 book *Did Jesus Live 100 B.C.?*.[28] Peter Schäfer has since shown that this temporal setting stems from Jesus having been incorporated into a Talmudic legend about Joshua Ben-Perahio, who served as the president of the Jewish court circa 100 BCE. In the legend, Ben-Perahio flees Judea to Alexandria due to the persecution of rabbinic sages by Judean King Yannai. At an Alexandrian inn, Ben-Perahio is appalled to see his former disciple disparage the appearance of a female innkeeper. Ben-Perahio excommunicates the former disciple, who then goes astray. In later Talmud manuscripts, this former disciple is identified as Jesus, pursuant with Jesus being the epitome of the "frivolous Jew who went astray" in Jewish tradition.[29] To be consistent with the Talmud, then, Jews believed Jesus to be a student of Joshua Ben-Perahio, thus coming of age circa 100 BCE.[30] This example illustrates how a Yiddish folk belief about Jesus originated out of a technicality rather than a polemic.

The belief that Jesus can be redeemed by Torah study appears to have originated out of a similar technicality: Medieval Jews were initially familiar with a generic legend about Torah study redeeming a sinful wandering dead man, and then Jews identified this man as Jesus, pursuant with Jesus being the epitome of the "sinful dead" in Jewish tradition. In support of this idea, Jews regularly labeled generic sinners as Jesus even into modern times. For example, Jewish parents in Eastern Europe might threaten a misbehaved boy by calling him *Yoshke Pandre* and reciting the following folk rhyme:

> *Yoshke Pandre ligt in shney, az me shmayst im, tut im vey.*
> *Yoshke Pandre ligt in blote, az me shmayst im, hot er kharote.*
> *Yoshke Pandre iz a goy, az me shmayst im, shrayt er "oy."*

> [Translation:]
> *Yoshke Pandre* lies in snow, when he is whipped, he feels woe.
> *Yoshke Pandre* lies in silt, when he is whipped, he feels guilt.
> *Yoshke Pandre* is a *goy* [misbehaved Jew], when he is whipped, he
>   shouts "*oy.*"[31]

Given that this Jewish tendency to label generic offenders as Jesus dates back to antiquity and survived into the modern era, this tendency would have also existed in the Middle Ages. Let us then turn our attention to the main legend of the wandering dead that appears throughout the medieval Jewish literature, which I will dub "The Rabbi and the Dead Man," and trace how Jews could have retroactively labeled the "dead man" in this legend as Jesus.

"The Rabbi and the Dead Man" has been recorded in the Hebrew and Yiddish literature at least seventy times between the early medieval and early modern periods.[32] Scholars such as Myron Bialik Lerner and Rella Kushelevsky have already analyzed this legend in depth, so here I will

CHRIST IN YIDDISH TRADITION | 33

just provide a very brief overview. The most primitive transcriptions of the legend follow a rabbinic sage who encounters a sinful dead man suffering in *gehenem*. The dead man is overburdened, described as either carrying a heavy load on his shoulders or gathering sticks for burning fellow sinners. He implores the rabbi to seek out his living son, teach the boy Torah and how to recite Jewish prayer, so that this dead man will be freed of his suffering in *gehenem*. Here is a concise early medieval transcription of the legend, as told from the perspective of first-century Rabbi Yohanan Ben-Zakkai:

> Once I was walking along a road and encountered a man who was gathering wood. I spoke to him with peace but he did not return the peace. He came to me and said that he was dead and not alive.
>
> I asked him, "If you are dead, why do you need wood?"
>
> He said to me, "Rabbi, listen to me until I tell you one thing. When I was alive my friend and I were engaged in sin. When we came here we were sentenced to burn. I gather wood to burn my friend, and he gathers wood to burn me."
>
> I asked him, "How long is the sentence?"
>
> He said to me, "When I came here I left my wife pregnant and I know the child is a male. Please care for him from the time he is born until he is five years old. Take him to the rabbi's house to learn the Torah, and when he says '*borkhu es adenoy ha'mevoyrokh*' [the Jewish call to prayer and Torah reading], I will be lifted from this punishment of *gehenem*."[33]

Essentially, the legend is a Jewish exemplum illustrating how a son's Torah learning and Jewish prayer can atone for his dead father's sins.

This unassuming legend came to have a profound effect on Jewish life in high medieval Ashkenaz. As we saw earlier, people were consumed by the idea that late sinners do penance through restless wandering—in purgatory (according to Christians) or *gehenem* (according to Jews)—and that they can only rest if living people provide them with suffrage. Both Christians and Jews developed customs for interceding on behalf of their deceased loved ones.[34] The high medieval Church, we saw, authorized priests to offer three Masses on Christmas to spare the repentant dead from returning to suffer in purgatory following their Christmas

Eve visit to earth. The high medieval "Synagogue," in turn, instituted the liturgical recitation of Kaddish, an Aramaic hymn of praises of God, on Saturday nights to spare the repentant dead from returning to suffer in *gehenem* following their Sabbath visits to earth. In the earliest rabbinic texts to promote this Saturday-night Kaddish custom, from the twelfth and thirteenth centuries, an updated version of the "Rabbi and the Dead Man" legend is appended to the custom description. It still entails a son freeing his dead father from *gehenem* by learning Torah and reciting a blessing (*borkhu*), but this time, the blessing includes lines from Kaddish.[35] The legend effectively became a Jewish variant of the burgeoning Christian legends about Masses and prayers redeeming the wandering dead of their sins, thereby teaching Jews how to redeem their own wandering dead relatives with Torah and Kaddish.[36]

We also find another new detail in the updated version of the legend. The dead man is implied to be Jesus. Jesus is not overtly named in any of the rabbinic transcriptions of this legend, because rabbinic literature has a convention of avoiding Christological names. Instead, the rabbinic convention is to passively refer to Jesus as the *oyse ho'ish*, which is Hebrew for "that man."[37] One lengthy high medieval transcription of "The Rabbi and the Dead Man," circa 1100, begins as follows:

> It once happened that Rabbi Akiva was walking through a cemetery. He encountered a man who was naked, black as coal, and carrying a heavy load of thorns on his head. Rabbi Akiva thought that this man, running like a horse, was alive. The rabbi ordered him to stop, and said to him: "Why must *oyse ho'ish* do such hard work?"[38]

The dead man is awkwardly referred to as "*oyse ho'ish*" throughout the rabbinic transcription, including when he speaks in the first person. For instance, the dead man explains to the rabbi that "*oyse ho'ish* is dead" and that "there is no relief for *oyse ho'ish*," making it clear to Jewish readers that this dead man is Jesus. Instead of gathering sticks or carrying a burden on his shoulders, the *oyse ho'ish* is described as carrying thorns on his head, further identifying Jesus by his iconic crown of thorns. When the rabbi goes to town to seek out the *oyse ho'ish*'s son, he learns that this "son" does not abide by the mitzvahs (commandments) of the Torah—an obvious metaphor for Christians:

Rabbi Akiva asked about the dead man's son. The townspeople told him that he is uncircumcised: "We did not even bother fulfilling the mitzvah of his circumcision." Rabbi Akiva immediately circumcised him and put a book of Torah in front of him.[39]

The rabbi wastes no time bringing the *oyse ho'ish*'s son back to Judaism. He takes the son to study Torah and recite Kaddish, and thereby relieves the suffering of the father, the *oyse ho'ish*. As the tale concludes:

Oyse ho'ish immediately came to Rabbi Akiva in a dream, and said "May it be God's will that you rest in *ganeydn* [heaven], for you saved me from the punishment of *gehenem*."[40]

What is Jesus doing in this legend—why would Jews have ever wanted to convey a message that it is possible for Jesus to be purged of his sins and freed from *gehenem*? David Shyovitz analyzed this Jesus version of the legend in his 2015 study of the origin of the Mourner's Kaddish. He argues that, in order for the custom of reciting Kaddish for the dead to take off, Jews would have needed to be convinced that no sin that their loved ones committed is too great for Kaddish to redeem. Studying Torah and reciting Kaddish can help *anybody* avert an eternal fate of suffering in *gehenem*—even the very epitome of he who deserves to suffer eternally. The epitome of he who deserves to suffer eternally in *gehenem* is, of course, Jesus. As Shyovitz puts it, the allusion to Jesus in this legend conveys the message that "*all* sinners in hell can eventually make it into heaven," because by identifying the sinner as Jesus, the tale "constructs a portrait of the sinner least likely to ever be freed from his torments— and then argues, in a shocking twist, that [the studying of Torah and] the recitation of the Kaddish can redeem even him."[41]

It is now clear that Jesus's role in Yiddish Christmas folklore did not originate as a polemic against Christians celebrating his birth. Instead, the origin can be summarized as follows. As Christians spread legends about dead sinners wandering in purgatory, Jews spread their own version of this type of legend. Jews translated the Christian concept of purgatory into the Jewish concept of *gehenem*—and Jews translated the Christian concept of a "dead sinner" into the Jewish concept of the most notorious dead sinner, Jesus. Thus, on Christmas Eve, as Christians told stories about dead sinners being redeemed from purgatory, Jews told stories about Jesus being redeemed from *gehenem*. This Christmas Eve *redemption* of Jesus was clearly not a polemical inversion of the Nativity celebration, in which case Jews would have maintained that Jesus is irredeemable. On the contrary, the Nativity celebration was not the Jews' main concern on Christmas Eve. Simply put, when Jews heeded the midwinter tumult about relieving the sinful wandering dead, an incidental image to come to Jewish minds was the familiar "Rabbi and the Dead Man" legend of Torah study relieving the sinful wandering *oyse ho'ish*.

An Interreligious Dialogue

This all said, Jews living amid Christian hegemony never stripped their Jesus folklore of its anti-Christian sentiment. While Jews had economic privileges under feudalism relative to peasants, they were nevertheless entrapped in an oppressive society that viewed Jesus as divine and Jews as filth.[42] The Yiddish stories about a sinful Wandering Jesus would have served a self-empowering, anti-Christian polemical function on Christmas Eve. Christians believed Christmas Eve to be given over to the Devil, and the Christian conception of the Devil was inextricably intertwined with the Christian conception of the Jew. Christians traditionally viewed Jews as insults to Christ for sticking by the Torah and as oppressors of Christians through economic manipulation. In high medieval Christian art, Jews were consistently portrayed as horned devilish figures with grotesque features—Devil worshippers, the Devil's assistants, or devils themselves.[43] The demons that Christians feared to work under the Devil on Christmas Eve were therefore "Jewish," at least implicitly, since being Jewish was effectively synonymous with being a malevolent anti-Christian Other.[44] In a thirteenth-century Nativity play performed in Benediktbeuern (Bavaria), the Antichrist who denies the virgin birth is named "Archisynagogus"—clearly Jewish. Medievalist Christopher Lee argues that the Devil himself in this Nativity play "sounds very much like Archisynagogus," and that the play's moral about the midnight birth of Christ overcoming the Devil is essentially about Christianity overcoming Judaism.[45] Other medieval Nativity plays cast King Herod as the Devil's representative on earth, an obvious symbol of a Jew.[46] The devils in a thirteenth-century Nativity play from Chaumont are explicitly described as Jewish.⁴⁷ It is clear, then, that while both Jews and Christians believed that devils from hell (or purgatory/*gehenem*) haunt the earth before midnight on Christmas Eve, Christians interpreted these allegories of evil as Jews, and Jews interpreted these allegories of evil as Jesus.

Christians explicitly interpreted at least one of the wandering penitents who sought rest on Christmas Eve as Jewish. The most well-documented wandering penitent in Christian folklore was a Jew known as Ahasuerus, Cartaphilus, Buttadaeus, among other names—collectively known by scholars as the "Wandering Jew."⁴⁸ Christians customarily believed that the Roman banishment of Jews from Jerusalem, which rendered the Jews a wandering diasporic people, was punishment for the Jews' maltreatment of Jesus. The landbound Christians hence told stories about some Jew being doomed to wander as punishment for deriding Jesus. Although most of these stories are lost in oral history, we can glean some details about the Wandering Jew via a 1606 report from Hamburg that describes an alleged "Wandering Jew sighting":

> The Wandering Jew was seen just a few years ago in Sundewitt, not far from Beuschau. He was carrying a basket with moss growing out of it. He only rests on Christmas Eve, when he seeks out a plough in the field. Only on that is he allowed to sit.⁴⁹

This report establishes the key detail that the Wandering Jew sought rest on Christmas Eve, just like the other wandering penitents described earlier. Scholars of Christian folklore have accordingly long understood the Wandering Jew legend as a variant of the other Christmas legends about the rest-seeking dead.⁵⁰ The Wandering Jew legend was particularly popular in early modern Scandinavia, where Christians practiced a custom of hiding all their tools on Christmas Eve to prevent the Wandering Jew from defiling them.⁵¹

The Wandering Jesus and the Wandering Jew thus existed as a pair—as part of an effective polemical exchange in which Jews and Christians implicitly argued that the other was the true Christmas demon. Christians feared the return of a Jew doomed to wander as punishment for deriding Jesus, and Jews feared the return of a Jesus doomed to wander as punishment for false teachings to the Jews. Christians believed that the

Wandering Jew eats feces (a classic anti-Jewish trope),[52] and Jews believed that the Wandering Jesus lives in feces. From this perspective, it is apparent that the Christmas stories Jews told about a menacing Jesus did not stem from Jews being removed from the mainstream Christmas culture. Rather, Jews and Christians formed a single, foul Christmas culture of telling chilling stories about the wandering sinners whom they each feared most. It is worth noting the asymmetry between these sinners: Christians feared a Wandering Jew, while Jews feared a Wandering Jesus rather than a Wandering Christian. Historian Ivan Marcus emphasizes that "medieval Christian antisemitism was directed at medieval *Jews*. Jewish animosity was directed at *Christianity* and its sancta that Jews associated with biblical idolatry and filth."[53]

The covert Christmas Eve exchange between Christians and Jews can be understood as a jab in a prolonged interreligious dialogue that traversed the year. Let us take a brief walk through the calendar year to establish the broader context of what went on between the two groups at Christmas. Unlike Christmas, which was relatively unimportant from a religious perspective, the entire basis of Christianity rested upon Easter. Christians and Jews traditionally renewed their respective foundational myths in the spring, when Europeans celebrated the return of longer days. The Jewish spring festival was Passover, which commemorated God liberating the Jews from slavery in Egypt following the sacrifice of the Passover lamb. For Christians, Jesus represented the new Passover lamb, sacrificed for the salvation of humanity. Christians identified the festival's ritual bread as a representation of Jesus's affliction (Eucharistic hosts), while Jews counteridentified it as a representation of the Jews' affliction in Egypt (matzo), making a point of arguing so in the opening proclamation of their Passover meal "*ho lakhmo anyo*" [*This* {matzo} is the bread of affliction]. Israel Yuval interprets the entire liturgy of Easter and Passover as an antagonistic interreligious exchange.[54] Christians, for example, traditionally spent Good Friday repeating how the Jews were responsible for the death of Jesus. They would chant a series of reproaches ("*Improperia*") charging the Jews with being ungrateful to God for delivering them out of Egypt, and for feeding them manna from heaven, and so on. Jews covertly responded to the list of reproaches with a counterchant in their own Passover liturgy, "*Dayeynu*" [It Would Have Been Enough], expressing gratitude for the very gifts from God that

Christians claimed the Jews did not appreciate. The pair of Passover and Easter can be viewed as a theological spark in an interreligious dialogue.

This dialogue also had a physically violent spark. Despite dubious claims that Christians were historically violent toward Jews on Christmas, Christians are well-documented to have been violent toward Jews on Easter, dating back to the dawn of Christianity. In addition to the ordinary Eastertime stoning of Jews, many of history's largest violent riots against Jews occurred on Easter.[55] While the Jewish minority was not able to reciprocate the same level of violence, Jews are well-documented to have violently harassed Christian peasants during the end-of-winter Jewish festival of Purim.[56] Purim was when Jews commemorated the downfall of their archenemy Haman, and scholars have established that the figure of Haman functioned as an alias for Jesus among Jews in Christian Europe.[57] (The Haman version of the Yiddish folk rhyme about Jesus lying dead in muck is *"Homen ha'roshe ligt in dr'erd / Mortkhe ha'tsadik rayt afn ferd"* [Haman the Wicked lies dead in muck / Mordecai the Righteous rides high on a buck].)

Easter celebrations traditionally included anti-Jewish Passion Plays in which Christians violently reenacted the suffering that "the Jews" inflicted upon Jesus. Jews, in turn, hosted violent anti-Christian Purim plays that culminated with Jews assaulting the actor playing Haman. Eighteenth- to twentieth-century European sources indicate that this actor was often a real (paid) Christian garbed in exaggerated Christian imagery.[58] The earliest of these sources are Church records forbidding Christians from playing Haman, but Christian folk attestation from interwar Poland indicates that Christians nevertheless continued to do so.[59] Take, for example, the following Polish attestation:

> The Jews [. . .] paid a Christian to let them flog him with branches, and to spit on him. Such a rented Christian they called Haman. [. . .] They led him, pushing and beating him with reeds—like Jesus.[60]

Christians got their violent revenge at Easter. When they could not obtain a physical Jew to serve as a target of assault, Christians used an effigy of Judas instead: Among the most well-documented early modern Easter folk rituals was the "Burning of Judas," in which Christians burned an effigy of Judas on a stake, popularly known as "Burning of the Jew."[61] In turn, a Purim ritual that the Church had condemned since late antiquity was for Jews to bind an effigy of Haman to a wooden cross and burn it.[62] This Jewish "Crucifixion of Haman," in combination with general Jewish violence toward Christians on Purim, led high medieval Christians to spread the word that Jews ritually murder Christians around Easter to reenact Jesus's crucifixion, fueling further Christian violence toward Jews.[63] The respective anti-Christian and anti-Jewish violence of Purim and Easter—rites of passage for aggressively drowning out the winter—can be interpreted as a violent climax of the Jewish–Christian interreligious dialogue.

Another spark in this dialogue took place fifty days after each of Passover and Easter in yet another pair of major religious festivals. Shavuos and Pentecost marked the revelation of the brightest time of year. For Christians, Pentecost commemorated the Holy Spirit descending upon Jesus's followers at Mount Zion, hence the revelation of the Eucharist and birth of Christianity. For Jews, Shavuos commemorated the theophany of God at Mount Sinai, hence the revelation of the Torah and birth of Judaism. Christians, as a matter of course, denied that the Torah is still binding as they celebrated the arrival of the New Testament on Pentecost. Their German folklore maintained that the Messiah whom the Jews still await will be the Antichrist, and that he will arrive together with devilish Jews (the legendary "Red Jews") to bring about the apocalypse. Jews, in turn, celebrated their still-binding Torah on Shavuos as they denied that any new covenant will be sealed before the true Messianic Age. Their Yiddish folklore maintained that the Messiah whom they still await will be a righteous descendant of King David (who had ruled united Israel), and that the purported Red Jews who will accompany him will be the lost tribes of the Israeli nation.[64] These rivalrous interpretations of biblical and messianic revelation gave rise to competing summer-holiday practices. In high medieval Ashkenaz, Christian boys were confirmed to the Church on Pentecost by ingesting their first Eucharistic hosts. Jewish boys, in turn, began their first day of synagogue schooling on Shavuos by ingesting cakes and eggs inscribed with Torah verses.[65] (When Christians later delayed the boy's confirmation to puberty, Jews developed the pubertal bar mitzvah ceremony as an effective successor to the Shavuos ceremony.)[66] In the early modern period, Christians marked Pentecost by decorating their churches with greenery. Jews, in turn, marked Shavous by decorating their synagogues with greenery and counteracting the Christian devotion to the Church with their most vigorous Torah study of the year, traditionally lasting the entire night.[67] Shavuos and Pentecost thus formed a pair for each group to assert commitment to their respective covenant with God.

Was the Christian celebration of the Nativity also part of an inter-religious dialogue? We know that the birth of Jesus crossed the mind of medieval Spanish Jewish mathematician Abraham Bar-Hiyya (c. 1065–1136). Bar-Hiyya wrote that Christmas is not the true birthday of Jesus but rather a Christianization of pagan midwinter celebrations. This Christianization, according to Bar-Hiyya, rendered Christians to believe that Jesus (whom Bar-Hiyya refers to, of course, as the *Tole*) was born on December 25 in the year 0 CE. Bar-Hiyya converted this Julian calendar date to the Jewish date of the ninth day of the month *Teyves* in the year 3761.[68] An early medieval Hebrew text incidentally lists the ninth of *Teyves* as a fast day for Jews. Citing Bar-Hiyya, several nineteenth-century scholars argued that Jews had instituted a fast of the ninth of *Teyves* as a "Jewish" commemoration of Jesus's birth, to mourn all of the tragedies that befell Jews as a consequence of Jesus being born.[69] These scholars were apparently incorrect, because prior to the nineteenth century, Jews described the ninth of *Teyves* as a fast for mourning the death of Simon Peter (who "heroically" separated Christianity away from Judaism).[70] Nevertheless, the nineteenth-century scholars raised awareness about an association between the ninth of *Teyves* and Jesus's birth. Some Jews came to interpret the main Yiddish term associated with Christmas, *nitl*, as an acronym for *noyled ishu tes l'Teyves*, "Jesus was born on the ninth of *Teyves*."[71]

If not the ninth of *Teyves*, what about the 24th of December—can the Yiddish Christmas stories about Torah study providing rest to a Wandering Jesus be interpreted as a Jewish counterpart to the Christian celebration of Jesus's birth in an interreligious dialogue? Well, it is difficult to imagine that the earliest Jews to retreat from their holy books before midnight on Christmas Eve were even partly intending to counter the midnight Christian celebration, since we have seen a clear pattern of Jews responding to Christian theology by reaffirming their devotion to Judaism and Torah. If Jews held a counterfestival to the midnight celebration of Jesus, then it began at midnight. Medieval

Christians traditionally marked midnight with the recitation of the Latin prayer "*Te Deum*" to exclaim triumph over the Devil, initiating a marathon of Masses in honor of Christ.[72] The Jewish tradition was similar. An early fifteenth-century Jewish text recounts that Jews recited the Hebrew prayer "*Oleynu*" aloud on Christmas night.[73] Jews customarily recited "*Oleynu*" to convey triumph over demonic forces,[74] and Israel Yuval has shown that "*Oleynu*" functioned as a Jewish counterdeclaration to "*Te Deum*."[75] Additionally, a sixteenth-century Jewish text deems the long winter nights following the winter *tkufe* (i.e. Christmas Eve) to be an ideal time for Torah study,[76] analogous to the Christian marathon of Masses following the winter solstice. Into the modern period, rabbis continued to advocate for Jews to hold midnight Torah study sessions while Christians celebrate Midnight Mass.[77] It is therefore evident that, once the midwinter danger passed after midnight, Jews and Christians commenced a theological debate about the superior mode of religious energy (studying Torah versus celebrating Mass). Before midnight, Jews and Christians engaged in a symbolic debate about the nature of the dangerous wandering sinners from whom they withheld this energy (Wandering Jesus versus Wandering Jew). Christians had the louder voice, but Jews were not silent in this shared Christmas culture.

Of course, the narrative that Jesus was born on Christmas may have reinforced Jesus's presence in Yiddish Christmas folklore. Nonetheless, the concurrence of the birth narrative with this presence appears to have begun as a coincidence. Similar coincidences are abundant in history— for instance, the Christian association between Jews and the Devil originated out of an incidental biblical mistranslation to suggest that Moses had horns,[78] and the Jewish association between Haman and Jesus originated out of an incidental biblical mistranslation to suggest that Haman was crucified.[79] It is not out of keeping that the Jewish association between Christmas Eve and a Wandering Jesus originated out of an incidental identification of Jesus as a wandering midwinter revenant (as per the depiction of Jesus in the "Rabbi and the Dead Man" legend), which then came to form a polemical dialogue with the Christians who associated Christmas Eve with a Wandering Jew. Jews and Christians played a parallel role in forming a grim Christmas Eve culture, and Jesus's role in Yiddish Christmas folklore was merely a byproduct of this culture.

Conclusion

Scholars conventionally assume that the casting of Jesus as a Christmas demon in Yiddish folklore was a polemical inversion of Christians celebrating his birth. The assumption is based on the image of a major Christian holiday ostracizing a scoffing Jewish minority. This image turns out to be misguided. Jesus's presence in Yiddish Christmas folklore was actually a consequence of Jews participating in an embedded popular culture on Christmas Eve that had little to do with the Nativity celebration. The figure of a sinful Wandering Jesus existed in Yiddish folklore outside of Christmas, parallel to the figure of the sinful Wandering Jew in the folklore of Christian languages. Since people feared wandering sinners to return on Christmas Eve, this was the night when the Wandering Jew and the Wandering Jesus engaged in their effective showdown. This is not to say that Jews never interpreted their Yiddish Christmas folklore as subverting the midnight Nativity celebration, but that Jews did not originally introduce Jesus into the folklore for this purpose. Jews were simply afraid of the bleakest night of the year—the night when everybody feared the most frightening demons they could imagine. Christians insisted that these demons were anti-Jesus Jews. And Jews insisted that this demon was Jesus himself.

3

Nidelnacht and *Nitl-Nakht*

On Christmas Eve 2020, a debate arose on Twitter regarding the etymology of *nitl*, the main Yiddish word associated with Christmas.[1] The debate was ignited when Nick Block, a professor of Jewish Studies at Boston College, whimsically wished his Twitter followers, in Yiddish, "*a gut nitl*" [happy *nitl*].[2] Upon receiving replies inquiring about this Yiddish word *nitl*, Block suggested that it is a diminutive of the Yiddish word *nit*, "not," such that the word *nitl* conveys the unimportance of Christmas among Jews.[3] An hour later, Block received a reply from Arun Viswanath, grandson of leading Yiddish linguist Mordkhe Schaechter (1927–2007). Viswanath claimed that the etymology that Block presented is merely a folk etymology.[4] The true etymology, according to Viswanath, is that *nitl* is a shortening of *nitl-nakht* [*nitl* night], which in turn derives from a Middle High German term for Christmas Eve, *Nidelnacht*.[5] Viswanath added that it is "odd" that this etymology "only recently has come to light," attesting to "the power of popular folk etymology."[6]

Within minutes, Viswanath's tweet received pushback from a rabbinic scholar writing under the Twitter handle @OrNistar. This scholar pointed out that *nitl*, in its earliest appearances in medieval rabbinic literature, did not include the -*nakht* suffix and therefore cannot be a shortening of *nitl-nakht*. The true etymology of *nitl*, he put forth, derives from the Latin *natalis*, "birthday," just like the term for Christmas in Portuguese (*Natal*), Italian (*Natale*), Spanish (*Navidad*), and French (*Noël*). The phonological shift from *a* to *i* (*natal* to *nitl*), he posited, arose as a pun with the Hebrew *nitle*, "hanged," since the earliest rabbinic references to *nitl* associate it with Jesus's pejorative nickname *Tole*, "Hanged One."[7] Viswanath maintained that the *Nidelnacht* etymology is "the most simple explanation that doesn't require bizarre jumps in logic."[8] The Middle High German term *Nidel*, however, meant "milk cream," which is a less intuitive source for a Yiddish word for Christmas than birthday or hanged. Viswanath ultimately conceded that the etymology of *nitl* is "murky and less snappy" than he had initially thought.[9]

This Twitter debate revived discourse on the etymology of *nitl* that took place among Yiddish scholars a century earlier. At the beginning of the twentieth century, scholars took for granted that the term *nitl* must derive from the Latin *natalis*.[10] Then, in 1923, folklorist Max Grunwald (1871–1953) suggested that the word *nitl*, known to most Jews in the form *nitl-nakht*, more plausibly derives from the German *Nidelnacht*.[11] Grunwald cites the Swiss tradition of *Nidelnacht* as a superstitious winter night when folks smother each other in milk cream to ensure that the house will be blessed for the coming year.[12] The following year, Yiddish linguist Max Weinreich (1894–1969) suggested that, while the Yiddish *nitl* undoubtedly derives from the Latin *natalis*, the phonological shift from *a* to *i* (*natal* to *nitl*) derives from the "Germanic form" of *natalis*, *Nidelnacht*.[13] Weinreich cites the comprehensive *Deutsches Wörterbuch* dictionary, which defines *Nidelnacht* as any of the seven nights before Christmas.[14] However, Weinreich later retracted his claim in his posthumously published book *History of the Yiddish Language*, in which he acknowledges that *Nidel* is not the Germanic form of *natalis* but rather means milk cream.[15] Writing that the etymology of *nitl* is a "hard nut to crack," Weinreich concludes that the phonological shift from *a* to *i* must have been a corruption of *natalis* with *nitle* (the Hebrew term for hanged) and unrelated to *Nidelnacht*.[16] Yet, other scholars have noted a late medieval Jewish transcription of *nitl* spelled "*nidl*," raising doubts that the Yiddish *nitl-nakht* and German *Nidelnacht* are unrelated.[17] In the 2015 book *Origins of Yiddish Dialects*, linguist Alexander Beider matter-of-factly writes that the word *nitl* "is of German origin" and derived from *Nidelnacht*.[18]

We thus arrive at the third question on our agenda: Is the Yiddish *nitl-nakht* indeed related to the German *Nidelnacht*? A cursory analysis suggests not. We know from rabbinic sources that high medieval Jews in northern France were already referring to Christmas as *nitl*. These earliest textual references to *nitl* are presented in conjunction with the word *keytsekh* for Easter (Latin: *Pascha*), a corruption of the Latin's Hebrew root *peysekh* with the Hebrew word *koyts*, "thorn," alluding to dead Jesus's crown of thorns. The texts explicitly describe *nitl* and *keytsekh* as holidays "for the sake of the *Tole*."[19] It therefore seems that the word *nitl* originated by Jews corrupting *natalis* with *nitle* in the Romance-language world, rather than from a shortening of the German *Nidelnacht*.

On the other hand, these early rabbinic sources specifically refer to *nitl* in the context of the rabbinic opinion that Jews should avoid business with Christians on Christian holidays.[20] Among modern Yiddish speakers, the term *nitl-nakht* referred not to an extraneous Christian holiday but rather a night when Jews refrain from religious activity. We saw that the Yiddish folklore associated with this night originated as a variant of a German folklore about refraining from religious activity, so it is unlikely that the nearly identical Yiddish and German names for the night were unrelated. The name "*nitl*"-*nakht* could have developed as a pun on the name *Nidelnacht* based on this night incidentally being the eve of the Nativity, which was known in the rabbinic literature as *nitl*.

This chapter builds on our findings thus far to advance the century-old debate about *nitl-nakht* and *Nidelnacht*. It proposes that these two names are not only of common etymological origin, but that the respective traditions of *nitl-nakht* and *Nidelnacht* are themselves of common origin. Despite all the discussion on the similar phonology of these names, scholars have not considered the similarity of their associated folkloric content; the discussions pertained entirely to comparative linguistics rather than comparative folklore. This chapter therefore begins by collecting evidence that there was a historical time when the Yiddish and German folkloric traditions associated with Christmas Eve were largely undifferentiated, forming a night known in both languages as *Nidelnacht*. It then investigates the circumstances that caused the Yiddish and German versions of Christmas Eve to diverge, which resulted in Christians and Jews focusing their Christmas Eve folklore on different supernatural visitors (Wandering Jew versus Wandering Jesus). The ultimate goal for this chapter, rather than simply arguing that the Yiddish name *nitl-nakht* derives from the German name *Nidelnacht*, is to argue that the Yiddish tradition of *nitl-nakht* derives from the German tradition of *Nidelnacht*.

Nidelnacht, Frau Holle, and the Jews

First, in order to justify the idea that there was a time when the Yiddish and German folklores about supernatural Christmas Eve visitors were undifferentiated, we need to establish the period when Jews began to believe that evil Jesus is among the visitors—this detail is obviously unique to a divergent Yiddish version. We turn to a 1999 study by Marc Shapiro on the early modern writings of Jewish-born converts to Christianity who sought to expose the anti-Christian elements of Jewish culture. Shapiro found that attestations of a Christmas folklore about a sinful Wandering Jesus are not unanimous and only gradually begin to appear over the course of the sixteenth century. He deduced that this folklore must have been a new innovation in the sixteenth century, because as the apostates were intent on conveying the full extent of anti-Christianity in Jewish culture, Christmas folklore about an evil Jesus is "something they would have jumped on had they been aware of it."[21] Shapiro's work hence suggests that any Yiddish Christmas folklore that was widespread before the early modern period was not in conflict with the local German Christmas folklore, or else the apostates would have exposed it.

What we now need to establish is, first, what this German Christmas folklore was, and second, whether medieval Jews did indeed share this Christmas folklore. Decks of cards did not make their way to Central Europe until the early modern period,[22] so medieval folks needed activities other than playing cards to bring light to Christmas Eve. We know that Germans threw around the term *Nidelnacht*, but what exactly did this term refer to? In recent centuries, *Nidelnacht* was among the less common names that Germans used for a supernatural night in the Christmas season. Contrary to religious names like *Weihnacht* and *Christnacht*, the most common German name that modern folklorists collected for a Christmas night is *Rauhnacht* [Rough Night], with a common variant being *Rauchnacht* [Smoky Night] based on a practice of burning incense in stables and barns to drive off evil forces. Other names, such as *Klopfelnacht* [Knocking Night] and *Glöckelnacht* [Ringing Night], emphasize the knocking on doors and ringing of bells by children dressed in scary costumes. There is also the name *Losnacht* [Lot-Casting Night], which emphasizes the custom of telling fortunes for the coming year, and names like *Zwischennacht* [Between Night], *Innernacht* [Inner Night], and *Unternacht* [Under Night], which emphasize the liminal nature of midwinter.[23]

It is more difficult to know what the older name *Nidelnacht* [Milk Cream Night] originally referred to, since various conflicting folk explanations had developed by the time the field of ethnography took off in the nineteenth century.[24] Swabian folklorist Anton Birlinger (1834–1891), for example, defines *Nidelnacht* as a debauched night ruled by the Devil when folks are visited by a demon known as the *Nidel*.[25] Birlinger also suggests that *Nidelnacht* "might" have once referred to a night when processions of wandering revenants are sighted.[26] Conversely, Palatinate folklorist Lukas Grünenwald (1858–1937) describes *Nidelnacht* as a name for the winter solstice in Upper Bavaria etymologically related to *Nöttelestag* [Unlucky Day].[27] Birlinger too notes the winter solstice to be especially linked to the name *Nidelnacht* in Swabia,[28] but this opinion is not unanimous among folklorists. Swiss folklorist Ernst Ludwig Rochholz (1809–1892) simply defines *Nidelnacht* as a folk name for each of the twelve nights of Christmas.[29] Other Bavarian folklorists describe *Nidelnacht* as a night when folks seek a reward from the Devil in exchange for abstaining from religious activity.[30]

We seem to arrive at the medieval roots of *Nidelnacht* through the work of Bavarian folklorist Max Höfler (1848–1914). Höfler studied the food offerings that people left out to appease the supernatural Christmas Eve visitors, the most common being creamy milk porridges. Noting that *Nidel* is a Middle High German term for milk cream, Höfler deduced that the name *Nidelnacht*, which he dates to the fourteenth century,[31] originally referred to a night when *Nidel*-based foods were offered to supernatural visitors.[32] The practice of leaving offerings for supernatural visitors at midwinter was very prevalent in the Middle Ages, as evidenced by ample condemnation of this practice in ecclesiastical sources.[33] In order to understand the medieval *Nidelnacht*, then, we need to turn our attention to the German folklore associated with these offerings.

In a landmark 2014 study, Ronald Hutton demonstrated that medieval folks did not leave these offerings for the visiting wandering penitents who sought rest on Christmas Eve.[34] Rather, the medieval sources describe people leaving these offerings for a group of supernatural women led by Frau Holle, variously known as Holda or Hulda.[35] Holle is a feminine folkloric ancestor of the modern Santa Claus, who amalgamated with St. Nicholas in the early modern period. The belief in a visiting maternal figure at midwinter long predates Catholic saints and goes back to pagan times. The Anglo-Saxon pagan name for Christmas Eve was

Mōdraniht, "Mother's Night."[36] The custom of setting an overnight table of food offerings is one of the few well-documented hallmarks of the pre-Christian Yule.[37] Historian Claude Lecouteux explains the function of this ancient midwinter tradition:

> The movement of this host of women was connected to [. . .] omens. If the visitors were satisfied with the food offerings, they would bring prosperity and fertility to the household. Thus taking shape in the background was a calendar-based rite belonging to the mythology of beginnings: whatever happens on this date foreshadowed what would happen over the New Year. [. . .] This custom was observed throughout the entire Middle Ages, as the clerical literature testifies.[38]

People identified the leader of these supernatural women as Holle by no later than the thirteenth century. This dating is indicated by Cistercian monk Rudolf's unsuccessful attempt to reclaim this tradition as a cult of Virgin Mary, writing circa 1250 that "on the night of the Nativity of Christ, they [Christians] set a table for the Queen of Heaven, whom the folks call Frau Holda."[39] According to the 1468 Bavarian manual *Thesaurus pauperum* [*Treasury of the Poor*], this table included bread and milk.[40] Some medieval sources describe Holle remaining active for all twelve nights of Christmas, and in certain regions people left out the offerings on the twelfth night, the night of Epiphany (Middle High German: *Giperchtennacht*). In these regions, Holle was known as Perchta or Berchta, which can be translated as "Lady Epiphany."[41]

Although the medieval sources do not say much about Holle herself, the tradition of offering her bread and milk continued in parts of German Europe into the modern era, allowing folklorists to record details that were passed from mother to daughter within the last few centuries.[42] Most notable of these details is that, whereas people today leave plain cookies and milk for Santa Claus, people historically left fancier braided breads and milk porridges for Holle.[43] (Some sources also apparently describe people leaving her noodles, as the terms *Nidel* and *Nudel* were sometimes used interchangeably.)[44] There was a large folklore associated with both the braided bread and milk porridge offerings. People offered the braided bread in the context of Holle expecting girls to have their hair neatly braided. If a girl left some hair unbraided, Holle punished the girl by tangling her messy hair into mats, with this tangled hair popularly known under names such as *Hollenzopf* ["Holle-braided" hair].[45] In order to please Holle, people left braids of hair on display as a Christmas Eve offering to her, customarily in the symbolic form of braided breads.[46] As to the milk porridge offering, people traditionally believed that the condition for the house to be blessed for the coming year was to hear Holle slurp it. There was also an elaborate folklore about how the position that the spoon is found in the bowl the next morning can be used as a fortune teller for the coming year.[47] The Berchta version of Holle was viewed as more malevolent: Berchta would allegedly slit open the bellies of people who misbehaved and stuff their intestines with refuse. People customarily consumed some of the greasy milk porridge prior to Berchta's visit so that her knife might slip off their belly.[48]

It is important to note that Holle/Berchta folklore was not Christian folklore. Ronald Hutton describes this folklore as "utterly un-Christian,"[49] and stresses that the medieval Church viewed it as "a superstition held by silly and ignorant women."[50] It follows that tales of Holle/Berchta were not restricted to the mouths of Christian folks. It is difficult to ascertain the extent of Holle's presence in medieval Yiddish folklore, since Holle existed as a mainly female oral tradition that rabbis had no reason to record in the Hebrew literature. Holle is, nonetheless, mentioned in one of the oldest extant Yiddish texts: a fourteenth-century Yiddish glossing of folk medicinal invocations, one of which involves asking "Holda" for permission to break off a leaf in her yard.[51] Medieval folks believed that falling snow is the result of Holle shaking her featherbed out into her yard, and modern Eastern European Jews retained an idiom that describes falling snow as feathers being shaken out of a featherbed.[52] Scholars have previously noted that medieval Jews believed in Holle, but in the context of believing in her as a general maternal figure. These scholars only mentioned in passing that people believed Holle to be active at Christmas.[53] We are left to establish whether medieval Jews and Christians shared the same folk practices pertaining to leaving offerings for Holle on *Nidelnacht*.

There does not, unfortunately, seem to be any direct documentation of medieval Jews offering milk porridges to Holle. While there is a documented modern Yiddish folklore about Lilith ("Mother of Demons") chasing milk on Christmas Eve,[54] there is no surviving source that confirms that medieval Jews identified Holle as this milk-seeker. Likewise, while early modern Jews are well-documented to have consumed milk fat on Hanukkah to honor heroine Judith,[55] there is no extant paper trail linking this custom back to medieval Holle. There is, however, circumstantial evidence that medieval Jews offered braided breads to Holle, as these breads retained their etymological roots after being Judaized into offerings for the Sabbath Queen. The name "Holle bread" became "*khale* bread" (often spelled in English as "challah bread"), with the word *khale* (חלה) being a biblical Hebrew term for a loaf offering. The name "Berchta bread" became "*berkhes* bread," associated with the Hebrew word for blessing, *birkes* (ברכת).[56] Why might medieval Jews have originally offered these breads to Holle/Berchta? In a thirteenth-century rabbinic Hebrew manuscript, an explanation is provided for why Jews should not shave off matted hair before entering the ritual purification bath (the *mikve*): The mats are caused by a "demon," rendering them dangerous to cut off.[57] In a fourteenth-century Hebrew manuscript that cites this explanation, a rabbi clarifies that this matted hair is known commonly (i.e. in Yiddish) as *Holle locke* ["Holle-curled" hair].[58] It is discernible, then, that medieval Jews shared the common belief that the tangling of unbraided hair into mats is the work of Holle. Like Christians, Jews had motivation to please Holle with braided breads when she visited on *Nidelnacht*.[59]

We can dig deeper into the Jewish engagement with Holle by scrutinizing the rabbinic description of her as a "demon." Medieval Christian clerical sources repeatedly brand Holle as a witch,[60] as clerics expressed frustration with Christian devotion to her at Christmas. One twelfth-century cleric even laments that children prefer singing about this witch than singing the *Ave Maria*.[61] The fact that rabbis likewise demonized Holle suggests that they may have had a depaganization motive in Judaizing Christmas "Holle bread" into Sabbath "*khale* bread." In support of this idea, there is evidence of medieval rabbis Judaizing another offering that Jews made to Holle—not a Christmas Eve offering, but one that people made to Holle throughout the year. As many folklorists have recorded, maternal Holle presided over vulnerable infants while they were exposed to baby-preying demonesses (whom Christians called *lamiae* and Jews called Lilith). Once christened, Holle allowed the infants to be safely "flung back and restored to their cradles," recorded by John

of Salisbury as early as the twelfth century.[62] In order to liberate a child
from Holle in the absence of formal christening, the child could be provided with an informal name as a pseudochristening.[63] For Jews, this
pseudochristening necessarily meant providing the infant with a non-
Judaic (Germanic/Yiddish) name, since non-Jewish Holle would not accept a Hebrew name. A well-documented medieval Ashkenazic Jewish
folk ritual for providing babies with non-Hebrew names was the *Hole-
kraysh*, "Cry Out [to] Holle," in which Jewish children lifted a baby while
shouting "Holle" before granting him or her a secular name.[64] Rabbis
apparently Judaized this custom by distorting "*Hole-kraysh*" (הולקרייש)
into "*khol-kraysh*" (חולקרייש), "Cry Out [a] Secular [Name]," as it is written in the Hebrew literature.[65] Max Weinreich argues that Jews quickly
forgot about Holle's role in the baby-naming ritual and merely came to
view it as protection against infant-snatcher Lilith.[66] This Judaization
would explain the modern Yiddish folklore about Lilith rather than
Holle seeking milk on Christmas Eve, in conjunction with Lilith's role as
"ruler of the *tkufe*" in Jewish mystical tradition.[67]

Returning to the braided bread, an early rabbi to Judaize "Holle
bread" into "*khale* bread" was Israel Isserlein. Isserlein was the most influential rabbi in eastern Austria in the first half of the fifteenth century;
he taught students from across Ashkenaz. He is also the first person documented to have laid "*khale* bread" on the Sabbath table.[68] It is relevant
that, when passively referring to Christmas in one of his carefully scribed
Hebrew texts, he uses the spelling *nidl* (נידל) instead of the traditional *nitl*
(ניתל) that puns with *Tole*.[69] Isserlein's spelling corroborates that Jews
were using the term *Nidelnacht* for Christmas Eve in his community.
We can get a sense of the local Yiddish Christmas folklore in Isserlein's
community by consulting the Book of Customs (*Seyfer ha'minhogim*)
written by Isserlein's contemporary Isaac Tyrnau. Like Isserlein, Tyrnau
lived in the Vienna area in the early fifteenth century. This was a work
of rabbinic literature, so Tyrnau obviously did not record the disdained
popular custom of offering braided breads to Holle on *Nidelnacht*. There
is, however, one midwinter practice that was apparently deemed "Jewish" enough for Tyrnau to record: The night of *nitl* was the one night
of the year when Jews recited the prayer "*Oleynu*" aloud rather than
quietly.[70] As we have seen, this practice was a Jewish counterpart to the
Christian recitation of "*Te Deum*" on Christmas Eve—"*Oleynu*" and "*Te*

Deum" each marked triumph over threatening Otherly forces. Such a practice further corroborates that there were attempts to Judaize popular Christmas Eve practices in Isserlein's setting.

Taken together, it is clear that medieval Jews were engaged with the supernatural Christmas folklore of the German milieux. As such, the simplest explanation for why the names *nitl-nakht* and *Nidelnacht* sound similar is that they have a common origin, stemming from a time when Jews and Christians shared a common midwinter folklore about Holle that priests and rabbis scorned. The debate on the etymology of *nitl-nakht* hence takes new shape under the premise that the tradition of *nitl-nakht* did not originate as a Jewish war on Christians observing the Nativity (*natalis*) but rather out of Jews and Christians jointly participating in an irreligious Christmas Eve (*Nidelnacht*). Perhaps the Yiddish name *nitl-nakht* arose as a Judaization of *Nidelnacht* (with "*nitl*" interpreted as a derogatory poke at the *Tole*), analogous to the Judaization of "Holle bread" into "*khale* bread" and the "*Hole-kraysh*" into the "*khol-kraysh*."[71]

Nitl-Nakht Diverges from *Nidelnacht*

At the end of the Middle Ages, Jews and Christians transitioned from being visited by Holle to being visited by demonic symbols of each other. Our question now is why it took until the early modern period for this divergence to transpire. We know that people since the high medieval period believed the wandering dead to return on Christmas Eve (in addition to Holle and her entourage), and that the Jewish legend of the wandering dead Jesus dates back to this high medieval period. So why did it apparently take several centuries before Jews began to widely promote the Wandering Jesus as one of the supernatural visitors of Christmas Eve?

Let us assess the social context. Among the most pronounced innovations in folk culture to take place at the end of the medieval period was the burgeoning of secular performative routines outside places of worship—a hallmark of the Renaissance. The prime example was the Christian Carnival that ushered out winter, marked by public parading, masquerading, and staging a secular Carnival play. This Renaissance performative culture had a major influence on Yiddish folk culture. Jews transformed their traditional end-of-winter festival of Purim into a Jewish Carnival, featuring a masqueraded *purimshpil* [Purim play] as an analogously structured (and analogously vulgar) Yiddish version of the German *Fastnachtsspiel* [Carnival play].[72] Outside of Carnival, Renaissance performative routines often took the form of a house visit by a costumed actor (known in German as an *Einkehrbrauch*), which was likewise incorporated into Yiddish folk culture. On Passover, early modern Ashkenazic Jews ended the meal by opening the door for an actor dressed as Elijah the Prophet.[73] Since Christmas was not exempt from the proliferation of secular performative routines, it would make sense for us to explore the innovations in the Christmas folk culture of Renaissance Ashkenaz and assess how they may have impacted and been adapted by Jews.

We shall begin by noting that the Catholic Christmas season since the Renaissance traditionally opened with a house visit from St. Nicholas on the night of December 5 (St. Nicholas Eve). An actor dressed in a bishop's robe and long white beard delivered gifts to praying children if they passed a series of tests.[74] Abraham a Sancta Clara (née Johann Ulrich Megerle; 1644–1709) provides a detailed account of this tradition. He describes an "ancient practice" of St. Nicholas quizzing children on what they learned at school and how they behaved over the past year in order to earn their gifts.[75] (He further remarks that the actor who plays Nicholas is trained to act dignified "so that the children don't get upset if Nicholas is drunk and falls down the stairs.")[76] Unlike the lighthearted plays of Carnival, a Sancta Clara notes that Nicholas's goal "is to frighten the children [. . .] so that they are discouraged from immoral behavior," adding that Nicholas is customarily accompanied by "devils."[77] This goal was in keeping with the Germanic disciplinary style of *Kinderschreck*, that is, using threatening figures to instill fear in children. An anonymous disapproving account from the late eighteenth century details the fear that befell Catholic children on St. Nicholas Eve:

> Dragging their feet, the young supplicants slowly approach the dreaded Nicholas. The bishop opens the conversation with gestures. He turns majestically to the children, who are constantly bowing, and he intones with a lowered voice: "I already know—I know too well—what you have learned and what you have not learned in the past year. I know all about

your irresponsible pranks and disobedience toward your papa and mama. You will (*threatens with rod*) be punished as fits, if you cannot recite your prayers properly."

But before they can do so, the barking Krampus rumbles toward the children, forces them still and scatters their gushing words as they are pressed against the walls of the hall, unheard by the bishop, and the echo fills the praying boys and girls with fear and terror.[78]

Who, pray tell, is the Krampus? This monster was one of the many variants of St. Nicholas's devilish assistants that have been documented across Europe. He functioned as a particular type of *Kinderschreck* figure that would eat up misbehaved children, known as a *Kinderfresser* [child gobbler]. Since the *Kinderfresser*'s costumes were designed to take on the most frightening characteristics imaginable to Christian children, the *Kinderfresser* was virtually identical to the stereotypical Christian portrayal of the devilish Jew. The typical *Kinderfresser* bore a blackened face, dark animal hides, and goat horns.[79] A famous Renaissance depiction of a *Kinderfresser* still stands today at the sixteenth-century stone foundation in Bern known as the *Kindlifresserbrunnen* [Little Child-Gobbler Fountain]. Scholars are divided as to whether this fountain was originally designed to depict a Christmas demon or a Jew,[80] but as described earlier, it stands to reason that Christmas demons and Jews were effectively synonymous. The Krampus from the Austrian Alps is the most famous of St. Nicholas's *Kinderfresser* pals known today, whom Madison Tarleton describes as a "horned, devilish, child-snatching, malicious figure [. . .] donning common antisemitic and anti-Jewish features."[81]

The visit from St. Nicholas and company was only the beginning. According to a 1677 pamphlet, appearances of devilish *Kinderschreck* figures on German streets multiplied over the course of Advent.[82] Then, on the climactic night of Christmas Eve, Christian parents adapted the visit from Frau Holle into another *Kinderschreck* tradition: scaring children with stories about returning wandering dead penitents.[83] Early modern Germanic sources describe Holle as the leader of the returning wandering dead, and they portray the milk porridge offering and its "magical replenishment" as a ritual transaction with the dead.[84] This development appears to be responsible for the name *Nidelnacht* losing its association with Holle. Renward Cysat (1545–1614) of Switzerland describes people only offering milk cream to the wandering dead and not Holle.[85] The Berchta version of Holle remained popular beyond her association with the wandering dead, but Berchta too evolved as she was transformed into a grotesque *Kinderschreck* figure. An actor traditionally portrayed Berchta with an appended long nose and other coarse Jewish stereotypes as a witchy female counterpart to the male *Kinderfresser*; she is identified in an eighteenth-century Bavarian woodcut as the *Butzen-Bercht*, "Bogey Berchta."[86] In regions where Berchta was known as Perchta, the offering of milk (German: *Milch*) was known as *Perchtenmilch*, which folks left out for Perchta's entourage of devilish "*Perchten*" capped with stereotypical Jew horns.[87]

It is hence apparent why Yiddish Christmas folklore diverged from the Christians' Holle/Berchta folklore following the end of the Middle Ages. Jews were doubtlessly uncomfortable with the craze of using ugly anti-Jewish tropes to spook children. Jews needed to reclaim these traditions in such a way that they could fit into their own Yiddish culture.

The Christian tradition that evidently troubled Jews the most was the one pertaining to the most explicit Jew. Folklorist Bengt af Klintberg describes the Wandering Jew as a "bugaboo" that Christian parents invoked to scare their children on Christmas Eve.[88] Christian parents told their children the frightening story of a Jew who, due to deriding Jesus, was punished by God to wander without rest—except tonight, when the Jew lurks in a plow outside the home, posing a danger to any Christian child who dares to step outside.[89] Jews, we will see, developed their own Christmas *Kinderschreck* tradition to counter the anti-Jewish *Kinderschreck* traditions. Jewish parents told their children the frightening story of the Wandering Jesus on Christmas Eve: from his illegitimate birth, through his astrayment from Judaism and his deceitful charlatanism, to his hanging and fate of wandering in excrement in *gehenem*—except tonight, when Jesus returns to earth to wander in excrement outside the home, posing a danger to any Jewish child who dares step outside.

The earliest recorded allegation of Jewish anti-Jesus sentiment on Christmas, which comes in 1463 from non-Jewish Austrian Professor Thomas Ebendorfer (1388–1464), does not include specific details of a Yiddish Christmas folklore. Ebendorfer spent more of his life condemning how his fellow Christians appeased Holle than condemning the diverging Christmas customs of Jews.⁹⁰ We must then turn to the passages written by the early modern Jewish apostates who exposed the secrets of their former Christmas folklore, as collected by Marc Shapiro. Johannes Pfefferkorn (1469–1523) provides the earliest description in 1511. He begins by describing how Jewish parents read aloud the *"Tholdos Jescho"* on Christmas Eve. *Tholdos Jescho,* which is Hebrew for "The Chronicles of Jesus" (usually transliterated into English as Toledot Yeshu), is a known variant name for the *Mayse Tole,* the Jewish version of the story of Jesus. Following the reading, Pfefferkorn writes, parents picked up the story where the text leaves off. They augmented the finale—dead Jesus wandering the excrement of *gehenem*—with a chilling epilogue about dead Jesus wandering the excrement of earth. Pfefferkorn explains:

> They [Jews] believe and maintain that the lord Jesus, due to his apostasy and false teaching, is punished by God to wander through all the excrement or latrines in the world on this night [Christmas Eve]. I learned this in my youth and believed it. On the evening of *Weihnacht,* I urinated outside the latrine chamber out of fear and worry of the hanged Jesus.⁹¹

We find a similar narrative in the reporting of another Jewish convert to Christianity, Ernst Ferdinand Hess, in 1598:

> The *mamser* [bastard] crawls through all latrines, that is, the whore's child is forced to travel through all excrement and latrine chambers. Therefore, you instill great fear and fright in your young children that they do not go out to the latrine chambers on that night [Christmas Eve], even if they need to go very badly.⁹²

It is confirmed—Jesus played the role of a *Kinderschreck* figure in early modern Yiddish Christmas folklore. It fits that Daniel Barbu, a prominent scholar of Jewish folklore about Jesus, interprets Jesus in these passages as a "bogeyman meant to inspire fear among children."⁹³

By the end of the sixteenth century, a generation of Jewish adults emerged who had learned in their youth that Jesus is among the wandering penitents who return at midwinter. It is at this point in time that Jewish apostates begin to report their former kin ascribing their midwinter merriment to warding off a Wandering Jesus.⁹⁴ Our earliest report comes from apostate Samuel Friedrich Brenz in 1614.[95] After Brenz recounts that the "*Maese Thola*" [*Mayse Tole*] is "read on *Christnacht* in great secret inside [the Jews'] houses,"[96] he describes how Jews use a classic demon repellent, garlic, as a prophylactic:

> The Jews devour much garlic, especially on *Christnacht*. If asked the reason, the answer is that the *Tole*, that is, the Hanged One, is dishonored [. . .]. And they tell their children that God inflicted upon Jesus that on *Christnacht* [. . .] he must crawl out of latrines.[97]

Brenz then goes on to explain why Jews celebrate on Christmas Eve:

> On *Christnacht*, the Jews make merry and eat and drink to excess. The reason they give is that a house full of reading and praying provides the *Tole* with better rest and allows him to crawl into the corners of the house.[98]

Brenz's account is corroborated by another, provided two years later from Jewish-born apostate Dietrich Schwab:

> Jews are not allowed to study or pray at the time of *Weihnacht*, which they call *Nittel*, that is, the Festival of the Hanged One. The reason is that they believe that Christ is in terrible pain on this night and therefore [by not studying or praying] he has no rest or respite.[99]

We thus find that the distinctly Jewish "*nitl*"-*nakht*—the night when Jews granted respite to themselves to deny respite to Jesus—was born by the dawn of the seventeenth century. The anti-Jewish tropes embedded in public Renaissance *Kinderschreck* traditions resulted in Jews reclaiming Christmas as their own anti-Christian festival.

We can glean additional information about the early modern *nitl-nakht* from a *Mayse Tole* manuscript printed in Strasbourg in 1471. This manuscript is presumably similar or identical to what Jewish parents read to their children on Christmas Eve. In contrast to medieval manuscripts of the *Mayse Tole* that end with Christians lamenting Jesus's defeat on Good Friday or *keysekh* [Easter],[100] this early modern manuscript ends with Christians lamenting Jesus's defeat on *Weihnacht*. The manuscript defines *Weihnacht* as the night (*nacht*) when Christians cry (*wein*) to lament Jesus's defeat.[101] Early modern Jewish calendars likewise spell *Weihnacht* as *wein-nacht*, that is, "crying night" (Yiddish transliteration: *veyn-nakht*).[102] It is clear that Jews claimed the merriment of Christmas as unique to them, while Christians were left to spend the longest night of the year crying over Jesus's demise. Jews even came to explain the word *nitl*, under a revised spelling (ניטל instead of ניתל or נידל), as the night when Jesus was "taken away" from the world (i.e. died)—linked to the Hebrew *notal* (נטל) for "took."[103]

By the early modern period, then, Jews could no longer celebrate the same *Nidelnacht* as Christians. Jews needed to believe that *they* were the ones who had reason to celebrate on Christmas Eve, contrasting a pitiful Christian *wein-nacht*.

A Germanic Interreligious Dialogue

The Jewish apostates who provided the quoted reports were obviously not providing objective accounts of Yiddish Christmas folklore. They deliberately sought to contrast the holy Christian *Weihnacht* and *Christnacht* with a markedly unholy Jewish *nitl-nakht*—without acknowledging the unholy Christian *Nidelnacht*. In reality, Christmas Eve was very similar between early modern Christian and Jewish folks: It was a night of merriment. Thuringian folklorist Franz Magnus Böhme (1827–1898) explains how the popular culture of "*Weihnacht*" included not-so-holy gambling:

> At the time of *Weihnacht*, the people of Thuringia would play with a homemade toy (*Torl*) and gamble for nuts. [. . .] This wooden *Torl* had four sides, each marked with a Latin letter that indicated the winning or loss: A = (win) all, H = (win) half, o = nothing and S = set, i.e. the player must set nuts back into the pot. Each player flicked the toy with their thumb and middle finger, causing it to spin on the table until it landed. The side on which it landed determined the player's fate.[104]

The familiar "dreidel" that the Jews gambled with at midwinter was a mere variant of this popular European toy.[105] In Yiddish, the letters marked on the four sides were ג (*g* for *gants* or *gor* = all), ה (*h* for *halb*

= half), ג (*n* for *nit* = nothing), and ש (*sh* for *shtel* = put).[106] Yet the apostates do not mention that Jews and Christians *both* gambled on Christmas Eve. Brenz reports that "Jews make merry and eat and drink to excess" on Christmas Eve as if Christians did not do the same. In a sense, these Christians-by-choice were rewriting the Christmas folk narrative to reassign the unholiness of Christmas to the Jews.

The early modern divergence in Christmas folk traditions between Christians and Jews was therefore not only a divergence in the identity of a *Kinderschreck* figure. Christmas Eve had always been unholy, and in the early modern period, Christians and Jews began to pin this unholiness on each other.

The endeavor to dissociate Christmas unholiness from Christianity was center stage in the Protestant Reformation. Martin Luther (1483–1546) sought to put an end to the un-Christian Christmas folklore that pervaded Christian communities and replace this unholiness with solemn caroling. He was a vocal critic of the folk devotion to Frau Holle, as well as the association of seasonal gift-giving with St. Nicholas instead of Jesus's birth.[107] The Reformation thus promoted an alternative seasonal gift-giver, a "baby Jesus" known as the *Christkindl* (whom we briefly met earlier). This new tradition comprised a girl or young woman dressing as the *Christkindl* and traversing houses to deliver Christmas Eve gifts. To the dismay of Protestant leaders, however, the female *Christkindl* was quickly integrated into the broader *Kinderschreck* traditions of Christmas Eve, merging with fellow lady figure Holle who led the sinful wandering dead.[108] By the late seventeenth century, our sources indicate that the female *Christkindl* was customarily accompanied by a male *Kinderfresser* named *Knecht Ruprecht* [Servant Rupert] who did her dirty work. In a 1668 Nuremberg Christmas procession play, Ruprecht succinctly tells his master that "I, your servant Ruprecht, will brush down [the children who have been bad] and beat them."[109] By the late eighteenth century, records from the Rhenish Palatinate speak of a male escort to the *Christkindl* other than *Knecht Ruprecht*—a covert St. Nicholas himself, disguised in fur and identified as *Pelznickel* [Nicholas in Fur].[110] Johann Christian Hasche (1744–1827) writes that *Pelznickel* was known to "slap girls on their bare bottoms with rods" if they misbehaved.[111] A Christian pamphlet that circulated at the turn of the eighteenth century condemned how the female *Christkindl* had become intertwined with her evil male counterpart and the ghosts of Christmas, resulting in children being terrified of the visiting baby Jesus.[112] The Reformation was therefore far from successful in eradicating Christmas unholiness among the Christian folk, as it had instead caused Christian children to fear a visit from a sinister Jesus on Christmas Eve, just like Jewish children.

With Jesus now effectively a *Kinderschreck* figure for Christians, Jews had the perfect argument for making the case that it was actually the Christians, not the Jews, who were responsible for the unholy Christmas folklore that was going around. Jews had been trying to dissociate themselves from Christmas unholiness ever since the publication of apostate Brenz's unflattering narrative of what Jews do on Christmas Eve. A year after the publication of Brenz's account, a Jew named Solomon Zebi Hirsch published a Yiddish defense that vehemently denied the reported anti-Christian element of Yiddish Christmas folklore. In what Marc Shapiro deems "sheer dishonesty,"[113] Hirsch insists:

> It might happen that a Jew eats garlic on *Christnacht*, since the Christians celebrate for several days and do not deal with us. However, this is not because of *Yishue* the Nazarene. Who would believe such foolishness? [. . .] That we supposedly eat and drink to excess and make merry on *Christnacht* is a complete lie. [. . .] It can sometimes happen that Hanukkah falls at the same time. We eat and drink then, but not because of the foolishness that the apostate said.[114]

Jew-defender Johann Wülfer (1651–1724) elaborated on Hirsch's work in a 1681 Latin translation prepared for Christians. To counter the German reports by Jewish-born Christians that sought to expose Jewish unholiness on Christmas Eve, Wülfer appends a Hebrew report by a Jew who seeks to expose *Christian* unholiness on Christmas Eve:

> On this night, women or girls walk up to the houses and ring bells in their hands. The children are consequently swept by fear and scream bitterly. Their fathers comfort them and tell them, "Have no fear, it is only the *Christkindl*. Go and approach him, and pray to him, and he will not hurt you. On the contrary, he will give you gifts, fruits and sweet things or good clothes" [. . .] but the next day the children say, "Yesterday I was terrorized by the *Christkindl*, and if I hadn't prayed he would have killed me."[115]

The author then asserts that the only reason why some Jewish children may be familiar with a sinister Jesus who visits on Christmas Eve is that they learned of it from their Christian peers. His report was nevertheless insufficient for putting an end to the fad of pinning the Christmas unholiness on the Jews. Jewish apostates continued to write their own German reports to expose what went on in their childhood communities. In 1715, Jewish-born Lothar Franz Fried described how, on "*Geburt Christi*" [Night of Christ's Birth], "no Jew in the entire world is allowed to study any book other than [the *Mayse Tole*]." Instead of studying, Fried writes, Jews play cards, indulge in garlic, and mock the "*mamser ben hanida*" [bastard son of a menstruant, i.e. Jesus].[116] Fried adds that despite all this debauchery, "no Jew sleeps with his wife" on Christmas Eve, because a child conceived on this night would be corrupted to become a "Christian."[117] Two years later, Jewish-born Paul Christian Kirchner reported that Jews play cards and dice through the entire Christmas season for the purpose of mocking Jesus. Several Christians-by-birth confirmed the apostate reports. Johann Jakob Schudt (1664–1722) reports having seen Jews out and "debauched" on the streets of Frankfurt late into the night of Christmas Eve 1712.[118] Andreas Würfel (1718–1769) of Nuremberg reports that Jews engage in this outrageous behavior for five to six weeks, first during Hanukkah, and then for the sake of "*nittal*."[119] Johann Andreas Eisenmenger (1654–1704) of Frankfurt claims to have seen it all: Jews not studying Torah because they hate Christ; a young Jewish boy screaming that he is afraid to go out to the privy; and a Jewish student discussing the *Mayse Tole* with his rabbi.[120]

According to Jewish historian Adolf Eckstein (1857–1935), such accusations went to an extreme on Christmas Eve 1767. On this night, a Jewish apostate by the name of Sensburg attempted to expose the Jews' hedonistic Christmas Eve parties to Christian authorities in Bamberg. At Sensburg's behest, the authorities launched a raid of the town's Jewish homes. Yet the local Jews got wind of the matter ahead of time. They managed to clean up their cards and pull out their holy books before the soldiers arrived, thus avoiding any trouble.[121]

Even the name *nitl-nakht* became a source of trouble for Jews. In 1770, Jewish-born Caspar Joseph Friedenheim reported that Jews refer to "*Christabend*" [Christ Evening] as "*Nittelnacht*." Friedenheim creatively explains this name as a distortion of a Hebrew word for "night of birth," *niled*, into a word that means "hanged night."[122] As Friedenheim spells *Tole* as "*Dola*,"[123] he is effectively claiming that Jews distorted the word *niled* into *nidel* to form the term *Nidelnacht*. This claim is certainly ironic, given that the term *Nidelnacht* was widely used among Christians. The reality of Christmas Eve is that it was common for both Christians and Jews to undermine any holy significance of the evening. They were united in identifying it by an "unholy" name, whether it be *Nidelnacht*, *nitl-nakht*, or other names that contrast with a holy name like *Christabend*. And apparently, they were also united in foisting their individual embarrassments about this Christmas unholiness onto each other.

Conclusion

We have finally arrived at a complete origin theory for *nitl-nakht*, the Yiddish version of Christmas Eve. A long-held scholarly assumption was that the Yiddish folklore pertaining to *nitl-nakht* originally had something to do with the Nativity, known in Latin as *natalis*, reinforcing the idea that *nitl-nakht* etymologically derives from *natalis*. What we uncovered here is quite the opposite. In the medieval period, Christians and Jews appear to have practiced largely undifferentiated midwinter folk customs on the night known as *Nidelnacht*. These customs, which included appeasing Frau Holle with bread and milk, provoked conflict between common folks and religious authorities, but not necessarily between Christians and Jews. It was only in the early modern period when a clear antagonizing element arose in Christmas folklore. Christians and Jews each began to weaponize Christmas as an attack on the other. First, they instituted variations in a shared *Kinderschreck* tradition of spooking children by establishing symbols of the other as the spooky *Kinderschreck* figure. Then, they each blamed the other as responsible for the *Kinderschreck* tradition itself. Nevertheless, despite this antagonistic divergence between the German *Nidelnacht* and the Yiddish "*nitl*"-*nakht*, the two conceptions of Christmas Eve essentially maintained their commonality at their core. Christmas Eve was a night when all folks released their inhibitions and rebelled against religious routine. The irreverent *nitl-nakht* was just one side of Christmas's irreverent Jewish–Christian coin.

4

An Eastern European Jewish Christmas

At the turn of the nineteenth century, the leading rabbi of Europe lost his patience with Jews celebrating Christmas. Moses Sofer (1762–1839), a founder of strictly Orthodox Judaism, was irritated that his fellow Jews would take a night off from their Torah study to carouse and play games. Such behavior had no place in Jewish culture on any occasion, let alone on a holiday that did not belong in the Jewish calendar.[1] Sofer did not appreciate that Jews had no choice but to vacation from their study on Christmas Eve, or else their archenemy Jesus would be relieved of his suffering and unleash his wrath on the Jewish people. Yiddish Christmas lore circulated among the common folk, and elitist rabbis did not always take it seriously.[2]

Rabbis were not only troubled by the Christmas Eve carousing, but they were also confused. Some rabbis tried to come up with a rational explanation of how this Jewish Christmas behavior came about. Sofer's teacher, Nathan Adler (1741–1800), noted that Jews traditionally abstain from Torah study and sex when in mourning. Adler therefore suggested that Jews spend Christmas Eve mourning the lives lost due to the birth of Christ.[3] This explanation made little sense to Sofer. If Jews were truly mourning on Christmas Eve, the evening would involve other mourning customs, and certainly not merriment. Sofer was also perplexed by why Jews suddenly resumed their Torah study at midnight. In a Hebrew letter, Sofer expressed his frustration that he had never heard an "acceptable" explanation for why Jews did not study Torah on the eve of "their" (Christians') holiday. He went on to propose his own explanation. Jews historically set their books aside on Christmas Eve, according to Sofer, so that they could go to sleep early. They would then be sufficiently rested to begin vigorous Torah study at the stroke of midnight. This practice, he writes, allows Jews to avoid the poor image of being asleep while Christians are celebrating Midnight Mass. The Jews' other Christmas Eve practices, such as abstaining from sex, are "nonsensical" and should be abolished.[4]

In keeping with this view, Sofer attempted to eradicate the frivolous Christmas festivities in his community. He explicitly prohibited card-playing on Christmas Eve, threatening a fine as penalty. Sofer explains in another Hebrew letter that he was successful at putting an end to this cardplaying, but he was far from successful in convincing Jews to go to sleep early. No longer allowed to play cards, the Jews are said to have become enveloped in Yiddish gossip and arguments during their Christmas Eve carousing. Sofer was so frustrated with this behavior that he ultimately reinstated an authorization to play cards on Christmas Eve as the lesser evil. Sofer's view came to be that only the most serious Torah scholars must avoid playing cards, conceding that there was no stopping the Jewish masses from reveling on Christmas Eve.[5]

Sofer's report serves as attestation that Christmas Eve merriment was remarkably deep-seated in the Yiddish folk culture of his time. It further demonstrates continuity following the earlier apostate reports from the early modern Germanic Ashkenaz region: Sofer is reporting from the end of the early modern period near the eastern border of Ashkenaz (by the junction of Austria, Czechia, and Slovakia), around the same time that Ashkenazic Jewry proliferated on the eastern side of this border following feudalism's shift eastward,[6] with Eastern European Jews ultimately coming to produce the Yiddish Christmas anecdotes that opened this book. Marc Shapiro notes that even many Torah scholars in Eastern Europe refused to study Torah on Christmas Eve, including Sofer's own leading students.[7]

The answer to the fourth question on our agenda, then—did Eastern European Jews really celebrate Christmas?—seems to be yes, albeit Jews understood their celebration as for the sake of Jesus's affliction rather than Jesus's honor. Nevertheless, given that the idea of Eastern European Jews celebrating Christmas is so contradictory to conventional wisdom, we cannot convincingly answer this question until we analyze a larger assortment of firsthand accounts of what Eastern European Jews did on Christmas. Historians usually rely on the Hebrew rabbinic literature to trace Jewish history, but such literature is not going to be very helpful here, since the rabbis who penned this literature were not always in the full loop of Yiddish Christmas folklore or willing to write about it publicly. As Marc Shapiro points out, "When one remembers how dangerous it could have been had the Gentile community found out" about the

Jews' anti-Jesus Christmas traditions, "it is obvious" that these traditions cannot "be illustrated through an examination of [the public rabbinic] Jewish sources."[8] To compound the issue, Jewish immigrants often flatly denied that they were engaged with Christmas in the Old World, meaning that we also cannot rely on the oral traditions that immigrants have passed down to contemporary Jews. Fortunately, around the turn of the twentieth century, a secular Jewish literature emerged parallel to the rabbinic literature. This secular literature, largely in Yiddish (and to a lesser extent Hebrew), includes nonfiction materials such as memoirs and ethnographic accounts of Yiddish folk life in Eastern Europe. These materials are almost entirely unexplored and can be invaluable for helping us uncover the secret Jewish Christmas traditions of Eastern Europe.[9]

This chapter reviews Christmas anecdotes from Yiddish folk life in Eastern Europe between the late nineteenth century and the outbreak of World War II. It argues that, while Eastern European Jews did not celebrate "Christ's Mass," they did celebrate Christmas in a general sense. Eastern European Jews had a deeply ingrained system of beliefs about vacationing from religious routine on Christmas Eve, rendering Christmas festivities a requisite part of Jewish life—and commonly regarded as the most fun part of Jewish life. This chapter ultimately shows that the Eastern European Jewish activities that went about on Christmas Eve should not be interpreted as an attack on a foreign Christian holiday, despite some Jews having justified it as such. The reality is that Eastern European Jews looked forward to Christmas as if it were a holiday compatible with their own Jewish culture.

Christmas Beliefs in Eastern Europe

Before we attempt to interpret the Christmas Eve pause that Eastern European Jews put on their studies, we need to make sure we understand their own rationale for this activity. Back in Germanic Ashkenaz, Jews believed that continuing their Torah study would provide relief to a Jesus who wanders the excrement outside their homes. Yet the fear of being attacked by physically wandering revenants did not pervade Eastern Europe like it did the West. Eastern Europeans were more infatuated with werewolves and vampires than wandering revenants. How did Jews incorporate their traditional Christmas folklore into the Christmas of Eastern Europe?

For context, it is relevant that Jews played an important role within the Slavic Christmas folklore of Christians. Folklorists have recorded a wide variety of magical rituals that Eastern European Christians practiced during their garlic-heavy Christmas Eve supper to protect against unclean forces.[10] Since Christians traditionally viewed Jews as filthy, many Christians believed that Jews function as shields that can absorb the unclean forces. Hence, Christians often viewed Jews as propitious at midwinter.[11] On the day of Christmas Eve, Christians in Eastern Europe customarily invited Jews to join their Christmas celebrations as a *polaznik*, that is, a stranger guest who brings good luck for the coming year.[12] Accordingly, Jewish memoirists frequently recall prewar Christmas Eve activities such as attending their Christian neighbors' Christmas Eve suppers, being treated to festive Christmas foods, and (according to one Yiddish memoir) joining Christians in attending Christmas Eve Masses.[13] When Jews did not accept these invitations, Christians still generally insisted that Jews supply them with a course for their Christmas Eve supper. Christians traditionally believed that Jewish-made foods had garlic-like protective power against demons.[14] Since Christians were not permitted to eat meat at this supper (due to the Nativity fast), Jews typically supplied Christians with jars of what Poles called *ryba po żydowsku* [Jewish-style fish], known in Yiddish as *gefilte fish*. Polish folklorist Franciszek Kotula (1900–1983) notes that Jews would provide Christians with *ryba po żydowsku* as a "gift,"[15] although Jews did not necessarily have a choice in supplying the fish gratuitously. Hirsz Abramowicz (1881–1960), a Jew from what is now Lithuania, explains:

> At *kaleyd* [*Kalėdos*; a Lithuanian term for Christmas], since Christians needed fish for the fast on *nitl*, the Jewish fisherman had to "give up the ghost" and provide for all landowners, police officers, forest clerks, community writers, village mayors and the like. Otherwise, they would all "pick on" him, not let him fish, and make a law that any fish he catches is an "illegal catch."[16]

Ryba po żydowsku remains a standard Christmas Eve dish among Polish Catholics today.[17]

For both Catholic and Orthodox Christians, the Christmas Eve supper traditionally commenced as soon as the first star appeared in the sky in the late afternoon.[18] Then, Christians spent the long hours between the early supper and the late church service making merry to ward off unclean forces. The merriment included musical caroling, although this caroling was very different from the contemporary Western conception of Christmas caroling. Folklorist Harry Senn (1939–2017) explains that these Eastern European Christmas carols had "nothing to do with the Christian Christmas."[19] He describes the Eastern European Christmas Eve as follows:

> Confederations of young unmarried men parade through Eastern European villages singing ritual hymns (called *colinde*) and performing dances, accompanied by musicians and others wearing animal masks. [. . .] Christmas Eve celebrations included participants in wolf costumes that raced through the onlookers teasing and tormenting them [. . .] to dramatize the abrupt appearance of wandering invisible spirits.[20]

Andrei Oişteanu adds that the tormented onlookers were sometimes dressed as Jews or the Devil, to dramatize the spirits chasing after filthy creatures.[21] The extent to which real Jews participated in the caroling is not clear. According to memoirist Jonah Rosenfeld (1880–1944), "Anybody who has lived in Russia knows of this [Christmas caroling] custom," and "Jewish children too put on masks and paraded the streets."[22] However, Rosenfeld's anecdote of Jewish masquerading takes place on Christmas Day rather than Christmas Eve. Most memoirs of Christmas Eve recount Jews simply giving out coins and treats to the Christian carolers who knocked on their doors (analogous to modern trick-or-treating). In Yiddish stories set on Christmas Eve, the carolers are typically described as drunk Christians dressed in fur and animal skins, and Jewish characters rarely go out to join them.[23] Some memoirs describe the carolers as peasants who brought wheat or barley to Jewish homes, delivering blessings for the new year.[24] The peasants sought Jewish-made prophylactic foods in return, and Jews were known to hand them braided *khale* (challah/*chała*) bread.[25] This braided bread remains a popular holiday treat in Poland today, known by the diminutive *chałka*.[26]

Our question is what went on inside the Jewish doors while the Christians were caroling outside. Just as Christians associated unclean midwinter forces with Jews, Jews associated the unclean forces with Jesus.

Jewish memoirist Salcia Landmann (1911–2002), from what was then Galicia and now western Ukraine, recalls that in addition to sharing the "Slavic popular belief" that "evil spirits and demons" roam on Christmas Eve, Jews also refrained from study on this night to avoid "honoring Jesus."[27] What does this mean?

Let us turn to a major Jewish ethnographic study conducted in Eastern Europe between 1912 and 1914, headed by Yiddish folklorist S. Ansky (1863–1920). A member of Ansky's team, Abraham Rechtman (1890–1972), recorded the following belief from a town in the Volhynia province of the Russian Empire (now western Ukraine):

> The "*Yoyzl*" (Jesus) was a Jew and studied Torah. [. . .] On the "*nitl*"-*nakht* [. . .] he is annually tried in the Heavenly Court. Therefore, if Jews engage in Torah study on that night, that can remind the court how he, the *oyse ho'ish*, studied, which can serve as a defense for him. Thus Jews must absolutely not study that night in any way, in order not to awaken merit in the Nazarene.[28]

This explanation for why Jews paused their study on Christmas Eve certainly seems convoluted. Yet it is perfectly consistent with Jewish mystical tradition, which was deeply interwoven with Yiddish folklore. A widespread mystical belief was that if a living Jew studies the same Torah passage that a deceased Jew once studied, the deceased Jew will repeat this Torah passage in his grave. The Heavenly Court will then reward this deceased Jew with a *tikn*—a spiritual rectification to be made fit for heaven (*ganeydn*)—so that he no longer suffers in *gehenem*.[29]

A search through Yiddish memoirs of Jewish men who grew up in Eastern Europe consistently turns up this same rationale for not studying Torah on Christmas Eve. For example, Solomon Simon (1895–1970), from the Minsk province of the Russian Empire, writes:

> The *Tole* was an apostate Jew, a big studier, a true scholar, therefore there is no learning in *kheyder* on the night of *nitl* [. . .] in order for the merit of the Torah not to support him and ease his suffering.[30]

Another memoirist, Harry Bloom (1887–1960) from Congress Poland, writes:

The students were completely free of studying on the so-called "*nitl-nakht*," in order to spite the "*oyse-ho'ish*" (*Yishu*), who would, God forbid, receive a "*tikn*" if we were to study.[31]

This belief is repeated throughout Yiddish memoirs.[32] It is even quickly mentioned as a common folk belief in an 1887 work of Hebrew rabbinic literature published in Warsaw,[33] which Isaac Rivkind cites as consistent with what Jewish boys learned at *kheyder* across Eastern Europe.[34] So there we have it. *Nitl-nakht* essentially functioned as the antithesis to the Jewish holiday of Shavuos, when Eastern European Jews studied Torah all night to outpour *tikn* after *tikn*. Notably, Jews also traditionally studied extra Torah on the anniversary of a Torah scholar's death in order to provide him with a *tikn*. It fits that Jews refrained from studying any Torah at all on the night of *nitl*—as described earlier, Jews understood the night of *nitl* as the night when Jesus was "taken away" from the world—although some Jews eventually embraced the mainstream narrative that Jesus was born rather than died on Christmas, as we will later see.

We now turn to the archives of the YIVO Institute for Jewish Research, which include responses to a 1926 ethnographic call for submissions on Yiddish Christmas folk traditions.[35] Jeffrey Shandler previously quoted some of these responses in his scholarship on Jews and Christmas, but we will reassess them here in light of the newly uncovered context. The responses reveal that Jews believed Jesus to be one of the "wandering invisible spirits" of Christmas Eve, as per Senn's above description. A YIVO informant from the Volhynian town of Trisk recalls children saying that "*Yosl Pondrik* flies around" on Christmas Eve.[36] Similarly, a YIVO informant who grew up in Galicia tells us that "on the *nitl-nakht* [. . .] we would not go to *kheyder* because '*Yosl Pondrik*' flies around on that night."[37] The belief that Jesus can fly derives from the *Mayse Tole*, which features a climactic aerial battle between Jesus and Judas after they each recite God's ineffable name and use its powers to fly.[38] Benzion Hoffman (1874–1954) summarizes this famous scene, which duly keeps with the theme of filth, as that Jesus "recites the ineffable name to fly like a bird in the sky, but Judas recites the name to fly even higher so that he can pee on him, causing [Jesus] to fall back to the ground."[39]

The folklore we have seen thus far comes from Jewish boys and men. What about the women? Since Jewish men spent much of their lives discussing Hebrew literature, Yiddish folklore was most strongly associated with women. We should expect women to have played an important role in the development of Yiddish Christmas folklore. And indeed, our informant from Trisk tells us that women taught him two potential consequences if a Jew did open a holy Jewish book (a "*seyfer*") to study on Christmas Eve. The first consequence, as one woman told our Trisk informant, is that Jesus would "hide in the *seyfer* and refuse to leave" and proclaim that he "also studied it."[40] This belief apparently developed in areas of Congress Poland as a parody of carolers traversing houses and refusing to leave until they received money, as evidenced by the description of a YIVO informant from Warsaw:

> There was no studying in either *kheyder*, *besmedresh* [study hall], or *yeshive* [higher-learning institute]. This was motivated by Christ having been a great scholar and having studied a lot. As soon as one would study on "*nitl*," he would ask for money for the time he studied.[41]

The second consequence of opening a *seyfer* on Christmas Eve, as another woman taught our Trisk informant, relates to Jesus's infamous association with excrement: "When one opens a *seyfer*, he 'befouls' it."[42] This belief apparently developed in southern Ukrainian regions where Jews knew *nitl-nakht* as *blinde nakht*, "blind night." Here the dark night's caroling processions featured blind minstrels playing the lira, a Ukrainian plucked-string instrument.[43] Abraham Goldberg (1883–1942), from the Podolia province of Russia, describes how on the *blinde nakht* "children did not go to *kheyder* or open any *seyfer*, because he [Jesus] flies around on that night and defiles the holy *sforim* [plural of *seyfer*]."[44] We hear more about *blinde nakht* in a response to a question posed in a 1943 issue of YIVO's American journal *Yidishe Shprakh* [*Yiddish Language*]. Lithuanian Jewish linguist Yudl Mark (1897–1975) asked if any readers had heard the term *blinde nakht* for *nitl*.[45] Philip Frimer (1895–1969), a Brooklyn painter from Podolia's capital city of Komenets, responded with "Well, sure, in Komenets and all of Podolia":

> On the *blinde nakht* we did not go to *kheyder* at night. Studying is forbidden on the *blinde nakht*. It is forbidden to even open a *seyfer*, or else he (the *Yoyzl*) will come and defecate in it. You don't believe me? "I tried to

be a wise guy," a young boy told me, "I opened my Uncle Israel's *seyfer*, and it had to be thrown out!"⁴⁶

(The 1997 Christmas episode of *South Park*, which follows a Jew who practices a Christmas tradition of singing about feces, turns out to be more historically accurate than the writers likely knew.)⁴⁷ Frimer goes on to explain that in Podolia, "a simple person did not know the word '*nitl*,' but *blinde nakht*—a baby in its cradle!"⁴⁸

Jesus was not only busy soiling or hiding inside holy books on Christmas Eve. He would also pollute any uncovered pots of liquids. As described earlier, Jews long believed that demonic forces pollute unprotected liquids during the four quarterly *tkufes*. They believed that "*tume*"—uncleanliness—reigns during these periods. They protected liquids from *tume* by placing pieces of iron atop the covered vessels, as iron was a classic European antidote for counteracting demonic pollution.⁴⁹ A YIVO informant from the Volhynian town of Lutsk describes the "night of *nitl*" custom of covering "all liquids with iron so that they are not desecrated by the *tume*."⁵⁰ Galician author Abraham Moshe Fuchs (1890–1974) provides a more detailed description in a 1924 Yiddish fiction story set on the *blinde nakht*:

> Tonight is the *blinde nakht*. The *Yoyzl* flies around the world tonight and desecrates everything, soiling Jewish homes with his wings. Jewish women drop a little piece of iron over flasks of water and a nail over cups of milk so that the *tume* does not reign supreme.⁵¹

The fear of *tume* was indeed closely associated with women. A 1959 Yiddish story mentions a prewar Jewish custom of "pouring out water on the night of the *tkufe* [to eschew contamination]," and an accompanying English translation is worded as that "women" pour out the water.⁵² Even the local Christians knew that women were the main Jewish *tume* fighters. In a 1920 issue of the American *Lutheran Companion*, Christian missionary John Resnick (1874–1924) presents his understanding of the Jews' "Blind Night" in his heavily Jewish-populated Ukrainian hometown:

> The orthodox Jewess never fails to put some piece of iron into her kitchen utensils—this is to prevent the child Jesus, who is supposed to take a

flying-tour on that very night over the whole earth, from coming into her home and defiling her pots and pans.[53]

How exactly would Jesus pollute unprotected pots and pans? Moshe Sambatyon (1913–1986), from what is now northern Moldova, recalls that on the night of *nitl* the "*oyse ho'ish* floats in a 'cauldron of boiling excrement' in the air and pollutes the mouths of babies,"[54] but it turns out that the pollutant that Jesus would drop into liquids was something other than feces. Dov Sadan (1902–1989) reports that on the *blinde nakht* in his Galician hometown, Jews needed to turn casks of water upside down, or cover them with linen, or else they would wake up the next morning to find "a red stripe or a red ribbon—a sign of blood."[55] Likewise, a 1917 English-language American story by Romanian-born Jewish author Edward Eliscu (1884–1959) provides the following description of the "Blind Night":

> It was the night that he, whom the Gentiles worshipped, was wont to fly over the earth, and wherever he discovered uncovered articles he would leave a mark of blood. Therefore, the women folks were especially instructed to see to it that all vessels containing milk, cream, fats, preserves and other things eatable, were kept covered and a piece of iron placed thereon, otherwise the streak of blood would appear and render the food unfit to eat.[56]

The belief that Jesus drops his blood as a pollutant is an inversion of the Christian belief that Jesus's blood is a cleanser. It was also associated with the pan-European belief that all water turns to wine at midnight on Christmas Eve. A YIVO informant of Yiddish Christmas folklore from a town north of Warsaw explains that "all liquids are covered with a little piece of iron, as it was believed that if liquids are not covered they are transformed into Jesus's blood."[57] Meir Wilkansky (1882–1994), a Hebrew author from the Vilna province (where *Yoshke* was known as *Yoske*), adds the following narrative:

> The gentiles believe in the divinity of *Yoske Pandre*. That we crucified him. They made the day of *nitl* their own holiday. But we are the ones who know: On the night of *nitl*, all water turns to blood; and this can only be prevented by placing iron over the water beforehand.[58]

Yet not all Jews knew that this blood belongs to Jesus. The Yiddish folk-lore documented further west (in Prussia and western Congress Poland) describes the Christmas Eve pollutant as Lilith's menstrual blood.[59] Jews traditionally believed that Christmas Eve is given over to Lilith's hus-band Samoel (i.e. the Devil),[60] and the belief that Lilith (rather than Jesus) drops blood may be related to the enduring Germanic belief that the main Christmas Eve visitor is a supernatural woman. Jews first iden-tified blood as a Christmas Eve pollutant, as well as a pollutant on the other three *tkufes*, all the way back in the high medieval period, long before Jesus entered the folklore. Some Christians too believed that flowing water turns to blood on Christmas Eve, just as they believed it does on other solstices and equinoxes.[61] The belief originally arose to make sense of the red spots that appear shortly after midsummer on the plant known as St. John's Wort. High medieval Christians believed these spots to be drops of blood from the beheading of John the Baptist, so they covered wells during the summer solstice to prevent the water from being contaminated with St. John's blood.[62] High medieval Jews likewise came to believe that blood is dropped at midsummer, claim-ing this blood to have flown out of the rock that Moses smote during the exodus from Egypt (Numbers 20:11).[63] The association of the *tkufes* with flowing blood ultimately resulted in yet another Yiddish Christmas folk belief, this one particularly widespread in northeastern Europe: If a knife is stuck into the earth on Christmas Eve, blood will pour out.[64] Yiddish folklorist S. Ansky interprets the belief as follows:

> If a knife is stuck in the earth on the night of Christ's birthday (*nitl*), blood spills out. Do I even need to explain what underlies this belief? Obviously, the Jew feels that the earth has soaked up so much Jewish blood since the birth of Christ that blood pours out wherever the earth is pierced.[65]

It is not clear whether many Jews shared Ansky's interpretation of this belief, as Ansky is in the middle of defending the anti-Christ element of Yiddish folklore rather than providing an objective testimony. What is clear, however, is the pertinence of Christmas to Eastern European Jews. Jews did not merely note Christmas in their calendars. An enormous web of Yiddish folk beliefs about Christmas was deeply entrenched in Eastern European Jewish culture.

The Most Wonderful Time of Year

Given all of the harrowing reasons to avoid religious routine on Christmas Eve, Eastern Europe Jews made merry instead, succumbing to the human drive to bring light to this long night. A look through the Yiddish literature reveals that Jews, like Christians, viewed Christmas as the most wonderful time of year. This attitude was especially prevalent among men, who enjoyed a singular vacation from Torah study while their wives exhorted about *tume*. Isaac Rivkind notes that, with the exception of ultrahardline rabbis like Sofer, "even those observant Jews who were opposed to playing on Hanukkah would permit playing on *nitl*."[66] He explains:

> The custom to make merry on *nitl* was accepted by just about everybody, even the most religious and observant. It goes without saying that the simple and common folks also participated in the merriment. Many of the great Jewish sages, from the great rabbis to the most pious mystics— who would never otherwise touch a card in their entire lives, who were devoted entirely to Torah and worship—would make merry on *nitl* and play all sorts of games.[67]

This merriment is fondly recalled in many Yiddish memoirs of Jewish men from Eastern Europe. A memoirist from the Polish town of Stashev singles out *nitl-nakht* as a special joy of his youth, when "it was a mitzvah to play with dreidels or even . . . cards."[68] A memoirist from the Volhynian town of Ratne likewise singles out "the night of *nitl*" as an exceptionally joyous occasion, when his otherwise angry and abusive teacher at *kheyder* would entertain gleeful students with dominoes.[69] Yechezkel Kotik (1847–1921), from the Belarussian town of Kamenets Litovsk, recalls that the merriment began on Hanukkah and peaked on *nitl*, when "it was a mitzvah to play cards and not study any Torah at all."[70] Naftoli Gross (1896–1956), from the Galician town of Kolomaye, affirms that his teacher played cards with students on *nitl-nakht* "for the sake of fulfilling the mitzvah."[71] Those who knew *nitl-nakht* as *blinde nakht* convey similar enthusiasm. Philip Frimer (1895–1969) from the Podolian city of Komenets writes that "on the *blinde nakht* we used to play all sorts of games and cards."[72] Closer to Kiev, David Cohen

(1895–1972) of Shpole describes the *blinde nakht* as a night "of great jubilation" in which "all sorts of games and debaucheries are allowed."[73] Dovid-Leyb Naymark (1891–1960), from the Polish city of Shedlits, expresses the Jewish joy of Christmas Eve at length:

> The *kheyder*-boys regained consciousness and breathed a sigh of relief. Despite the piercing frost outside, the boys were swept with warmth. Quite something! Not only was there no studying for the entire evening, but the *rebe* [teacher], the strict and pious *rebe*, allowed cardplaying, something that he otherwise looked down upon as *bitl toyre*, the greatest sin.[74]

David Frischmann (1859–1922) from Lodz expresses this joy further:

> *Nitl* was my favorite holiday of them all. I would wait for it all year long. [. . .] It was a mitzvah, an honest mitzvah *not* to study. [. . .] My whole little heart would quiver and flutter and my soul would almost jump from my body due to so much delight. And not only not studying [. . .] but also playing cards![75]

There was no other Jewish holiday on which cardplaying was so universally permitted let alone encouraged, not even joyous occasions like new moons and Purim. And not even Hanukkah. As Samson Erdberg (1891–1962) of northern Poland points out, the only day of Hanukkah on which it was considered a "mitzvah" to play cards was the one that might overlap with *nitl*.[76] Zalmen Kotler (1874–1953) of eastern Galicia laments that "we [*kheyder* boys] could not even be happy on the [other] days of Hanukkah" because studying had to continue.[77] Jewish boys were customarily let out of *kheyder* early on each afternoon of Hanukkah (just before sunset),[78] but they were still required to adhere to the Torah and recite Hebrew prayers at home, and might even be called back to the *kheyder* to resume study afterward.[79] On the contrary, Tobias Golombek (1903–1977) emphasizes that "the only way Jews 'participated' in the holiday [of Christmas] was that children were free from studying on the '*blinde nakht.*'"[80] A notable recurring theme in Yiddish memoirs is that boys would attempt to prolong the night's merriment by skipping *kheyder* on Christmas Day or earlier on the day of Christmas Eve.[81] As one memoirist puts it, Jewish boys "wished that the [*blinde nakht*] would last the entire winter."[82]

The Jewish Christmas merriment was not restricted to *kheyder* boys. It extended to venerable Torah scholars. A woman describing memories of her pious grandfather in Poland notes that "I never saw him doing anything at home other than studying—except the night of *nitl*."[83] Jewish scholar Samuel Krauss (1866–1948) explains that all Jews, young and old, "zealously worship the game" on Christmas Eve, adding that "it goes without saying that this does not happen without feasting."[84] Nor did it happen without heavy drinking. An 1867 article in an Odessa-based Yiddish paper describes the atmosphere in a town study hall (*besmedresh*) on Christmas Eve: Jews bingeing on beer and vodka while playing cards and casting lots.[85] A memoirist from the Belarussian city of Slutsk recalls a drunk pious Jew dancing on Christmas Eve who proclaimed that "tonight is the *nitl-nakht* and it is a mitzvah to dance as much as the heart desires."[86] Belarussian-born Zalman Shneour (1887–1959) simply defines *nitl* as the holiday when pious Jews gather together to drink and sing.[87] Shmuel-Mortkhe Zeltshen (1885–1960), who lived in the Russian interior in his young adulthood, recalls a year (1905) when Christmas coincided with the tenth of the Jewish month of *Teyves*. In Jewish tradition, the tenth of *Teyves* is a solemn day for commemorating the Babylonian siege of Jerusalem. Yet the Jews are said to have gotten just as drunk on this Christmas Eve as they would get on Purim. Zeltshen describes that he thus "learned that *nitl* even overrides the tenth of *Teyves*."[88] While rabbis such as Sofer advocated for Jews to return to their studies at midnight, it is likely that many Jews took the drunken party straight to bed, as evidenced by the rabbinic texts urging Jews to continue to resist sex after midnight.[89]

The Jewish Christmas Eve parties were not segregated from the Christian festivities. As we saw, Eastern European peasants traditionally spent the night intermixing with Jews, eating Jewish foods, and masquerading as Jews to ward off unclean forces. Jewish memoirist Golde Gutman (1906–1983), from what is now northern Moldova, recalls how Jewish women and girls mingled with masqueraded Christian carolers:

> An old gentile pours some wheat onto the floor and gives a blessing for the new year. The gentiles sing and frolic, tapping sticks on their faces.

Some wear beards and *peyes* [Jewish sidelocks]; others simply go crazy with coarse noses and lips and colored glasses. Their leader, a nice boy, is dressed as an officer, like an emperor. Next to him is a beautiful girl, the emperor's wife, draped with all sorts of ribbons.[90]

Gutman does not seem perturbed by the carolers' Jewface and antisemitic costumes, viewing them as part of the Christmas fun. She explains that, in return, her mother reminded her to "lay an iron nail on top of the can of oil so that the *goyishe Yoyzl* doesn't defile it."[91] Rusyn memoirist Teodor Gocz (1929–2018), from a village near the eastern Polish–Slovakian border, recalls that Jews would even get "angry" if the Christian carolers did not visit and rejoice with them for Christmas.[92] On the other hand, Jewish memoirist Joachim Schoenfeld (1895–1995), from what is now southwestern Ukraine, provides a less enthralled account of the carolers. While he praises that Christians "treated their Jewish colleagues to kutyiah" (a sweet grain dish that marked the start of the Ukrainian Christmas Eve supper),[93] he criticizes how they would disrupt the Jews' private Christmas Eve parties and go after their booze:

> Although the Jews wanted only to be left alone, most of the carolers had the temerity to knock at the Jewish doors, and when allowed in performed anti-Semitic plays mocking Jews. They brought in the crèche [figures representing the Nativity scene] and demanded, for their carol singing, vodka and money, which they received as a form of ransom, so that they could be gotten rid of.[94]

Since he writes in English, Schoenfeld omits mentioning that Jews had their own fun mocking Jesus. Many Yiddish accounts describe Jews gathering away from the carolers to recount their captivating story of the life of Jesus, the *Mayse Tole*. One informant describes how, in the late nineteenth century,

> a tiny light would flicker near the stove in the *besmedresh*. Jews, young and old, would gather around a table, and one would read aloud the legend of "*Yoysef Pandre*."[95]

A similar account is found in the memoirs of a Jewish boy from Galicia:

With curiosity and awe we would await the *"blinde" nakht*, when the *"Yoyzl"* was born. Jews were not allowed to study and the *kheyder* was closed. On that evening, we would gather outside the *kheyder* and tell all sorts of fantastic stories about the *"Yoyzl,"* about the evil force that ruled over the night.[96]

An additional memoirist recalls that "the young folks play cards or 'dreidel' while the old Jews tell the *Mayse Tole*."[97] The Christmas season was accordingly the time when Jewish children first learned about Jesus. A memoirist from a town north of Warsaw, in describing *kheyder* boys learning about *"Yosl Pondrik,"* points out that this learning took place in "the time of *nitl*."[98] Zvi Kanar (1929–2009), from a Polish town further south, remembers that "on the day before *nitl*, the *rebe* [teacher] at *kheyder* would pull out a book and tell us all about the *oyse ho'ish*."[99] Benzion Hoffman (1874–1954) from Latvia writes that "we had so much fun listening to the *rebe* read us the *Mayse nitl* [*Mayse Tole*]," highlighting the part of the story where "Jewish women throw cabbage heads at 'him' [Jesus] and kill him [by hanging him on a cabbage stalk]."[100] (The Hebrew reading of the Scroll of Esther on Purim, which recounts Haman's demise by mere hanging on a tree, was paltry in comparison.) Women also participated in the telling of the *Mayse Tole*. Israel Julius Aschheim (1851–1925) of California recalls that he was told this story "on each recurring Nittel night by my sainted [European] grandmother, when she rocked me on her lap."[101]

The Christmastime stories that Jews told about Jesus were directly intertwined with the Christmas Eve merriment. Jewish-born Alexander Alekseev (1820–1895) reports that, on the *blinde nakht* in his Podolian hometown, Jews played cards to "ward off" Jesus during his *tume*-filled trip around the world.[102] Benzion Hoffman elaborates that "playing cards strengthens the night's *tume* and thereby intensifies 'his' [Jesus's] punishment in the afterlife."[103] Chaim Zhitlowsky (1865–1943), from Russia's Vitebsk province, provides an alternative explanation of why cardplaying harms Jesus:

> *Yoyzl* [. . .] seeks annual forgiveness so that he can be allowed to return to earth. He shows that his *tume* did not have power over the Jews, the proof being that Jews are in the *besmedresh* studying Torah. But what do

we [Jews] do? We close our holy books and play cards. He is humiliated and dragged further into *gehenem*.[104]

Hoffman and Zhitlowsky's rationales for Jewish Christmas merriment are consistent with mainstream Jewish mystical beliefs about *tume*. Conversely, many of their fellow "Litvaks"—Jews from what is now mostly Belarus, Lithuania, southern Latvia, and northeastern Poland—did not subscribe to mysticism. Nonmystical Litvaks did not maintain the stories about an evil flying Jesus who defiles the world on Christmas Eve, nor did they maintain the dogma that studying Torah on Christmas Eve would relieve Jesus's suffering in *gehenem*. Some hardline Litvak rabbinic sages, known as Misnagdim ["opponents" (of mystics)], insisted that studying in Litvak *yeshives* continue through Christmas Eve.[105] Nevertheless, many Litvak folks managed to justify a Christmas Eve vacation from study via the Jewish principle of *letsonuse d'avoyde zore*: permission to engage in jestful activity on the condition that it is to make fun of idolatry and gentile worship.[106] They maintained that it is permissible to recount the *Mayse Tole* and engage in unholy behavior on Christmas Eve, on the grounds that this behavior mocks the coinciding night's Christian celebration of the Nativity. Isaac Dov Berkowitz (1885–1967), from the Belarussian city of Slutsk, provides such an anecdote. He describes that he learned the *Mayse Tole* at *kheyder* on the day of *nitl*, "the day of the *Yoyzl*,"[107] and then gives the following explanation for why he played cards that night:

> On this night the gentiles go to church, pray and bow to the idol of the *Yoyzl* and ring the bells. And we Jews made a rule that we are not allowed to study Torah on the night of *nitl* [to contrast with the idolatrous devoutness], and, with nothing to do for the entire night, we can play cards.[108]

Kalman Marmor (1876–1956), from the Lithuanian town of Mayshigola, similarly reports that frivolous Jewish cardplaying contrasts with devout Christian idolatry:

> My grandfather never played cards. I was therefore astonished when he told me one evening that I should not study but rather play cards with him. This happened on the night of "*nitl*." My grandfather explained to

me that the "*Yoyzl*" was born on that night, a former Jew who claimed to be the Messiah. The Christians believe in this claim. Jews, however, [. . .] know that the Messiah is yet to arrive. Jews therefore do not study any Torah on this night of *nitl* but instead engage in such frivolous activities as cardplaying.[109]

Hence, Christmas Eve merriment was so pervasive in Eastern European Jewish folk culture that even nonmystical Litvaks were unable to avoid this behavior, justifying it as an intellectual statement instead of rejecting it. Replacing Torah study with merriment on Christmas Eve was simply a fact of life for Eastern European Jewish folks.

An Extensive Yiddish Christmas Folklore

Given the popularity of Christmas in Yiddish folk culture, it follows that Yiddish had an extensive folklore about Christmas beyond the beliefs and merrymaking traditions that have been described thus far. I will use this section to describe some other features of Yiddish Christmas folklore. For one thing, the word *nitl* was a topic itself in Yiddish folklore. The Yiddish word *nit* means "not," and an "*l*" suffix in Yiddish denotes a diminutive, so Jews typically interpreted the Yiddish name *nitl* as a diminutive of "nothing night."[110] Alternatively, some maintained that the "*l*" stands for *lernen* [studying] such that *nitl* is shorthand for *nit lernen* [not studying] or *nit torn lernen* [not allowed studying].[111] Others maintained that *nitl* is an acronym for *nit idn torn lernen* [Jews not allowed studying] or *nit idn toyre lernen* [Jews not studying Torah].[112] Based on these folk etymologies, it is clear that Jews considered the word *nitl* to be a fun nickname for the Jewish celebration on Christmas Eve, rather than a term for the Christian celebration of the Nativity. Jews knew the Christian celebration by its formal Russian name *Rozhdestvo* [Nativity] or Polish name *Boże Narodzenie* [Divine Nativity]. The name *nitl*, conversely, is usually presented in quotation marks in Yiddish sources to indicate its informal Jewish cheekiness.

By definition, the celebration of *nitl* differed from that of *Rozhdestvo* and *Boże Narodzenie* only in terms of the rationale for the celebration. This point is illustrated in an 1867 article from an Odessa-based Yiddish weekly. A commentator from a traditional Jewish family recounts his first Christmas Eve hosted by assimilated, Russian-speaking Jews. He describes his delight upon observing their lavish feasting, boozing, dancing, and card games. He was pleased that these assimilated Jews had retained the Jewish tradition of "warding off the *tkufe*." It was only upon learning that these Jews called their celebration *Rozhdestvo* that he began to realize that this celebration was not in honor of the Jewish *nitl*. He defines *nitl* as "not studying in order to suppress the fate of a 'certain someone' on the Day of Judgment."[113] Whereas traditional Yiddish-speaking Jews viewed *nitl* as their own Jewish holiday (that is not grounded in rabbinic Judaism, akin to the Jewish May Day *lag b'oymer*),[114] they expressed disdain for the coinciding night's Christian celebration. Some Polish Jews distorted the name *Boże Narodzenie* into *beyz-geboyrenish*, "angry birthie." Other Jews, particularly Litvaks, retained their traditional distortion of *Weihnacht* into *veyn-nakht*, "crying night," to reclaim Christmas Eve as a night of joy for Jews and a night of crying for Christians.[115]

Yiddish Christmas folklore includes proverbs about the spookiness of the long night. These proverbs include *"nitl iz a beyz lidl"* [*nitl* is a menacing little song] and *"nitl iz a beyze leyd"* [*nitl* is a menacing affliction].[116] When a Jewish mother would be asked the age of a child who was born on this menacing night, she would customarily respond with the apotropaic saying *"nitl mit lib* [*nitl* with love], my child is x years old."[117] Other Yiddish phrases about *nitl* were more playful. In a town near Bialystok, Jewish children would sing along to the sounds of Christmas Eve trumpet blasts with the lyrics *"tatelu, mamelu, es dem kugelu!"* [daddy, mommy, eat the kugel!].[118] Yiddish expressions about *nitl* continued to evolve right up to the outbreak of World War II. An article published in a Warsaw newspaper after Christmas 1935 distinguishes two types of Jews who walk the streets on Christmas Day: those who hold their heads high and those who sulk. The former are the winners of the previous night's "mitzvah-fulfilling game of cards." The latter, the losers, are whom the article dubs "the suckers of the *nitl-nakht*."[119]

Other facets of Yiddish Christmas folklore sought to address a major problem posed by not studying on *nitl*: The Talmud states that the world will fall apart if Jews stop studying Torah for even one minute.[120] One resolution to this dilemma quoted the rabbinic phrase *"mineg yisroel toyre"*: Observing a Jewish custom is itself equivalent to Torah adherence.[121] Other Jews explained why the world does not end on Christmas as follows. It is daytime in America while it is nighttime in Eastern Europe. Therefore, when Jews in Eastern Europe put their books aside on Christmas Eve, American Jews are studying Torah and thereby keeping the world alive.[122]

Then there are Yiddish legends set on Christmas. Some of these legends are variants of spooky non-Jewish Christmas legends; others are original Jewish formulations. An example of the former (non-Jewish) type of legend tells of a tailor working late one Christmas Eve who was visited by a *zmore*, a malevolent female night creature (etymologically related to the "mare" in "nightmare"). The *zmore* tangled the tailor's thread so that he could not work. Angry, the tailor cut the thread in half and threw it out the window. On Christmas morning, he woke up to find outside his window an old woman cut in two. The *zmore* never bothered the tailor again.[123] An example of the latter (Jewish) type of legend tells of Eastern European Rabbi Shmuel Eidels (1555–1631), commonly known as the Maharsho. This legend, based on the early modern apostate-initiated raid of Jewish homes, goes as follows. One Christmas Eve, a resentful Jewish apostate attempted to expose the Maharsho's irreverent Christmas Eve behavior. Christian authorities headed over to the Maharsho's home to corroborate that he was not studying as usual. Meanwhile, a rabbinic book fell out of the Maharsho's bookshelf, which the Maharsho subsequently reshelved. Yet the book fell out a second time, and a third time, at which point the Maharsho believed it to be a sign of fate and began to study. Christian authorities arrived to see the Maharsho studying like any other night, greatly embarrassing the Jewish apostate.[124] A variant of this legend replaces the Maharsho with Chaim of Volozhin (1749–1821), the pioneer of the Misnagdim who famously opposed the Christmas Eve practice of abstaining from Torah study, thereby providing an origin story for why he would continue to study.[125]

Perhaps the most elaborate contributions to Yiddish Christmas folklore come from Hasidim—that is, pious popularizers of Jewish mysticism. Despite being Torah scholars, Hasidic rabbis fully embraced the popular culture of adjourning Torah study for Christmas Eve as per their populist style. Franz Kafka notes in his diaries that his friend Jiří Langer (1894–1943), who became a follower of a Hasidic rabbi in Galicia, was permitted to break from studying Torah at Christmas to read his friends' secular novels.[126] In contrast to the staunch Misnagdim who insisted that Torah study must continue on Christmas Eve, many Hasidic rabbis even allowed their disciples to make merry when Christmas Eve coincided with the Sabbath.[127] A Yiddish legend purports to be the origin of such Sabbath leniency: A Hasidic rabbi once insisted that his disciples continue studying Torah through Christmas Eve when it coincided with the Sabbath—but the rabbi changed his mind upon finding a disciple swimming in tears over not being able to play games that year.[128]

The mysticism of Hasidism divides the world into two sides:

1. The *sitre d'kdushe*—the side filled with *kdushe* [holiness]
2. The *sitre akhre*—the "other side" filled with *tume* [uncleanliness]

Hasidim understood Christmas Eve as a night when the *sitre akhre* is at its peak. Since studying Torah is associated with *kdushe*, Jewish mystics interpreted the custom of not studying Torah on *tume*-filled Christmas Eve as "not adding *kdushe* to the *tume*."[129] How did Hasidic rabbis justify this unholiness? Those of the Lubavitch movement proposed that adding *kdushe* would give dangerous vitality to the *tume*.[130] A tradition associated with Galician Hasidic rabbi Sholom Rokeach (1781–1855) was that Jews must be at peak spiritual closeness with God in order to fight the *tume*, and one cannot reach this closeness if the mind is busy studying Torah.[131] Polish Hasidic Rabbi Shmuel Bornstein (1855–1926) proposed that the unclean Jesus attracts and absorbs the *tume*, thereby purifying the Jewish nation, and the *kdushe* of Torah study would burn the *tume* apart from Jesus (an inversion of the Slavic Christian belief that Jews attract and absorb uncleanliness on Christmas Eve).[132] In addition to the vast Hasidic folklore about refraining from study to mitigate the danger of *tume*, the belief that all Jewish apostates were conceived on Christmas Eve is popularly attributed to the founder of Hasidism, the Baal Shem Tov (1698–1760).[133] The association of this belief with Hasidism is attested to in the seminal Yiddish satire of Hasidism by Isaac Joel Linetzky (1839–1915), in which a character mocks an inept Hasidic rabbi as having been conceived "right on the *blinde nakht*."[134] Astonishingly, then, Yiddish Christmas folklore was so pervasive in Eastern European Jewish life that it even managed to find itself associated with a stratum of rabbis.

Conclusion

So, did Eastern European Jews really celebrate Christmas? If we define "celebrating Christmas" as celebrating the birth of Jesus, then of course they did not. If we understand Christmas more broadly, however—as a festival for bringing light to midwinter darkness—then it cannot be denied that Eastern European Jews did celebrate Christmas. The Jewish Christmas anecdotes that we saw are not thoughts about an external Christian holiday. Eastern European Jews had an enormous folklore about Christmas within their internal Jewish culture, comprising beliefs, customs, legends, proverbs, and a great deal of merriment. From a broader perspective, Jews and Christians were enmeshed in a single Eastern European Christmas culture that encompassed the two groups exchanging festive foods and covertly poking fun at each other. They agreed that Christmas should be reserved as the merriest time of year, when responsibilities are vanquished and playtime is earned. They only disagreed on why.

5

The Reinvention of *Nitl-Nakht*

In the early twentieth century, Abraham Goldberg (1883–1942), an influential figure in the American Zionist movement,[1] declared that Jewish
nationalists were losing the war against assimilation. Goldberg, in a
Yiddish essay, points out Christmas as a prime example of the disaster
evoked by Jews assimilating into the New World. Despite American Jews
not converting to Christianity, he writes, assimilation has caused many
of these Jews to turn their back on their Jewish heritage by celebrating the Christian holiday of Christmas. He describes how the American
children of Jewish nationalists attend public schools, where they craft
Christmas decorations, sing Christmas songs, and receive sweet treats
from their teachers as Christmas gifts. The reason that Christmas brings
joy to American Jewish children, Goldberg explains, is the Christmas
vacation from their school and studies. All year long, children "yearn
for the freedom to play." When Jewish children are given time off school
for Christmas, it "necessarily becomes a holiday for them." Goldberg
describes how he recently witnessed Jewish children beaming with joy
on Christmas Eve. He wanted to scold these children for insulting their
Jewish heritage by embracing Christmas. But he decided it would be
no use, since the children's joy of being free from their studies would
override any lecture that Goldberg could give them. For this reason,
Goldberg writes, "the war against assimilation in the New World is a
difficult, if not impossible one."[2]

In light of what we have seen previously, Goldberg's argument does
not make any sense. The very hallmark of Christmas Eve in Jewish tradition was a vacation from studies to play. Yet Goldberg presents this
phenomenon as a novel consequence of New World assimilation that is
contradictory to Jewish tradition. Does Goldberg deny that Jews were
engaged with Christmas in the Old World? No—but he provides an
account of the Old World Jewish Christmas that is at odds with what
we have seen to be the case. In the Old World, according to Goldberg,

Christmas Eve "was completely different. For [Jewish] children in the Old World, it was a night of terror." He explains that Christians would "rage with fury" on Christmas Eve, such that "seas of Jewish blood have been poured, the innocent blood of our ancestors." Instead of playing on Christmas Eve, "the night was spent hiding at home terrified."[3]

To justify his claim, Goldberg provides terrifying memories of the Christmas Eve of his youth in his Podolian hometown. He describes Jesus flying around, who would defile any holy book that was opened. He avers that if a knife was stuck into the earth, blood would pour out. Here is an excerpt of his narrative:

> I will never forget the Christmas Eve, the *blinde nakht* of my youth. The lamp would burn dimmer that night, as if it too were frightened. *Blinde nakht*. It was as if a ferocious gentile barged into the house and carved out my eyes. On that night, a pale, young girl became blind. She wore a black kerchief and black clothes and held a lira in her hand and sang in a weeping voice: "Have mercy, I am blind. My eyes were carved out."
>
> I remember once thinking that I saw a gigantic woman approach our window and reach out her hand and wink at me: "Come! Come!" I thought she wanted to capture and chase after me. I ran crying to my mother and began to scream: "Hide me, an evil woman wants to capture me!" I was trembling like a leaf. My mother recited exorcism spells and said to me, "What is the big deal? Demons and evil spirits, God help us, have great power on this night. It is the *blinde nakht*."
>
> Meanwhile I could hear voices outside the window—something sad, dark, depressing. I began to swell up. It was as if a gentile funeral was taking place and constables were running around screaming "Kikes, take off your hats!" and lashing out whips.
>
> "Mama, I'm scared! It isn't going away!"—I screamed.
>
> My father stepped in. "Look at how he trembles and upsets his mother. The child is terrified of the gentiles' caroling. Bring something out to them, Brayna. Give them some braided bread and a few pennies."
>
> My mother undressed me and laid me to bed, ordering me to read my bedtime Shema prayer with great fervor. I recited the prayer out loud. Once I finished reading, I hid my face under my blanket and held my breath.
>
> It was a night of terror.[4]

This narrative does not, in fact, support Goldberg's claim of Christians terrorizing Jews on Christmas Eve. Goldberg acknowledges that Christians were not truly terrorizing Jews, but rather, it was all in his imagination. His description of demons and evil spirits having power on Christmas Eve, including a child-snatching woman, was not unique to the Jewish imagination—it was a belief that pervaded Christmas folklore across Europe.[5] Yet Goldberg portrays the darkness of Christmas as having been unique to Jews, and denies that Jews engaged in any merriment to bring light to this darkness.

Goldberg was not alone in describing Christmas Eve as a historical night of darkness for Jews and only Jews. Another prominent figure in the Jewish nationalist movement, Abraham Golomb (1888–1982), denounced North American Jews who celebrate Christmas as forgetting "the ingrained Jewish national feeling of elusion and terror associated with the '*nitl-nakht*.'"[6] He describes how, in the Old World, Jewish hearts would tremble upon hearing the midnight ringing of the church bells. He explains that these bells invited wild Christians into Jewish towns, and that "their 'consecrated wine' is our [Jewish] blood."[7] Yiddish journalist Daniel Charney (1888–1959) concurs: "Have we already forgotten that the folks celebrating Christmas in Europe cut up many more Jewish children than the number of Christmas trees that Jews trimmed in America this year?"[8] These violent representations of the Old World Christmas lead us to the fifth question on our agenda: How did Jews come to regard Christmas as historically dangerous? Or more specifically, why did Jewish immigrants insist that the younger generation of Jews had forgotten about a historical time when zealous Christians would rampage against terrified Jews on Christmas Eve—when in reality, Jews historically spent Christmas Eve playing games, while Christians also made merry to alleviate their own fear?

To answer this question, this chapter puts the New World reimagining of *nitl-nakht* into context. As the societal purpose of Eastern European Jewry became less clear in the nineteenth century upon the fall of feudalism and growth of the modern state, Jews were faced with the so-called Jewish Question: *What should become of the Jews in modernity?* Over two million migrated to the New World between 1881 and 1924, mostly to the United States (particularly New York City), although some settled in other lands throughout North and South America, Western

Europe, South Africa, and Australia, and an additional hundred thousand journeyed to Palestine. This chapter argues that Jewish immigrants, in searching for an answer to the Jewish Question and setting out a vision for a distinctive Jewish future, required a new foundational myth to distinguish themselves in a secular society. As a part of this pursuit, they devised a new Yiddish folklore about the Christmas of the Old World—in which the supernatural danger of Jesus tormenting the Jews was reinvented into a rational danger of Christians tormenting the Jews.

Yosl Pandrek Exits Yiddish Folklore

The decline of supernatural Christmas folklore among Jews was concomitant with a decline of supernatural Christmas folklore among Christians—a consequence of what Max Weber (1864–1920) calls the "disenchantment of the world."[9] As the rationalism and science of the Age of Enlightenment dismantled traditional folk beliefs about demonic forces, enlightened Jews stopped literally believing Christmas Eve to be given over to a demonic Jesus. But it is not immediately clear why Jewish immigrants shifted their Yiddish discourse about the Old World Christmas away from Jesus altogether.

In the 2007 book *From Rebel to Rabbi*, Matthew Hoffman (1968–2020) reviews a subquestion of the Jewish Question that he dubs the "Jesus Question": *How should modern Jews view Jesus?*[10] The pioneer of the Jewish Enlightenment in Germanic lands, Moses Mendelssohn (1729–1786), advocated for Jews to be integrated into Christian society and speak German instead of Yiddish. He sought to eradicate the traditional bitter view of Jesus that the *Mayse Tole* dictated.[11] Many of Mendelssohn's followers not only put an end to their disdain for Jesus, but they abandoned Judaism entirely by converting to Christianity, including four of Mendelssohn's six children. One answer to the Jesus Question was, hence, to replace derogatory folklore about Jesus with effectively worshipping Jesus.[12] Other enlightened German Jews did not go so far as convert to Christianity, but rather liberalized their Judaism. The main founder of Reform Judaism, Abraham Geiger (1810–1874), popularized the movement by asserting that Jesus was a Reform rabbi. Geiger branded Reform Judaism as the true religion of Jesus, unlike Christianity, a stray religion that had become merely about him.[13] Still other enlightened German Jews attempted to construct the Jewish people as a nation rather than a religion. Heinrich Graetz (1817–1891), in writing the first comprehensive history of the Jewish people, included Jesus as a respectable figure in Jewish history. Graetz attributed Jesus's strengths to his Jewish background.[14] As these enlightened, German-speaking Jews discarded their derogatory view of Jesus, they necessarily discarded their Yiddish Christmas folklore about *Yosl Pandrek*.

We know from our earlier discussions that Yiddish Christmas folklore about *Yosl Pandrek* persisted in Eastern Europe right up to the outbreak of World War II. The Enlightenment did attract Jewish followers in Eastern Europe, known as Maskilim. As Christian violence toward Jews spiked in Eastern Europe, however, it became clear to many Maskilim that Eastern European Jews would never be integrated into Christian society to the same extent as in Western Europe.[15] Instead, many Maskilim turned to Jewish nationalism. Zionists vouched for the development of a Hebrew-speaking nation in the Land of Israel. Anti-Zionists envisioned themselves as an everlasting Yiddish-speaking diasporic nation. Neither retained their Yiddish Christmas folklore about Jesus. A seminal figure in the Yiddish national movement was Chaim Zhitlowsky (1865–1943). Zhitlowsky preached that in order for Jews to form a sophisticated European nation, they must abandon their derogatory Yiddish Christmas folklore about "*Yoyzl*" and revise their demeaning view of Jesus.[16] Another pioneering Yiddish nationalist, Benzion Hoffman (1874–1954), reiterated that enlightened Yiddish speakers "certainly cannot continue to say that on Christmas Eve the air is 'filled with [Jesus's] *tume*.'"[17] For Eastern European Jewish intellectuals, the "low culture" of mocking Jesus did not have a future in their vision of a civilized Jewish nation.

Matthew Hoffman notes a key difference between how Eastern and Western European Jews responded to the Jesus Question: Those from Eastern Europe needed to address the ongoing violent persecution of Eastern European Jewry that was being committed in Jesus's name.[18] Many Eastern European Jewish émigrés responded to the Jesus Question by reclaiming Jesus as a Jew through irony. They emphasized that the figure used to ignite antisemitic violence was a Jew himself. The two most prominent American Yiddish authors to use this trope were Sholem Asch (1880–1957) and Joseph Opatoshu (1886–1954).[19] A seminal example from Sholem Asch is his 1909 Yiddish story "On a Carnival Night." This story is set during a Christian Carnival under the shadow of a crucifix in early modern Rome. The action begins when Jesus dramatically descends from his cross and walks over to the city's gates, where the true Messiah is chained. Jesus, whom the narration refers to as "the Jew from the city of Nazareth," begs forgiveness from the Messiah for the antisemitic atrocities being committed in his name. He subsequently heads over to the streets to join his fellow Jews in the humiliating "Jew Race" of the Carnival.[20] With this story, Asch refutes the conventional Jewish view of Jesus as a betrayer of the Jews. Instead, Jesus descends from the cross to prioritize his Jewish identity over the unjustified divinity that Christians have granted him. An example of this revised depiction of Jesus from Joseph Opatoshu is his 1925 Yiddish story "The Trial." This story is set in contemporary Poland in the days leading up to Easter. In a church tower, Christians put on trial a Judas effigy dressed in Jewish garb and deem him guilty. The effigy suddenly comes to life and turns to his "brother," a gilded crucified Jesus. Judas asks Jesus why he stays silent, calling Jesus by his Hebrew name "*Yishu*." Jesus silently cries as Judas is yanked away and thrown out of the tower.[21]

Opatoshu does not agree with Asch's view of Jesus. Asch portrays Jesus as innocent and able to reconcile with his fellow Jews, whereas Opatoshu portrays Jesus as having done too little too late, with no hope left for Jewish–Jesus reconciliation. But Asch and Opatoshu are united in that they do not tell traditional folk stories about an evil *Yosl Pandrek* haunting the Jews on *nitl-nakht*. They rather tell literary stories about an apologetic Jesus, set on Christian holidays when Christians would physically persecute Jews in Jesus's name. The scatological Christmas folk stories about *Yosl Pandrek*, in turn, disappeared from any serious discourse of enlightened Yiddish-speaking Jews.

Santa Claus Enters Yiddish Folklore

As Jewish immigrants abandoned their folk culture of mocking Jesus, the figure of *Yosl Pandrek* faded away from Yiddish Christmas discourse. Yet the joyful memories of playing games on *nitl-nakht* apparently faded away along with *Yosl Pandrek*. Why?

Let us consider the following. With Jews now integrated citizens and no longer benighted in a Torah-intensive culture, the concept of *nitl-nakht*—a single time of year when Jews are granted a break from Torah study to experience humanistic joy—became obsolete, as Jews could now experience the joy of *nitl-nakht* every night of the year. This new secular Judaism contrasted with the minority of Hasidic Jews who retained their traditional lifestyle in the New World, as conveyed by the American Yiddish joke:

> Q: What is the difference between a Hasidic rabbi and a Reform rabbi?
> A: A Hasidic rabbi observes "*nitl*" once a year. A Reform Rabbi observes *nitl* every night of the year.[22]

This sentiment is illustrated in the Yiddish poem "*Nitl*" by Mikhl Aronson (1879–1963), published in a secular New York Yiddish newspaper on Christmas Eve 1920:

> NITL, NITL, IS TODAY.
> Do you know what this word means?
> This word is well-known
> in our home in the Old World.
>
> THERE IN OUR OLD HOME,
> this day is awaited all year long.
> The day is a holiday
> for all the *kheyder* boys.
>
> THE *KHEYDER* IS EMPTY ON THIS NIGHT,
> as is the study hall,
> and games of cards are played
> across Jewish homes.
>
> IT WAS INSTITUTED MANY YEARS AGO
> not to study on this night
> when Nazareth brought the world
> a "savior."

THAT WAS ALL IN THE OLD WORLD.
  Nitl is not known here.
  This word sounds foreign to Jews
  here in Yankee Land.

BUT "*NITL*" REMAINS IN STYLE HERE.
  Nitl here—is all year long.
  Not studying and playing cards
  is now all over the place.[23]

Secular Jews in the New World were hence not thinking about the *nitl* of their pitiful past. Commentator Moshe Starkman (1906–1975) explains that, as the word *nitl* fell out of use among Yiddish-speaking Jews in America, it was replaced by a new word: Christmas.[24] In nineteenth-century Western societies, the Christian conception of midwinter evolved from a spooky time of dissolute merriment into a commercialized extravaganza. Journalist Pesach Kaplan (1870–1943) explained this Western Christian holiday to his fellow Bialystok Jews in 1929:

> For our fathers and grandfathers, *nitl* was the evening when Torah study was adjourned and cards were played. In America, "Christmas" (*nitl*) is a much bigger holiday. And to great astonishment, Jews are just as engaged with "Christmas" as non-Jews, if not more.[25]

Western Jews engaged with this grand Christmas in various ways, in America and in other lands outside Eastern Europe.[26] Some Jews adopted the new custom of decorating a Christmas tree. For example, the main founder of political Zionism, Theodor Herzl (1860–1904), enjoyed decorating a Christmas tree with his children in their Vienna home.[27] (Anti-Zionist Hasidic Jews joked that Herzl's only virtue was that he retained the Jewish tradition of not studying on Christmas Eve.)[28] A Yiddish commentator in São Paulo explained in 1968 that Brazilian Jewish parents commonly "set up Christmas trees for their children" because "the decorations on the tree make them happy."[29] Other Jews attempted to merge the new Christmas with their traditional Hanukkah in what has been dubbed *Weihnukka* (in Germany),

khanukrismes (in Israel), and most recently Chrismukkah (in America), with the decorated Christmas tree sometimes dubbed a Hanukkah bush.[30] Still other Jews viewed this new Christmas as a Christian phenomenon and instead created analogs to modern Christian traditions within their own Hanukkah celebrations. For instance, Gershom Scholem (1897–1982) learned in his Berlin youth of a Hanukkah gift-bringer called the *Chanukkamann* [Hanukkah Man] as a unique Jewish analog to the gift-bringing *Weihnachtsmann* [Christmas Eve Man].[31] The meager cardplaying of *nitl-nakht*, meanwhile, was lost in the past.

The Jewish engagement with the *Weihnachtsmann* is particularly noteworthy. The *Weihnachtsmann* is the benevolent descendant of the supernatural gift-bringers of Christmas past—Frau Holle, St. Nicholas, the *Christkindl*, *Pelznickel*, among others—who ultimately converged into a single figure, known in English as Santa Claus (and occasionally known as Kris Kringle, an anglicization of the name *Christkindl*).[32] Given that Santa Claus was tremendously prevalent in Western popular culture, it did not take long for him to enter the Yiddish folklore of Jewish immigrant children. It was common for New World Yiddish stories to incorporate secular popular culture figures. Mickey Mouse, for example, was the protagonist of a myriad of Yiddish stories, poems, and songs in North and South America in the 1930s.[33] Santa Claus was no less prevalent in Yiddish discourse than Mickey Mouse: Jewish immigrants often commented that their children had completely forgotten about the traditional figure who makes miraculous visits in Yiddish folklore, Elijah the Prophet, in favor of Santa Claus.[34] The Yiddish commentator in São Paulo (above) adds that "Jewish children will tell you stories of 'Papai Noel' [Santa Claus] and the presents he brings, but when you ask them about the Hasmoneans [heroes of the Hanukkah story], they will surely think that is some sort of famous soccer team. . . ."[35]

The Jews who fled Eastern Europe following the collapse of feudalism were seeking upward mobility, and many saw socialism as the economic answer to the Jewish Question. Santa Claus became a recurring character in Yiddish stories with a socialist agenda.[36] A 1939 American Yiddish children's story entitled "Santa Claus Passed Out," for example, follows a poor man who must work as a store Santa to earn money for food. He passes out of hunger on the job. A child witness asks his mother, "If Santa Claus gives so much, why can he not give to himself?"[37] Other

socialist Yiddish stories condemn Santa as a symbol of capitalism who does not give equally to all. A 1930 Yiddish children's play performed in New York features Santa announcing "I deceive everybody, promising gifts but not delivering," at which point the child actors rip off Santa's beard and chase him off the stage.[38] A major Yiddish medium for highlighting injustice and advocating socialism was the American daily *Forverts* [*Forward*]. In its inaugural Christmas edition in 1897, a front-page fiction story entitled "Santa Claus" has Santa telling a poor Jewish orphan girl that he cannot give her any Christmas gifts. He explains that he only gives gifts to rich Christians with a mother and father.[39]

Other Yiddish-speaking Jews reclaimed Santa for themselves, based on the insider knowledge that the actors who portrayed Santa were often Jews.[40] One Yiddish legend, as recorded in early twentieth-century Johannesburg, tells of a Jewish boy irritated by a Christian boy who boasts of receiving gifts from Santa. Santa himself then approaches the Jewish boy and whispers in Yiddish, "Why bother with this Christian *sheygets* [gentile rascal]? What do you care if he believes in me?"[41] Another Yiddish legend, recorded in New York, tells of a Jewish boy who sits on Santa's lap at a department store. Once Santa confirms that the boy is Jewish, Santa tells the boy in Yiddish that he has a present for him. He pulls from his pocket a mezuzah, a scroll that Jews hang on their doorposts.[42] Yet another legend, recorded from America to Australia, tells of a Jewish child who explains to Santa that s/he celebrates Hanukkah. Santa replies with a Yiddish blessing, such as *"mazl un brokhe"* or *"a lebn af dayn kepele."*[43] The Yiddish reclamation of Santa Claus infiltrated multifarious aspects of New World Jewish life. For instance, a Yiddish advertisement for the Newark dental practice of Dr. Eli Gilman (1891–1935) featured an illustration of a grinning Santa alongside the Yiddish caption "even Santa Claus looks good with polished teeth."[44] Some Jews even spotted Santa praying in their synagogue—as in the case of a Jewish Santa actor in New York who did not have time to change before reciting Kaddish.[45]

The Yiddish engagement with Santa Claus illustrates the point that Jews moved on from their days when Christmas meant playing cards to ward off Jesus. In the New World, the person purported to traverse the world on Christmas Eve was not a menacing Jesus who delivers blood and shit but a jolly Santa who delivers gifts and joy. Many Jews turned

their attention to this exuberant Christmas of the New World without looking back at the feeble *nitl-nakht* of the Old World.

The Reimagining of *Nitl-Nakht*

Yet there was a predicament. The exuberant Christmas of the New World was a Christian holiday ungrounded in Jewish tradition. On Christmas 1904, a Christian reporter for the *New York Tribune* explained that Jews had simply de-Christianized a holiday that did not belong to them:

> In the homes of the poor Hebrews, as well as of the well to do, Christmas is being celebrated with never a thought that it is the birthday of Him whom their forebears crucified more than nineteen centuries ago. The fine old story of the stable in Bethlehem, the mother without sin, the star in the East and the wise men who came with rich gifts naturally is not told by the Hebrew mothers. Indeed, they have little or no lore about the day to tell their youngsters. Many of them have fallen back on the Santa Claus myth, and the Hebrew tots are just as pleased over it as Christian youngsters ever were.[46]

A Jewish reporter for the Yiddish *Forverts*, writing in 1922, corroborates that it was commonplace for Jewish children in New York to write letters to Santa Claus and decorate Christmas trees while ignoring any association with the holiday's Christological aspect.[47] This de-Christianization extended north of the border, as a Jewish reporter for the *Canadian Jewish Chronicle* wrote in December 1929 that Montreal department stores were filled with the Yiddish chatter of *"vilst geyn zen Santa Kloz?"* [wanna go see Santa Claus?].[48] Some older Jews felt that adopting these non-Judaic ways threatened a sustainable Jewish future based on cultural continuity. In a 1923 article, Yiddish literary critic Shmuel Charney (1883–1955), who had immigrated to New York a few years earlier, slams American Jews who "shimmy and foxtrot" around Christmas trees. He reminds readers that Christmas was "completely, completely different" back home. In the Old World, he writes, *"nitl"* was a night of fear—and a night when church bells tolled to mark a Christian, not Jewish, holiday.[49] Likewise, in a 1957 article, American hotelier William Stein (1896–1962) maintains that going out to Christmas parties is inconsistent with Jewish

tradition. "Christmas is not a Jewish holiday," he asserts, "because who can forget how Jewish children in the Old World were afraid to even go out on the street [. . .] on the night of '*nitl*'?"[50]

Let us consider the case of one of the earliest and most vocal critics of American Jews celebrating Christmas, Yiddish poet Morris Rosenfeld (1862–1923). In a December 1910 piece for the *Forverts*, Rosenfeld facetiously sympathizes with Jewish children who feel excluded from the new American Christmas. He describes poor Jewish children who are enticed by sparkling Christmas ornaments that they see in shops. He describes poor Jewish children who are jealous of their schoolmates gratuitously receiving toys from Santa Claus. And then he presents a solution:

> Has Jewish history not prepared a cure for this plague? Do Christmas and Hanukkah not fall around the same time? And is our Hanukkah not a greater holiday than their Christmas?

> -When you get slapped in one cheek and give forth the second—that is Christmas.
> -When you earn freedom by putting up a fight—that is Hanukkah.
> -A dismal, foolish dream of a sick epileptic mind—that is Christmas.
> -An illustrious historical fact—that is Hanukkah.
> -A pale, deformed, pathetic idol—that is Christmas.
> -A courageous, brave hero—that is Hanukkah.[51]

Rosenfeld was influential in transforming Hanukkah into a major American Jewish holiday to compete with Christmas.[52] In doing so, he also helped corrupt the collective Jewish memory of *nitl-nakht*. Rosenfeld composed several Yiddish Christmas poems that served to remind Jewish immigrants of Christmas's darkness—and associate this darkness with Christmas being the holiday of the Jews' oppressors. In his 1902 Yiddish poem "Christmas Eve Bells," Rosenfeld depicts the night's church bells as a calling to violent Christian persecutors:

> RING OUT, RING OUT, YOU CHRISTMAS EVE BELLS!
> Announce to the heaven and the earth,
> You have terrorized the world many times,
> You have provoked a sword many times!

RING OUT, AND LET ALL THE STARS
hide their sweet splendor;
Let the moon become dark
and not illuminate this night!

YOU PROCLAIMED THE DARKNESS
for many years and generations
Oh, woe, how did the world sin
that it must hear your noise![53]

Rosenfeld was not the first to associate the darkness of Christmas Eve with Christian persecution of the Jews. In fact, this association existed back in Eastern Europe. Eastern European Jews traditionally read the *Mayse Tole* on Christmas Eve, which ends with the rise of Christianity and Christian persecution of the Jews.[54] The association of Christmas Eve with Christian persecution became useful for Jews seeking to undermine the idea that Jews and Christians can celebrate Christmas in harmony. In an 1867 piece for an Odessa-based Yiddish paper, an anonymous commentator describes how Maskilim were very displeased with the "ridiculous" explanation that Jews gave for not studying Torah on *nitl*—that doing so would alleviate Jesus's suffering in the afterlife—so the commentator seeks to devise an alternative, rational explanation of this behavior. Importantly, the commentator seeks to explain the Jewish observance of *nitl* in a way that maintains its distinctive Jewish nature, so that it differs from the modern Christian celebration that was increasingly attracting enlightened Jews.[55] The explanation that the commentator proposes ultimately resonated very strongly with Eastern European Jews amid growing Christian persecution. It is summarized in a blurb that appeared in Warsaw's premier Yiddish daily *Haynt* [*Today*] in December 1934:

> Where does the custom of refraining from study on the night of "*nitl*" originate? In old times, mobs of Christians would organize a hunt for Jews and beat them mercilessly on this night. It was therefore dangerous for Jews to go out on the streets. Rabbinic authorities enacted a ruling to refrain from study, every *kheyder*, *yeshive* and *besmedresh* must close, and all Jews should stay at home.[56]

Jews in Eastern Europe therefore came to believe that there was once a historical time when Christmas Eve was physically dangerous for Jews. And upon immigration to the New World, Jews repurposed this belief to distinguish the Christian Christmas from the frightening Jewish *nitl*. As succinctly conveyed in a letter to the editor of the *American Israelite* following Christmas 1879: "Jews ought to cry instead of being glad on Christmas, for in olden times many of our people were murdered on that day."[57]

Stories that Christmas was once dangerous for Jews became standard Yiddish "fakelore," to quote a term coined by Richard Dorson (1916–1981).[58] This development was concomitant with Jewish immigrants remembering the Eastern European *shtetl* (the Yiddish word for "town") through a romanticized lens. In searching for a sustainable group identity, many Jewish immigrants sought to reinforce the togetherness of the *shtetl* that seemed to be dwindling away amid New World assimilation. In reality, Jews and Christians regularly interacted and shared much in common in the *shtetl* of the past—ranging from mingling at the weekly market to decorating colored eggs at Easter[59]—but like other immigrant groups, Jewish immigrants focused their memories on a "usable" past that could allow them to define themselves as culturally distinct.[60] According to the collective memory of Jewish immigrants, Jewish and Christian life in Eastern Europe was dichotomous and without commonality. The only roles of Christians in Jewish life were disruptions of the peaceful *shtetl* culture of Torah adherence (akin to the fiction of *Fiddler on the Roof*). David Roskies has argued at length about how Jewish neoromantics devised a new Yiddish folklore that was "mostly fake [. . .] carefully selected and ideologically reshaped,"[61] with the reinvented conception of the *shtetl* being a simplistic fantasy world, "static and unchanging [. . .] everywhere the same [. . . and] as if the Jews existed in glorious isolation from [Christians]."[62] Dan Miron describes how there is not "even a trace of Christian culture or religion in the manifold projections" of the imagined *shtetl*. He explains that Yiddish stories portray Eastern European life as "divided between Christians and Jews, the former comfortably occupying its hilly, airy upper part and the latter squeezed into the lower part."[63] Accordingly, Jewish immigrant memories of the old Christmas did not consist of Christians and Jews spending Christmas Eve in the same way (i.e. telling spooky stories, exchanging festive foods, playing games, drinking, and dancing). Instead, these memories comprised a divide between the bright, vibrant Christian celebration of the birth of their savior, and the dark, frightful Jewish *nitl-nakht* spent protecting against the Christian savior.

Jewish immigrants thus sought to establish a cultural identity in the New World based only on what lay on the Jewish side of the Jewish–Christian dichotomy. Selected elements of their former life in Eastern Europe were, as Roskies argues, "repackaged as an authentic expression of the [Jewish] folk,"[64] while the "unusable" elements were blocked out of the Jewish collective memory. The spinning top that Jews historically used for gambling on *nitl-nakht*, the dreidel, was sentimentalized as an artifact of Hanukkah that had nothing to do with Christmas. The letters *n/g/h/sh* that marked the four sides to indicate the player's winnings, conventionally designating *nit/gants/halb/shtel*, became instead strictly known as an acronym for *nes godl hoye shom*, "a great miracle happened there," referring to the miracle of Hanukkah.[65] In the imagined past of pioneering Yiddish author Sholem Aleichem (1859–1916), the "best of all the Jewish holidays" on which Jewish boys "do not go to *kheyder*" and "play dreidel" is hence not Christmas but Hanukkah.[66] Jewish immigrants additionally promoted Purim as yet another occasion for Jewish merriment. The historical Yiddish version of the masqueraded European Carnival play (the *purimshpil*), in which Jews vulgarly cursed and assaulted a Christianized Haman, was sentimentalized as an endearing Jewish cultural tradition stripped of its crass anti-Christianity.[67] Jewish immigrants encouraged their children to play dreidel on Hanukkah and masquerade on Purim for the sake of carrying on this authentic expression of the Jewish people. Jewish immigrants did not, conversely, encourage their children to play or enjoy themselves on Christmas Eve, because Christmas merriment lay on the Christian side of the dichotomy in the Jewish imagination. A 1941 American Jewish motherhood guide advises telling Jewish children that "while their Christian friends get gifts only on Christmas, the Jewish calendar has two holidays—Hanukkah and Purim—when gifts are the order of the day."[68]

Jewish immigrants did remember that they would not study Torah on Christmas Eve. Since Torah study was remembered as bliss, a night without Torah study could only be deemed a misfortune. Usable memories of this misfortune included the sounding of church bells that mark a Christian holiday, a fear of a menacing Jesus who drops blood, and an influx of rowdy antisemitic carolers into the *shtetl* to celebrate the menacing Jesus at the resounding church. *Nitl-nakht* thus existed in the distorted Jewish folk memory as a terrifying night when Jews feared bloodthirsty Christians. And conveniently, this reimagined *nitl-nakht* was the perfect cultural artifact for Jewish immigrants such as Morris Rosenfeld to pass down to their children, to teach them that celebrating Christmas is contrary to their Jewish heritage.

A Modern Foundational Myth

Following the Morris Rosenfeld generation of American Yiddish writers that rose to fame in the late nineteenth century, a second generation arrived in New York in the early twentieth century. This second generation formed a new Yiddish literary movement called *Di yunge* [The Young Ones], whose goal was to push the role of New World Yiddish literature beyond its conventional uses of evoking nostalgia and preaching socialism. *Di yunge* sought to deploy Yiddish for literary modernism. In this pursuit, the founder and de facto leader of the movement, Mani Leib (1883–1953), wrote a Yiddish sonnet entitled "*Nitl*" that could not be any more different than Mikhl Aronson's perky poem of the same name. Published in 1952—over thirty years after Aronson's poem—Leib presents a dark scene of ringing church bells that incite mobs of knife-bearing Christians while terrified Jews hide inside.[69] Another modernist Yiddish poet, Hersh Leib Young (1892–1976), presents a similar unsettling scene of a roaring wind that extinguishes lamps on "the silent *nitl-nakht.*" Church bells toll under the shadow of a wooden crucifix, with the figure on the cross coyly described as the "guardian of the dead."[70] In Yiddish modernism, the dark night of *nitl* became a literary symbol to express the historical horrors of Christian violence.

Some Jewish immigrants acknowledged that the folklore about past Christmas Eve violence was ahistorical. American Jewish immigrant Ephraim Auerbach (1892–1973) asks, "How could we have possibly known whether it was dangerous to go outside if we were so busy hiding inside?"[71] Nevertheless, Eastern European Jewish émigrés commonly invoked the darkness of *nitl-nakht* to symbolize the persecution they overcame, providing a mythical origin story for the modern free Jewish nation. In an illustrative example from Christmas 1928, a Jewish immigrant in New York recounts how, when asked by his son why they do not have a Christmas tree, he responded with a lengthy explanation of their heritage:

> In my *shtetl*—I explained to him—Christmas was called *nitl*. This time of year was always frosty and snowy. The tiny houses of the *shtetl* stood covered with snowy hats, the windows frosted over, the panes completely white. [. . .] We spent the entire night sitting in the house, too afraid to go outside. [. . .] Late at night, we heard the church bells start to ring and I was too scared to say even one word. It seemed to us that the fear was creeping in through the tiny windowpanes.[72]

The narrator eventually concludes that,

> on the night of *nitl*, the gentile hearts were poisoned with hatred for Jews; so now, on the night of Christmas, Jewish hearts are dampened. [. . .] Christmas is not our holiday and we must not celebrate. Those who celebrate do not understand the meaning of Christmas.[73]

The relevant foundational myth of the Jewish people was hence no longer the exodus from Egypt following slavery. It was now the exodus from the *shtetl* following Christian intrusion on *nitl-nakht*, spawning a nation averse to Christmas. Jews had always been a people reliant on myths of historical persecution to motivate resiliency amid being caught between the dominant strata of society.[74] This reality dates right back to their origins in ancient Judea, as a residue of a developed nation of Israel caught between three imperialized continents. It continued through their diasporic days caught between the peasant masses and the domineering nobility. And it culminated with their arrival in the New World, as an upwardly mobile urbanized people impeded by a hostile gentile establishment. Throughout their long history, Jews were persistently profitable enough within their broader societies to evade annihilation, yet alien enough to elude assimilation into those societies, accumulating experiences of abuse on occasions that they were deemed disposable. Myths of persecution, true or not, allowed Jews to make meaning of their misfit status and maintain their distinctiveness in situations where assimilation became more feasible. As sociologist Morton Weinfeld puts it, "An ideology of omnipresent antisemitism is part of modern Jewish identity and international Jewish experience."[75]

Thus came the Jews' latest myth of historical persecution, this one addressing the situation of Christmas. This myth was chiefly conveyed in the intellectual New York Yiddish daily *Der Tog* [*The Day*]. Its inaugural editor, famed wordsmith Herman Bernstein (1876–1935), regularly employed the name *blinde nakht* in his Christmas editorials to emphasize the blinding darkness of the Old World Christmas (despite Bernstein being a Litvak who likely did not grow up with this term). Here is an excerpt from his Christmas Eve editorial of 1915:

> Do you remember the *blinde nakht*?
>
> When the *blinde nakht* approached, Jews would retire into their houses and avoid setting foot on the streets. They often trembled in fear of an ambush, since it was a mitzvah for the good Christians to beat or murder Jews on the night when their savior was born. Our sad Jewish history is full of bloody chapters of the *blinde nakht*. Massive, terrifying slaughters happened on that night.[76]

It shortly becomes clear that Bernstein is employing *blinde nakht* as a symbol of any darkness in the Jewish past:

> Being in this country, we have almost forgotten what once was. The *blinde nakht* now passes and we are free, without fear, without trembling. [...] In America we know nothing of the *blinde nakht*; let Europe be next in line![77]

This use of *blinde nakht*, or *nitl-nakht*, to symbolize the plight of the Old World was especially handy for Jews who migrated to Palestine. The reimagining of the Old World as a Jewish–Christian dichotomy was more relevant to Zionists than anybody else, as Zionists sought to recover the pure nation of Israel from contamination with Christianity. Early Zionists actually spent more time branding New Year's Eve (Yiddish: *silvester-nakht*) as historically dangerous for Jews than they spent on Christmas Eve. It proved particularly difficult to eradicate New Year's Eve merriment in the Land of Israel, where Jews still followed the civil calendar. (The Israeli *khanukrismes* craze did not become comparable to the *silvester* festivities until much later.) Nevertheless, there is no short-age of early Israeli attestations of the dangerous *nitl-nakht* of the Old World. According to Israeli folklore, *nitl-nakht* and *silvester-nakht* were the two nights when Eastern European Jews would hide at home and not study Torah in fear of drunk violent Christians. In this respect, Israelis often used the terms *nitl* and *silvester* interchangeably.[78] Consistent with Yiddishists redefining *nitl* as a Christian rather than Jewish holiday, and advocating that the word *nitl* is no more than a corruption of the Latin *natalis* [birthday], pioneering Zionists translated *nitl* into modern Hebrew as *khag ha'molad*—"Festival of the Birth [of Jesus]."

One Israeli description of the historical Eastern European *nitl* comes from Moshe Siegler (1914–1985), who grew up in the Galician town of Sasov. He writes:

> The word "*nitl*" evokes sorrowful thoughts of raging attacks against Jews by Christian mobs throughout place and time. Many violent riots were carried out on the *nitl-nakht* [. . .] and it was better for Jews to remain locked in their homes that night. [. . .] Jewish children were swept by fear when the church bells would ring on the *nitl-nakht*. [. . .] Christians would get drunk and wild [. . .] and beat up any Jewish bystanders. For this reason, children were not sent to *kheyder*, and adults [. . .] would also not go out in the hours when the gentile mobs raced into the church.[79]

Another Israeli immigrant, Pinchas Goldhar (1908–1991) from the Polish town of Stashev, incorporates the tradition of using iron for protection:

> The Jewish population lived in everlasting fear and dread, especially on the Christian holidays and in particular on "*Boże Narodzenie*" [Christ-mas], which fell at the time of Hanukkah, the time of greatest frost. The source of this fear was not an internal character of the Jews but rather an absolute helplessness and hopelessness of being able to defend oneself in the case of riot or unrest. The only thing we could do was not provoke the gentile by hiding in our basements and closing our doors and shutters with iron bars—until the fury passed.[80]

It is notable that Goldhar mentions Jews dreading the "Christian holidays" in general before focusing on Christmas. He was plausibly merging memories of Jews dreading anti-Jewish violence on Easter with memories of Jews defending against Jesus on Christmas. Aharon Zeev Ben-Yishai (1902–1977), from what is now near the Ukranian–Moldovan border, explains how the *nitl* defense mechanisms were no longer relevant upon arriving in Israel. He describes his first Christmas Eve in Tel Aviv:

> Bells didn't ring. Snow didn't fall. The windows weren't covered with frost, through which the *oyse ho'ish* instilled so much childhood fear. There wasn't the same mysterious fear, fear of being among the drunk gentiles whose tradition was to smash Jewish windows on the night of *nitl*. [. . .] If snow doesn't fall and bells don't ring—why would we need *nitl* here? Why would Jews still need to pause their lives?[81]

Nitl-nakht hence became a symbol of Jewish tenacity: By no longer having their lives interrupted by Christian persecution, Eastern European Jewish émigrés could proclaim to have conquered *nitl-nakht*, thereby laying a foundation for a bright, Christmas-less future in the New World.

Conclusion

Yiddish Christmas folklore took a sharp turn when it migrated out of Eastern Europe. Not only did a notion arise that Christmas was historically dangerous for Jews, but this notion became a de facto foundational myth for the modern Jewish people. It provided a vision for a Jewish future that is markedly different from the trajectory of Christians who celebrate Christmas. Jews needed to remember the one communal vacation in the historical Jewish year as its one unwanted disturbance in order to resist this vacation becoming the permanent state of future Jewry. The historical pair of fright and merriment associated with Christmas was therefore binarized within Jewish memory: Merriment was assigned to Christians, and fright was assigned to Jews. In accordance with the emblematic image of the *shtetl* being of peaceful Torah study, the emblematic image of *nitl-nakht* was of roaring church bells provoking a violent Christian mob that puts Torah study to a halt. Memories of Jesus dropping blood as Christians caroled Jewish homes were transformed into memories of Christians violently drawing Jewish blood. Memories of Jews using iron to protect against Jesus's uncleanliness were transformed into memories of Jews using iron to bolt doors and windows against raging Christians. Such a reimagining of *nitl-nakht* attests to the remarkable ongoing relevance of Christmas to Jews: The search for a Jewish national identity could not see the end of Yiddish Christmas folklore, but rather led to its reinvention to keep up with the Jews' changing circumstances. That is, as the historical *nitl-nakht* slipped away from the minds of Jewish children assimilating into the New World, their parents deemed the fear associated with *nitl-nakht* necessary for selective preservation—no longer for the purpose of warding off *Yosl Pandrek*, but now, for the purpose of warding off Santa Claus.

6

Peace on Earth, Good Will to Men

Another Yiddish Christmas tradition emerged in the early twentieth century. An annual satirical Christmas column would appear in the Yiddish *Forverts*, the New York socialist daily that circulated across North America. Christians in the New World branded Christmas as a time of serenity and compassion, so Christmas became the perfect target for Jewish socialists to deride as a travesty and hypocrisy in a sea of capitalism and injustice. Here is an excerpt from one iteration of this column, published a few days before Christmas 1922:

> Congratulations, Jews, congratulations to us all! Let us rejoice and be merry! The holy, kosher holiday of Christmas is here, the holiday of "peace on earth and good will to men." Only a few more nights until Christmas trees will sparkle in the homes of non-Jews and even many Jews, and the kind hearts of rich Christians will be filled with goodness and compassion for everyone and especially for . . . themselves. And, for the sake of this great compassion, they will rejoice around their tree, consume a good supper, and indeed—what's true is true—set aside a small donation to feed the mouths of the poor, in order to put their little conscience at ease.[1]

The audience of this Yiddish column comprised Jewish immigrants who were relatively unfamiliar with the New World's peaceful rendering of Christmas. For this reason, the column made recurrent analogies between this modern Christmas and the parallel occasion that Jewish immigrants were familiar with in their own Jewish tradition: the Jewish holiday of Yom Kippur.[2] Yom Kippur ("The Day of Atonement") was the traditional time when Jews sought peace and forgiveness from each other. The column, in facetiously praising the naive utopia of the modern Christmas, drew flippant parallels with the "Yom Kippur of our cozy days in the Old World,"[3] which Jewish socialists regularly ridiculed as ingenuine. To illustrate the hypocrisy of Christmas spirit, the column sometimes cited a classic Yiddish expression said to one's enemies on Yom Kippur—"I forgive you today, but I will get even with you tomorrow"—and reminded readers that as soon as Yom Kippur ends, Jews return "from serving the God of Heaven to serving the God of Money."[4]

The fact that the Yiddish press utilized a "Jewish" analogy to convey the concept of Christmas spirit is worthy of further attention. Historically, Christians and Jews celebrated a common self-indulgent Christmas that was hardly about peace and goodwill. In the modern Christian imagination, however, Christmas was a distinctively Christian holiday, based on the herald angels' proclamation of Jesus's birth: "peace on earth, good will toward men" (Luke 2:14). The *Forverts* column suggests that Jews too had a concept of peace and goodwill in their own imagination, on Yom Kippur rather than Christmas. Hence the sixth question on our agenda: Did "Christmas spirit" exist in Yiddish? We saw that many Jewish immigrants outwardly rejected the modern Christmas, but did its spirit manifest in Yiddish as "Yom Kippur spirit"?

To answer this question, we need to consider two parallel cultural transformations that took place in the New World in the late nineteenth century:

1. The Christian reinvention of Christmas from debauched to sentimental, rendering Christmas the heart of nostalgic Christian culture;
2. The Jewish reinvention of Christmas from debauched to terrifying, rendering Yom Kippur the heart of nostalgic Jewish culture.

This chapter argues that, as Christians reclaimed Christmas as a token of their imagined past, the Jews who resisted this new Christmas reclaimed Yom Kippur, the central holiday in their own imagined past. Jewish immigrants reinforced their distinctive identity by imagining a surrogate Christmas spirit on Yom Kippur, for Jewish nostalgics to idealize and Jewish socialists to criticize within the scope of an internal Yiddish culture. To make this argument, this chapter reviews Yiddish texts and films from the turn of the twentieth century onward, with a focus on those produced in New York (where the production of New

World Yiddish culture was concentrated), to demonstrate that the disparagement of the fearful *nitl-nakht* in secular Yiddish culture was accompanied by the centralization of a spirited Yom Kippur in this culture. This chapter thus reveals that, as Christians reclaimed Christmas as "authentically Christian," Jewish immigrants covertly sought to end the story of Christmas in Yiddish tradition and replace it with an alternative, "authentically Jewish" narrative centered on Yom Kippur.

Christmas and Yom Kippur

We shall first establish that the modern concepts of "Christmas spirit" and "Yom Kippur spirit" are two manifestations of the same idea. We begin by reviewing how these concepts first came about. The earliest events to bring about the spirited reinvention of Christmas date back to the Protestant Reformation, after the Catholic Church failed to eradicate the festival's purported pagan-like behavior. Martin Luther attempted to solemnize Christmas with sentimental Christian carols, but, as described earlier, his efforts were largely buried underneath the festival's irreverent folk traditions. Consequently, as Ronald Hutton describes, many Protestant churches conceded that "the battle had long been lost."[5] English Puritans concluded that Christmas is a pagan holiday and that nobody actually knows when Jesus was born.[6] The Church of Scotland formally condemned people who celebrate "the superstitious time of Yule."[7] Christmas celebrations became taboo in much of the early modern Western world.[8] A 1659 law in New England, for example, stated that "whosoever shall be found observing any such day as Christmas or the like, either by forbearing labour, feasting, or any other way [. . .] shall pay for every such offence five shilling as a fine."[9]

Christian folks were left with the midwinter blues. They could only romanticize about a historical time when they had a Christmas to fight off midwinter darkness. These romanticized memories of celebrating Christmas did not consist of debauched drinking and gambling, but of the solemn comfort and joy expressed in Luther-era Christmas carols. A most influential example of this romanticization comes from the fictional narratives of an imagined-past England by American author Washington Irving (1783–1859). In his 1820 essay "Christmas," the narrator describes how "of all the old festivals [. . .] that of Christmas awakens the strongest and most heartfelt associations." He portrays a nostalgic image of Christmas Eve as a cozy room "filled with the glow and warmth of the evening fire."[10] This image is reiterated in the opening verses of the 1823 poem that swept America:

> 'Twas the night before Christmas, when all through the house,
> Not a creature was stirring, not even a mouse;
> The stockings were hung by the chimney with care,
> In hopes that St. Nicholas soon would be there;
> The children were nestled all snug in their beds,
> While visions of sugar-plums danced in their heads;
> And mamma in her 'kerchief, and I in my cap,
> Had just settled our brains for a long winter's nap.[11]

Over in Germany, a sentimental "Christmas mood" (*Weihnachts-stimmung*) likewise formed in the early nineteenth century. Historian Joe Perry describes how Germans saw an increase in "nostalgia for a personal past of innocence and youth, embodied in exemplary experience of a 'real Christmas.'"[12] German Christians began to mark Christmas Eve by rejoicing around a decorated evergreen tree in a tradition attributed to Luther. Both Protestants and Catholics sang new sentimental carols based on a romanticization of Luther-era carols, such as the 1818 "*Stille Nacht*" [Silent Night] and the 1824 "*O Tannenbaum*" [O Christmas Tree].[13]

This sentimental reimagining of the Christian Christmas culminated in a large-scale revival of the holiday in the mid-nineteenth century.[14] Many people recognize English author Charles Dickens (1812–1870) as the founder of the revived Christian Christmas—Dickens was recently dubbed "The Man Who Invented Christmas" in popular culture.[15] The 1843 novella that initiated this Christmas revival, *A Christmas Carol*, is, on the surface, quite similar to the traditional Christmas ghost stories of England.[16] The key novelty of *A Christmas Carol* is that here the Christmas ghosts deliver a moral, a declaration of a "Christmas spirit" as a new type of warmth to fight off midwinter coldness. To briefly review, the novella follows miser Ebenezer Scrooge, a greedy moneylender embellished with negative Jewish stereotypes who personifies midwinter coldness: He underpays and mistreats his clerk; he refuses to spend time with his nephew; and he has no interest in sharing his wealth.[17] On Christmas Eve, Scrooge is visited by ghosts who show him that he is on a miserable trajectory toward a lonely death. The ghosts then teach Scrooge that the remedy for diverting this trajectory is to find goodness within himself, in the form of "charity, mercy, forbearance, and benevolence."[18] Scrooge's mentality is transformed. He gives his clerk a raise; he agrees to spend Christmas with his nephew; and he makes charitable donations. As Scrooge walks back from church, the narration states that he "had never dreamed of any walk, that anything, could give him so much happiness."[19] With this story, Dickens breaks from the convention of focusing Christmas ghost stories on the gloomy, cold backdrop of Christmas. He instead brings the warmth of compassion and generosity to the forefront of Christmas lore by depicting Christmas as "a kind, forgiving, charitable, pleasant time."[20]

A Christmas Carol sparked a tremendous transformation in the literary response to Christmas across the Western world. Christmas stories were no longer about frightening visits from demons, but rather about faith in the power of compassion and generosity. An 1889 American Christmas story defines the "true meaning of Christmas" as not to drink or gamble, but rather, "to give up one's very self—to think only of others—how to bring the greatest happiness to others—that is the true meaning of Christmas."[21] American President Calvin Coolidge (1872–1933) reiterated this point in his 1927 Christmas address: "Christmas is not a time or a season, but a state of mind. To cherish peace and good will, to be plenteous in mercy, is to have the real spirit of Christmas."[22] Such a spirit came to serve as the basis for a new Christmas that was emotionally deeper than the eerie Christmas of the past. The newly popularized prewinter holiday of Halloween, meanwhile, went on to inherit the former eeriness of Christmas.[23]

Christians branded the new spirit of Christmas as authentically Christian. It embodied the herald angels' proclamation of Jesus's birth that is read at church on Christmas Eve ("peace on earth, good will to men"). Washington Irving's seminal Christmas narrative highlights the holiday's church services as "extremely tender and inspiring" because they "dwell on the beautiful story of the origin of our faith."[24] Christians thus did not include Jews in their reclaimed holiday. As Jeffrey Shandler explains, Jews "served as a sign of the holiday's inappropriate commercialism" that corrupted its authentic Christian message.[25] The American weekly *Life*, for instance, included a December 1911 cartoon entitled "The Spirit of Christmas in New York" featuring a Jewish Santa Claus named "S. Clausenstein" with a dark skin tone, large nose, and evil expression. Clausenstein holds up a toy airplane and tells a group of Christian children, in his heavy Yiddish accent, "I vill give you this fine aeroplane fer only er kervorter down und er neekle er veek fer de balance of der year."[26] Nonetheless, sociologist James Barnett (1906–1992) argues that there is nothing truly Christological about modern Christmas spirit. He contends that "if Christmas did not make possible the realization of individual satisfactions and collective values, some other holiday would be used to achieve these ends."[27] What is that "some other holiday" that Jewish immigrants used for building spirit within their own modernized Yiddish culture? While Hanukkah is often seen as the "Jewish Christmas" in contemporary English-language Jewish culture, it played a minimal role in the Yiddish culture of the immigrant generation beyond offering some light merriment, as we will discuss later. But what about the deeper Jewish holiday of Yom Kippur?

Let us review the concept of "Yom Kippur spirit." According to the Talmud, God opens both the Book of Life and the Book of Death at the start of the new year, which roughly coincides with the autumn equinox. Jews are to devote the first ten days of their year to deep reflection, repentance, and righteousness so that their names will be inscribed in the Book of Life before the Books are sealed at the conclusion of day ten, that is, Yom Kippur.[28] Influenced by the high medieval European fear of divine judgment, Yiddish-speaking Jews called the ten days leading up to Yom Kippur the *yomim neroim*, "days of fear," and these days formed the darkest season in the Jewish calendar, metaphorically speaking.[29] According to Yiddish folklore, "*az m'blozt, vert kalt*"—as the shofar horn is blown to mark the *yomim neroim*, the days get colder.[30] Traditional Ashkenazic liturgy for these days centered on the chilling poem "*Unsane toykef*," a nearly line-by-line Hebrew analog to the Latin Advent poem "*Dies irae*" that emphasized fear and trembling in anticipation of judgment.[31] "*Unsane toykef*" describes the *yomim neroim* as the period in which God decides "who shall live and who shall die" in the coming year, and states that Jews can only divert the darkness of the severe decree (death) through the light of "repentance, prayer, and charity."

Martin Sable (1924–2015) makes an analogy between the Ashkenazic Yom Kippur and the modern Christmas. He suggests that modern Christmas spirit balances midwinter darkness analogously to how the Yom Kippur spirit of repentance, prayer, and charity balances the dark *yomim neroim*. In his analysis of *A Christmas Carol*, Sable argues that Scrooge embraces the remedies outlined in *"Unsane toykef"* to avoid being written into the Book of Death: After the ghosts show Scrooge his trajectory toward death, Scrooge expresses *repentance* toward his employee and nephew, engages in *prayer* at church, and gives *charity* to the poor. These three actions, according to Sable, form "the bases upon which Scrooge chose life," because Scrooge "so earnestly desired" being written into the Book of Life.[32]

Sable's argument is his own contrivance, but it does reveal a striking similarity between the modern Christmas and Yom Kippur. The analogy can be extended further. Historically, the urge to fight the darkness of the Christmas and Yom Kippur seasons obscured their religious message about goodness overcoming severity: Christian folks were preoccupied with supernatural defense to avoid torture by demons like the Krampus, and Jewish folks were preoccupied with supernatural sin removal to avoid being written into the Book of Death (which scholars have discussed elsewhere).[33] Modernity, however, transformed the seasons' formal religious message into a popular secular message about the weight of individual goodness. Christians turned to adopting compassion so that they would be written into Santa Claus's "nice list," showcasing faith in the words that conclude the Christmas Eve gospel reading, "peace on earth, good will toward men" (Luke 2:14). Jews turned to adopting compassion so that they would be written into the metaphorical Book of Life, showcasing faith in the declaration that begins the Yom Kippur Eve liturgy, "light shines on the righteous" (Psalms 97:11). In the 1994 book *The Wonders of America: Reinventing Jewish Culture 1880–1950*, Jenna Weissman Joselit explains how secularized American Jews transformed the *yomim neroim* from "days of fear" into "days of awe":

Casually observant most of the year, the American Jewish folk bestowed on Rosh Hashanah [the Jewish New Year] and Yom Kippur the reverential-sounding title of the "High Holy Days," underscoring their prominence. [. . .] Outfitted in brand-new suits and dresses, they crowded the synagogue, listening attentively. [. . .] The drama of the moment, though compelling, was not the only reason behind the High Holy Days' overwhelming popularity. Memory and its claims on the community also pulled American Jews into an embrace with sacred time and into the pews of the synagogue.[34]

The central synagogue event of Yom Kippur Eve was the recitation of "Kol Nidre," which proactively annulled any vows that would not be fulfilled in the coming year, "from this Yom Kippur to the next Yom Kippur"—essentially an acknowledgment that while mistakes are inevitably made throughout the year, Yom Kippur is a singular moment of serenity.[35] Jewish immigrants observed the "Kol Nidre" declaration set to an emotional melody that developed in early modern Europe (standardized by Lewandowski in 1871),[36] which Tzvee Zahavy interprets as the "anthem" that initiates a "marathon of meditative compassion and forgiveness."[37] Christians, in turn, observed the lines "peace on earth and mercy mild / God and sinners reconciled" in their central Christmas Eve hymn "Hark! The Herald Angels Sing," set to a powerful Mendelssohn melody in 1855, a decade after publication of *A Christmas Carol*.[38] Scholars understand these climactic moments of Christmas Eve and Yom Kippur Eve as central to reinforcing a timeless Christian and Jewish identity based on a perceived communal continuity. John Storey describes the reinvented Christmas Eve as "driven by a utopian nostalgia: an attempt to recreate an imaginary [Christian] past."[39] Annette Boeckler describes the "special moment" of Yom Kippur Eve as having "peculiar power to awaken Jewish identity," in which the "Kol Nidre" melody "triggers memories: of the year just past, of people who have died, of eras long gone."[40] Lawrence A. Hoffman elaborates on the spirit of this special moment:

> It draws on its evocative power to bring to mind our past, to remind us of the cyclical passing of the years and thus of the moments that mattered once and (through musical recapitulation) matter still. [. . .] It is not great music we are after in our sacred services, but just music that symbolizes for us: the Christmas carol of our youth or the strains of *Kol Nidre*, without which it would seem that Christmas or Yom Kippur does not even arrive.[41]

The resemblance between Christmas and Yom Kippur is grounded in the fact that they both coincide with the turn of their respective new year. Christmas scholar Lauren Rosewarne describes the turn of the new year as "a time inextricably linked to fresh starts and clean slates."[42] She notes that "a common theme in Christmas narratives is characters having the opportunity to press 'reset,'"[43] and that "benevolence is a critical step in a character's rebirth."[44] In modern Christmas-less Yiddish culture, Yom Kippur functioned as the parallel season for this spirit of benevolence. Just as Christians participated in church fundraisers on Christmas, Jews participated in charitable synagogue auctions on Yom Kippur.[45] And just as Christians sent greeting cards during the Christmas season wishing one another a "merry Christmas and happy new year," Jews sent Yiddish greeting cards during the *yomim neroim* wishing one another *"l'shone toyve tikoseyvu v'sekhoseymu"*: "For a happy new year, may you be written and inscribed [in the Book of Life]." Weissman Joselit notes that these Yiddish cards (called *shone-toyves*) "were often barely more than Judaized versions" of Christmas cards, yet they "took American Jewry by storm."[46]

This secular reinvention of Yom Kippur was a chief response to the many New World Jews who were adopting the spirit of benevolence on Christmas itself, which was deeply troubling for the first generation. David Isaac Freedman (1874–1939), a Jewish immigrant in Australia, worried in 1925, "How rare it is to see the Jew approaching the [Jewish] New Year in this spirit. [. . .] Christmas Day is the time they have chosen for this exchange of the token of mutual regard."[47] In America, too, Elliot Epsteen (1886–1957) described in 1914 how Jewish immigrants in America were concerned that "their children know much of Christmas, and nothing of Yom Kippur."[48] On the other hand, Icek Shmulewitz (1911–1986) reported for the Yiddish *Forverts* in 1961 that the secularized *yomim neroim* had turned many Jews away from Christmas:

> There are [secular New York] Jews who used to think that Rosh Hashanah and Yom Kippur were purely religious holidays. [. . .] They would send good wishes for the new year at the turn of the civil calendar year. [. . .] But such Jews, for whom the words *"l'shone toyve tikoseyvu"* were once foreign, now send their holiday greeting cards during the *yomim neroim*. [. . .] It is certainly better than celebrating Christmas. [. . .] Even the New

York Christians now know that the Jewish New Year begins not on the first of January, but on the first of the Jewish month of *Tishre*.[49]

Leo Robbins (1895–1957) reported for the *Forverts* as early as 1930 that "the post office calendar considers the Jewish *yomim neroim* as much a holiday season as the gentile Christmas and New Year," noting that the "American-style" *yomim neroim* are comparably commercialized with parties and entertainment.[50] Historian Judith Thissen explains that Jewish immigrants in New York "may well have considered celebrating the High Holidays in a Yiddish theatre or moving-picture house far more attractive than going to a regular immigrant synagogue."[51] Importantly, Robbins emphasizes in his *Forverts* report that despite many New York Jews celebrating Yom Kippur in "Chinese chop suey restaurants," the commercialized *yomim neroim* are a distinctly "Jewish" alternative to the commercialized Christian holidays:

> The "Jewish holidays," the *yomim neroim*, are the symbol of Jewish iden-
> tity for American Jews. It is the only time of year when the Jew makes an
> effort to present himself as a Jew, like his father or grandfather. He closes
> his shop, he doesn't go to work, and whether or not he is religious or buys
> a synagogue ticket, he shows the world that he is a Jew.[52]

Jews in turn transformed the shofar horn—which in Old World Yiddish folklore was a symbol of the arrival of winter coldness—into a symbol of the arrival of a "season of friendship, warmth and rejoicing," to quote a 1934 American Jewish paper.[53] The Christmas church bells became the new Jewish symbol of winter coldness. Whereas the *yomim neroim* were now known as the "Jewish holidays," Jews routinely accentuated the non-Jewish nature of the "Christian holidays." Reform Rabbi Abba Hillel Silver (1893–1963) of Ohio, for instance, pronounced in 1927:

> Christmas is an essentially Christian holiday as much as Yom Kippur is
> essentially a Jewish holiday. The fact that Christmas is the religious holi-
> day of the vast majority of the American people and that Jews are brought
> in close contact with the occasion through social intercourse or business
> does not in the least alter the fact that it is the supreme and most sig-

nificant festival of Christianity and that therefore Judaism has no share whatever in it.[54]

Taken together, we can establish that Jewish immigrants installed a holiday spirit at Yom Kippur that was essentially the same concept as Christmas spirit—not for the purpose of mimicking the Christian-claimed Christmas, but to repel it with a pronouncement of their own Jewish identity.

The Christmas Genre and the Yom Kippur Genre

We will now establish how Yiddish authors reclaimed Yom Kippur as a center of their secular culture, just as how Christian authors reclaimed Christmas as a center of theirs. Katharine Allyn See (1906–1994), who analyzed American Christmas stories written between the reinvention of Christmas and the First World War, argues that Christmas stories form a literary genre:

> The typical American Christmas story has, in varying degrees, certain characteristics, sufficiently marked, and sufficiently constant, to establish this class of stories as an independent, minor literary genre. Its central psychological motif is the balance of the themes of warmth and cold. Ordinarily warmth forms the primary, and cold forms the secondary, theme. Its message is that expressed in the original Christmas text, "Good will toward men."[55]

The most familiar Christmas story among contemporary Americans is that which forms the 1965 television special *A Charlie Brown Christmas*, which aired annually on American television for over fifty years. Set during a cold, snowy Christmas season, the story follows Charlie Brown searching for the true meaning of Christmas while his peers selfishly focus on commercialized aspects of the holiday that Jews introduced (flashy light displays, aluminum Christmas trees, merchandise from Santa Claus).[56] Charlie Brown only finds the true meaning of Christmas once he and his peers are reminded of the herald angels' proclamation of "good will to men" in the original Christian Christmas text. The children then come together to warmly sing "Hark! The Herald Angels Sing" in harmony amid the snowstorm.[57]

How did the Christmas literary genre manifest in the Yiddish literature—did it manifest as stories set on Yom Kippur? At first glance, it appears that the Christmas genre manifested in Yiddish on Christmas itself. Author Esther Kreitman (1891–1954), in pursuit of developing a sophisticated Yiddish literature, translated *A Christmas Carol* into Yiddish, published in Warsaw in 1929.[58] Seven years earlier, Kiev-based writer Lipe Reznik (1890–1944) translated the 1816 German Christmas novella *The Nutcracker and the Mouse King* into Yiddish, featuring new festive illustrations by Jewish designer Joseph Chaikov (1888–1979).[59] Other Yiddish authors wrote their own sentimental Christmas narratives featuring Jews. In 1950, Zaynvl Diamant (1904–1963) published a Yiddish story about a Jewish couple in Eastern Europe that is unexpectedly forced to take in a Christian woman for Christmas. After some tumult, the story ends with the Jews playing cards on *nitl-nakht* while the woman sings Christmas carols.[60] Another Yiddish author, Esther Miller (1890–1985), includes a sentimental Christmas memory in her literary memoir of her Belarussian hometown. On a snowy Christmas morning, Jewish socialists drop pamphlets from a rooftop that urge Christian peasants to revolt against their landlords. Despite the cold weather, Miller describes only warmth among the Jews as they watch the peasants pick up the pamphlets and form a Christmas vision of economic justice. She describes a Jewish girl as "enchanted by the white world around her, by the snowy trees and snowy people. Everything seemed like a beautiful white dream."[61]

Nevertheless, based on what we have seen earlier, it is clear that most Yiddish Christmas narratives were not filled with joyous holiday spirit. The influential Reform Rabbi Emil G. Hirsch (1851–1923) "reminded" American Jews as early as 1893 that "thousands lost their lives in the very night which had according to the gospel sounded the song of 'good will to man,'"[62] and it follows that sentimental Christmas narratives like those of Diamant and Miller were otherwise rare in modern Yiddish literature. One might expect that the spirit of the Christmas genre would have manifested as a Yiddish literary genre pertaining to the coinciding Jewish midwinter festival, Hanukkah. American Yiddish poet Morris Rosenfeld very much wanted Hanukkah to become the Jewish alternative to the modern Christmas. As we saw, Rosenfeld composed Yiddish poems highlighting the threatening darkness of *nitl-nakht* in an attack on Christmas. So too did Rosenfeld compose Yiddish poems highlighting the liberating brightness of Hanukkah, to promote a Christmas alternative. His 1897 Yiddish poem *"O ir kleyne likhtelekh"* [Oh You Little Candles] employs the motif of lighting Hanukkah candles amid darkness as a metaphor for attaining upward economic mobility amid poverty.[63] This poem became remarkably popular among Jewish immigrants across the New World, from Canada to Australia. As Christians reclaimed the concept of the Christmas carol by singing sentimental Luther-like carols, New World Jews sang *"O ir kleyne likhtelekh"* in at least six different sentimental melodies,[64] rendering it something of a "Yiddish version" of the modern Christmas carol. Other new Yiddish Hanukkah songs included Mortkhe Rivesman's 1912 *"Khanike, oy khanike"* [now popularly known in English as "Hanukkah, Oh Hanukkah"] and Mikhl Gelbart's 1927 *"Ikh bin a kleyner dreydl"* [in English, "I Have a Little Dreidel"].[65] Jews around the world also continued to sing *"Mo'oyz Tsur"* on Hanukkah, a Hebrew poem that was set to a Christian carol melody back in the Luther era itself,[66] functioning as a counter–Christmas carol grounded in Jewish history.

Hanukkah did not, however, take off as an effective Christmas in modern Yiddish culture. While it did develop into something of a "Jewish Christmas" in postwar English-language American Jewish culture, Ruth Gay (1922–2006) points out that "the immigrant generation could never have been made to believe that there was any equation between Hanukkah and Christmas."[67] It is true that Hanukkah's significance in Yiddish culture was boosted in the New World. In the 2013 book *Hanukkah in America*, Dianne Ashton argues that, while early Jewish immigrants "questioned Hanukkah's relevance in the New World,"[68] Yiddish writers such as Rosenfeld managed "to save the holiday from demise,"[69] paving the way for Jews to celebrate Hanukkah with "gifts, foods, songs, and concerts."[70] And it is true that some Jewish immigrants then projected a deeper Hanukkah into their imagined past. Boston immigrant Ben Gailing (1898–1999), for example, testifies that the Hanukkah candles in his Lithuanian hometown would "protect" Jewish boys from the dangers of *nitl*.[71] Nevertheless, whereas Hanukkah received heightened attention in modern Hebrew culture based on a symbolic association with Zionism, it achieved little attention in modern Yiddish culture beyond serving as a December alternative to Christmas.[72] Jews did not even take off work for Hanukkah, as this nonbiblical holiday had no real significance in Judaism following the Roman destruction of the Jerusalem Temple. (Scholars argue that the reason rabbis retained Hanukkah over time was simply to provide a Jewish alternative to the non-Jewish midwinter festivities, originally Saturnalia, later Christmas.)[73]

Jewish immigrants thus did not have the same motivation to attend grand Hanukkah concerts like how Christians flocked to Christmas gospel concerts—but on Hanukkah 1902, Jews crowded Carnegie Hall for an orchestral performance of "Kol Nidre," which the Yiddish press promoted with a promise to "transform Hanukkah into a Yom Kippur."[74] Likewise, a grand Yiddish concert held at Broadway's Town Hall Theater on Hanukkah 1922 did not include Morris Rosenfeld's "*O ir kleyne likhtelekh*" or any other Hanukkah songs, but it did include a heartfelt performance of Rosenfeld's "*Yonkiper tsu minkhe*" [Yom Kippur Afternoon].[75] Unlike the thin selection of Yiddish stories about Hanukkah,[76] Yiddish culture forged a deep nostalgia for Yom Kippur that paralleled Christian Christmas nostalgia. Matthew Frye Jacobson describes how Yiddish authors in America used Yom Kippur to express the resiliency of Jewish national identity:

> These are the scenes that most captured the unconquerable spirit of *Yiddishkayt* [Jewishness]: a once-pious woman, having fallen under America's ungodly spell, reawakens on Yom Kippur and once again feels at one with "the children of Israel . . . massed together in every corner of the globe." An Americanized, "fallen" woman of the ghetto reclaims her Old World self when the chant of the Kol Nidre, drifting up from a shul across the street, awakens in her a nearly pious "sadness in the soul." "I am not Jenny!" she cries. "I am Zlate."[77]

It goes without saying that Hanukkah did not have a comparable significance on communal identity in the Jewish immigrant imagination. Akin to how the typical Christmas story follows people in need of learning the forgotten true meaning of Christmas, the Yiddish Yom Kippur story emphasizes an analogously forgotten "true meaning of Yom Kippur." A prime example is the 1900 Yiddish story "If Not Even Higher" by I. L.

Peretz (1852–1915), which follows a skeptical Litvak who learns the meaning of the Yom Kippur season upon witnessing the virtuous deeds of a Hasidic rabbi.[78] This popular classic among Jewish immigrants could not have worked were it set on Hanukkah: Christmas spirit inherently translated into Yiddish as Yom Kippur spirit rather than Hanukkah spirit.

This is not to say that all Jewish immigrants viewed Yom Kippur with the same utopian lens with which most modern Christians viewed Christmas. Being an urban minority, Jews were on average more politically aligned to the left than Christians, and many left-wing Jews ridiculed Yom Kippur's utopian message. Around the turn of the twentieth century, Yiddish-speaking radicals in cities such as London, New York, and Montreal spent the solemn Yom Kippur fast engaging in antireligious *nitl*-style behavior at rented halls, such as feasting, dancing, and other merrymaking—far from what is preached in "*Unsane toykef.*" Rebecca Margolis explains that this "Yom Kippur Ball" tradition "provided the radical Jew with a shared community on Yom Kippur" without accepting the holiday's banal sentimentality.[79] As such, Yiddish authors did not only use Yom Kippur stories to idealize a spirit of peace and goodwill, but also to lampoon it. Some Yiddish authors simply used the Christian Christmas to lampoon this spirit—such as the satirical *Forverts* Christmas column, and the Yiddish Santa Claus stories discussed earlier—but Yom Kippur provided a distinctively Jewish backdrop for relaying such lampoons.

An example is the 1895 Yiddish story "Yom Kippur Eve" by socialist David Pinski (1872–1959) in Warsaw and published in New York. This story follows the owner of a cloth factory named Elye who, like Scrooge, mistreats and underpays his employees. On Yom Kippur Eve, Elye wants to avert the severe decree and avoid being written into the Book of Death, so he superficially offers drinks and cakes to his employees. The story's critique of empty Yom Kippur customs parallels how modern Christmas stories critique the holiday's materialism as overshadowing the true meaning of Christmas. Elye attempts to be redeemed by offering his workers something, but not even the Yom Kippur bonus that they so desperately need, highlighting the irony of how empty Yom Kippur customs completely miss the true meaning of the day.[80]

Other Yiddish stories portray Yom Kippur spirit as having been genuine back in the Old World, but left behind upon emigration. The 1923

Yiddish-intertitled silent film *East and West*, for example, follows an American Jewish girl who returns home to Galicia to find Jews praying and fasting on Yom Kippur—and this frivolous American hides an English novel in her prayer book and gorges food in the back kitchen.[81] Matthew Frye Jacobson explains that Jewish immigrant authors were faced with an "incompatibility of standard, enduring Yiddish narrative forms [such as those of I. L. Peretz] with cosmopolitan arguments."[82] As such, Yiddish Yom Kippur stories that engage with the cosmopolitan New World often draw parallels with Washington Irving's pre-Dickens Christmas stories: They garner nostalgia for a holiday of long ago that had since disappeared.

An example is the 1953 Yiddish story "The Yom Kippur Light Blew Out" by Rosa Palatnik (1904–1981), who immigrated from Poland to Paris in 1927. The story follows a young woman, Mirl, who recently arrived penniless in Paris with her two-year-old daughter and found a sewing job. On the day of Yom Kippur Eve, Mirl becomes nostalgic for the idyllic Yom Kippur of the Old World. She recalls the gloomy *yomim neroim* being lit up by bright synagogues and high-spirited Jews wishing one another *"gmar khsime toyve"* [a sealing in the Book of Life]. Mirl decides to attend a Yom Kippur Eve synagogue service in Paris, wanting her daughter to experience the joy of "Kol Nidre" that she herself had experienced in her youth. Mirl puts on a dress, festively decorates her apartment, and lights a Yom Kippur candle. Just before departing for the service, she receives a visit from a gentile messenger who assigns work to be completed by morning. Mirl is shaken. Her Yom Kippur spirit is shattered by this gentile who is as devoid of holiday spirit as Scrooge. With the Yom Kippur reverie extinguished, Mirl recalls her days and nights of poverty and hunger before she found this job. Wanting a better life for her daughter, she decides to forgo "Kol Nidre." She sets up her sewing machine and blows out the Yom Kippur candle. The serene bliss of Yom Kippur is left buried in the Old World.[83]

Thus, whereas English-language Christmas stories customarily end with the forgotten Christmas spirit being recovered in the modern world, the Yiddish version of Christmas spirit was deemed incompatible with the modern world. Only the Jewish authors who wrote in the language of the modern world were able to end their Yom Kippur stories with cosmopolitan optimism. A most popular non-Yiddish Yom Kippur story is the 1921 English-language story "The Day of Atonement," written by second-generation immigrant Samson Raphaelson (1894–1983). The story follows Jakie Rabinowitz, the son of an immigrant cantor in New York. Jakie runs away from home as a child and goes on to become a successful entertainer. He changes his name to Jack Robin, marries a non-Jew, and gets signed to star in a Broadway production that opens on Yom Kippur Eve. In a tragic turn of events, Jack's cantor father dies on the day of Yom Kippur Eve. Cantor Rabinowitz's final words are that his son will be forgiven if Jakie sings "Kol Nidre" in his place that evening. Jack, realizing that the meaning of Yom Kippur is making amends with others rather than pursuing personal dreams, makes the difficult decision to miss the opening night of his Broadway show. He delivers a spectacular performance of "Kol Nidre" at the synagogue. Jack's performance is so spectacular that he receives publicity among the mainstream entertainment industry, paving his way to stardom.[84] To author Raphaelson, it is possible for Jews to balance Yom Kippur spirit with the modern world, just as Christians balance Christmas spirit with the modern world. Such an ending would have been impossible for a New World Yom Kippur story written in Yiddish, since retaining Yiddish was incompatible with fully accepting the modern world. The Christmas genre translated into Yiddish as a Yom Kippur genre, but in a world where Yom Kippur was omitted from the civil calendar, the happy ending of the typical Christmas story did not always have a Yiddish translation.

The Christmas Film and the Yom Kippur Film

The 1921 story "The Day of Atonement" was remarkably successful. Author Samson Raphaelson adapted his story into the 1925 Broadway play *The Jazz Singer*, and in 1927 the play was adapted into the very first feature film with synchronized dialogue, also entitled *The Jazz Singer*. As sound film took off in the subsequent decade, Yom Kippur became a standard setting for films made in the Yiddish language (Yiddish Hanukkah films did not exist). Ruth HaCohen recently argued that the rapid social change of modernity caused Jewish immigrants to reflect on the Old World Jewish togetherness of Yom Kippur.[85] In what follows, I argue that Yiddish Yom Kippur films formed a genre at the heart of reinvented Yiddish culture, evoking sentimental value among Jewish immigrants analogous to what the later Christmas film genre would evoke among Christians.

For context, the typical family melodrama follows a protagonist who chooses to fulfill personal desires rather than following the family's wishes—until a family member falls ill, at which point the protagonist learns that family values are more important than personal dreams. In American English-language film, such a melodrama is often set on Christmas, ending with the protagonist returning home and singing Christmas carols with the family. Lauren Rosewarne argues that this "Home for Christmas" theme is central to the Christmas film: "to see family and to return to an ancestral house [. . .] where people from one's past—where ex-partners—often still reside."[86] Yet the original American English-language film to employ this theme was set on Yom Kippur rather than Christmas. In this seminal film, *The Jazz Singer*, the struggle between personal desires and family values takes the form of a Jew struggling between assimilating into the New World and maintaining Old World traditions. *The Jazz Singer* ends with the protagonist returning home to his family and his Jewish past for Yom Kippur—and the "Christmas carol" that concludes *The Jazz Singer* is "Kol Nidre."[87]

Yom Kippur melodramas shot in Yiddish generally followed the same formula as *The Jazz Singer*. In Yiddish melodramatic film, the standard struggle for the male is between becoming a secular musical star or remaining a Jewish cantor.[88] The standard struggle for the female is between marrying an assimilated womanizer or a traditional rabbi.[89] An example of both of these struggles is found in the 1939 American Yiddish film *Mothers of Today*. In this film set in New York, a brother and sister from the traditional Waldman family are respectively seduced by a sister and brother from the assimilated Boxer family. The film opens with traditional Mrs. Waldman blessing Sabbath candles, in contrast to Mrs. Boxer, who is a *"hayntike mame"* ["mother of today"] that spends the Sabbath out drinking and gambling (*nitl* behavior par excellence). The conservative Waldman children run off with the alluring Boxer children. Cantor Solomon Waldman forgoes his synagogue performance of "Kol Nidre" and strives to become a radio star, as per girlfriend Evelyn Boxer's suggestion. Annie Waldman abandons her arranged fiancé to run off with gangster boyfriend Hymie Boxer, who winds up in prison for murder. Following the shock of her children's troubles, Mrs. Waldman falls blind. It is at this point that the children all realize the mess they created and suddenly find Yom Kippur spirit. Hymie Boxer recites the Yom Kippur atonement liturgy in prison and blames his troubles on being raised without Jewish tradition. Solomon Waldman makes the decision to revive his cantorial career. The film closes with the two families joining together in the Waldman apartment as Solomon gleefully belts out "Kol Nidre."[90]

The resemblance between Yiddish-language Yom Kippur films and English-language Christmas films becomes even clearer when we directly compare a key exemplar of each of these categories of film: (1) the English-language Christmas film *It's a Wonderful Life*, which premiered on Broadway in the Christmas season of 1946; and (2) the Yiddish-language Yom Kippur film *Kol Nidre*, which premiered on the Lower East Side in the Yom Kippur season of 1939. These films have each been deemed iconic entries of their respective genres: *It's a Wonderful Life* is ranked #1 on the American Film Institute's list of "Most Inspiring Films of All Time,"[91] and *Kol Nidre* is "said to be one of the best musical film dramas made" according to the *American Jewish World* newspaper and a "great sensation" according to the Yiddish *Forverts*.[92] Importantly, *Kol Nidre* was made before *It's a Wonderful Life*, which means that the plot of the latter film did not influence the plot of the lesser-known former.

Both *It's a Wonderful Life* and *Kol Nidre* are character analyses that follow their respective protagonists from childhood, through young adulthood and into marriage. The protagonist of *It's a Wonderful Life* is George Bailey. George wants to follow his dream of traveling the world, despite his father wanting George to take over the family bank. The protagonist of *Kol Nidre* is Jenny Dorfman. Jenny chooses to marry the self-obsessed gambler Jack, despite her father wanting Jenny to marry the gentle young rabbi Yosele. George and Jenny's paths change course when their fathers suffer a stroke. George is forced to take over his father's bank, and George misplaces a large sum of money. Jenny realizes that her husband is not faithful nor financially reliable. With their dreams shattered, both George and Jenny come to view their lives as a failure. The films climax with a suicide attempt by the protagonist on the eve of their respective holiday: George attempts to jump from a bridge on Christmas Eve, and Jenny attempts the same on Yom Kippur Eve. George is saved by an angel (an incarnation of the "supernatural visitor" in Christmas folklore) who shows him how the goodness inside of him has helped others throughout his life. Jenny is saved by the sound of "Kol Nidre," the Yom Kippur chant that initiates an inward search for goodness. George and Jenny both learn to believe that a "wonderful life" does not consist of seeking self-pleasure, but rather, consists of the compassion needed to bring joy to others. George realizes he has been sharing this compassion with others throughout his life. He returns home to join his family and community in singing "Hark! The Herald Angels Sing." Jenny realizes that Rabbi Yosele has been sharing this compassion with others throughout his life. She subsequently marries him and reconciles with her family.[93] These two films are, to quote a Yiddish folk saying, "*di zelbe yente nor andersh geshleyert*" [the same story veiled differently].

Only a few months after *Kol Nidre*, another major Yiddish Yom Kippur film was released in America, *Overture to Glory*. This latter film is based on a modern Yiddish legend about Vilna cantor Joel David Loewenstein-Strashunsky (1816–1850), who is said to have abandoned his faith and family in Vilna to perform in the Polish opera *Halka* in Warsaw.[94] In the film, just before a performance of *Halka*, Strashunsky learns that his young son has died. He realizes that the interpersonal family connections that he had abandoned are more important than pursuing personal artistic dreams. The final scene of the film is an exemplary Yiddish version of the cinematic "Home for Christmas" scene: Strashunsky returns to Vilna on a stormy Yom Kippur Eve and enters his former Vilna synagogue, where he performs an impassioned "Kol Nidre" in front of his former wife and community.[95] Ruthie Abeliovich argues that this scene, along with the other cinematic "Kol Nidre" performances, provided Jewish immigrants with "a sort of medicine for their homesickness."[96]

The foundational myth for the modern Jewish people was hence not only the exodus from the *shtetl* following Christian intrusion on *nitl-nakht*, as proposed earlier—but also that Yom Kippur is the emblem of pure *shtetl* culture, and that it must be recovered from the corrupting non-Jewish world. This message is made explicit in the 1939 Yiddish film *A Letter to Mother*, in which the Jewish protagonist symbolically attends a Yom Kippur synagogue service on the immigration ship from Poland to America.[97] Such a message parallels that of Christmas being the foundation of modern Christian culture, as put forth in Washington Irving's seminal narrative idealizing Christmas church services that dwell upon "the origin of our faith."[98]

Christmas was, in fact, a standard premiere and special-showing date for American Yiddish theater and film productions that emphasized pure Jewish culture. These productions often centered on performances of "Kol Nidre" or the blowing of the shofar.[99] For Christmas Eve 1919, for example, New York's Yiddish Art Theatre prepared a special production of Sholem Aleichem's *Tevye the Dairyman*, the basis for the later *Fiddler on the Roof*.[100] A Yiddish film adaptation of *Tevye* premiered in Manhattan on December 21, 1939, with a special midnight screening on Christmas Eve.[101] This *Tevye* film premiere coincided with a flood of Christmastime *Kol Nidre* screenings across American cities. In the Bronx, for instance, *Kol Nidre* played continuously in the week leading up to Christmas 1939, culminating with a midnight Christmas Eve screening.[102] A year earlier, another popular Yiddish *shtetl* film, *Mamele*, had premiered in Manhattan on Christmas Eve 1938.[103] And yet another year earlier, Christmas Day 1937 saw the premiere of *The Cantor's Son*, billed as "the first great Yiddish musical talkie production in America."[104]

This latter film opens in the *shtetl* of Belz filled with Jewish men cordially studying Torah. Shloymele, the son of a Jewish cantor, runs off to America to become a secular star. But he becomes deeply nostalgic for Belz. He sends his earned money off to his cantor father in Belz so that the cantor can buy a new prayer shawl for the *yomim neroim*. For Shloymele's inaugural American radio performance, rather than sing a secular song, he chooses to sing the Hebrew prayer that concludes the Yom Kippur memorial synagogue service, "*Ov ho'rakhamim*." A synagogue committee hears Shloymele's performance and hires him to be the cantor for their *yomim neroim* services. Shloymele instantly becomes famous and takes a cantorial tour across America. He then returns home to Belz for his parents' fiftieth wedding anniversary. He is ecstatic to see that the *shtetl* of his youth has not changed at all. He decides to remain in Belz for the rest of his life.[105] In short, the film conveys a message that there is no trace of Christmas in the authentic Jewish *shtetl*. Mark Slobin describes *The Cantor's Son* as "a rhetoric of nostalgia" and that "the overall effect is to create a fantasy world of anti-assimilation and survival of Old World values."[106] According to Yiddish film, Jews must reject Christmas and return to their pure Judaic roots centered on Yom Kippur.

The Christmas film thus translated into Yiddish as the Yom Kippur film. Both film genres garner sentimentality for an idealized, domestic version of the respective holiday while implicitly decrying the hedonism of the premodern Christmas. The two types of film epitomize what literary critic Fredric Jameson calls "nostalgia films."[107] And yet, despite the overarching commonality between nostalgic Yom Kippur and Christmas films, they are inherently antithetical. According to Yiddish Yom Kippur films, observing the traditional Jewish holiday of Yom Kippur—as initiated by the nostalgic sound of "Kol Nidre"—is the antithesis to assimilating and in turn singing Christmas carols.

The Fate of the Yom Kippur Genre

What ultimately became of the Yom Kippur genre? Let us consider what happened to Samson Raphaelson after the success of his Yom Kippur play being adapted into the 1927 film *The Jazz Singer*. Raphaelson became an avid screenwriter and continued to adapt plays for the screen through the 1930s. His most acclaimed screenplay was an adaptation of the 1937 Hungarian play *Parfumerie*. The play follows two seemingly incompatible shop employees who ultimately realize that they are capable of getting along after discovering that they are each other's anonymous pen pals. Raphaelson very well could have followed in the footsteps of *The Jazz Singer* and set his screenplay on Yom Kippur. Such a setting would be symbolic of the plot's themes of interpersonal harmony and making amends. Instead, he kept with the Hungarian original and set the film on Christmas. *The Shop Around the Corner* premiered shortly after Christmas 1939 to rave reviews, including a rave review in the Yiddish *Forverts*,[108] and is today regarded as one of the greatest films of all time.[109] Released around the same time as the Yiddish Yom Kippur films *Kol Nidre* and *Overture to Glory*, *The Shop Around the Corner* launched a new genre of film, the Christmas film.[110]

Shortly after the release of *The Shop Around the Corner*, American Jewish songwriter Irving Berlin (1888–1989) prepared a new song for what would become the second major installment of the Christmas film genre, *Holiday Inn*. Berlin had immigrated to New York from Eastern

Europe as a child. Upon the premiere of *Holiday Inn*, his traditional Jewish background received special coverage in the New York Yiddish press.[111] The lyrics of his song were quite similar to the sentiments that Rosa Palatnik expressed in her Yiddish story about longing for the idyllic Yom Kippur of long ago: "I'm dreaming of a white Christmas, just like the ones I used to know."[112] Following Berlin's success, other American Jews continued to compose popular Christmas songs over the next two decades, creating Christmas's secular song genre.[113] Meanwhile, with Christmas films taking off, Jewish film studio chairman Charles Koerner (1896–1946) arranged for a screen adaptation of the 1943 Christmas story "The Greatest Gift"—which became the iconic 1946 Christmas film *It's a Wonderful Life*, launching the Christmas film genre in full force. The Yiddish Yom Kippur film genre, meanwhile, completely died out after 1940, alongside a sharp decline in secular Yiddish culture. That is, while Christmas and Yom Kippur were *both* reimagined around the turn of the twentieth century, Jews ultimately joined Christians in developing the reimagined Christmas while leaving their Yom Kippur–centered Yiddish culture behind.

The reimagined Yom Kippur did serve its purpose. Jews successfully erased Christmas from the perception of authentic Jewish culture, and they mainly targeted their Christmas songs and films at Christians. The concept that Jews celebrate Yom Kippur rather than Christmas continued to prevail in post-Yiddish American popular culture. In the 1977 Hallmark television special "Have I Got a Christmas for You," for example, Jews decide to work overtime on Christmas Eve to fill in for their Christian colleagues, in return for Christians having filled in for their Jewish colleagues on Yom Kippur Eve.[114] This plot reflected a real phenomenon that was documented among Jewish and Christian colleagues around the world.[115] The Yom Kippur–Christmas dichotomy is reinforced in the more recent series *The Marvelous Mrs. Maisel*, in which the assimilated Midge Maisel, who recurrently celebrates Yom Kippur right from the 2017 pilot episode, claims not to know the words to "White Christmas" because she's Jewish.[116] Most notably, a 1994 episode of *Northern Exposure* presents an adaptation of Dickens's *A Christmas Carol*, in which a miserly Jewish character undergoes a spiritual reawakening during a ghostly visit—on Yom Kippur Eve rather than Christmas Eve.[117]

While these English-language examples sustain the dichotomous Yom Kippur–Christmas model of holiday spirit, they are a far cry from the earlier Yiddish Yom Kippur films. They are directly engaged with the Christian Christmas; and looking beyond these examples, Hanukkah has arguably become more relevant than Yom Kippur in English-language Jewish culture due to Hanukkah's proximity to Christmas. Jews successfully erased Christmas from their imagined past, but they could not resist engaging with Christmas in their present. Joshua Eli Plaut explains that American Jews forged "an identity that is at once separate from the religious and historical dimensions of Christmas, yet convergent with its underlying spirit."[118] Once Jews were not restricted to a Jewish language, their Christmas spirit was not restricted to Yom Kippur spirit.

Conclusion

Christmas was once a holiday that both Christians and Jews celebrated, mainly in the form of drinking and gambling to ward off demons (colloquially known under irreligious folk names such as Yule, *Nidelnacht*, and *nitl-nakht*). But in the nineteenth century, Christians reclaimed Christmas as an artifact of their own religious history, claiming the central declaration in their Christmas Eve liturgy as its holiday spirit. Jews then disowned their association with Christmas. They instead claimed what Christians deemed "Christmas spirit" under the guise of "Yom Kippur spirit." The turn of the twentieth century thus saw the imagining of two dichotomized cultures: a Christian culture centered on a reimagined Christmas, and a Jewish culture centered on a reimagined Yom Kippur. Yiddish authors seeking to criticize absent values of peace and goodwill often did so in stories set on Yom Kippur rather than Christmas. The nostalgia of the modern Christmas film genre manifested in Yiddish via a Yom Kippur film genre. Morris Rosenfeld may have felt compelled to compose a Yiddish Hanukkah poem to take on the role of a Jewish Christmas carol, but this role was essentially already fulfilled by the traditional Yom Kippur "carol" of "Kol Nidre." In contrast to the success of the Christian reimagining of Christmas, however, the Yiddish reimagining of Yom Kippur was cut short by assimilation into the New World. Nonetheless, this Yiddish reimagining left a long-lasting mark on New World Jewish culture: the notion that Christmas is not authentic to it.

7

The Yiddish Christmas Literary Genre

We are ready to address the final question on our agenda: Why were Yiddish Christmas stories prevalent in the New World? It is clear why Yiddish Yom Kippur stories were prevalent—Jews wrote Yom Kippur stories for the same reason that Christians wrote Christmas stories—but why would Jewish immigrants have cared to read Yiddish stories about the holiday that they so staunchly disowned?

To answer this question, we need to establish the type of sentiments that are invoked in the Yiddish Christmas literature. Let us motivate our analysis by comparing two unrelated American poems about Christmas trees from the early twentieth century, one written by a Christian in English, the other written by a Jew in Yiddish. The first, a 1920 English-language poem by e e cummings (1894–1962) entitled "little tree," begins with the following lines:

> little tree
> little silent Christmas tree
> you are so little
> you are more like a flower
> who found you in the green forest
> and were you very sorry to come away?
> see   i will comfort you
> because you smell so sweetly[1]

The second, a 1902 Yiddish poem by Morris Rosenfeld (1862–1923) entitled "The Christmas Tree," reads as follows:

> Much poetry lies in the green Christmas tree
> It stays green when all is dead!
> I stand and look at it, and must tremble:
> It seems to me that it is red!

> Yes, red and wet from blood,
> I see in it the switch that futilely minces my skin.
> I see in it the anger, the malice and the hate:
> The love of the Christian.[2]

These poems illustrate how far Christians and Jews had come from the days when they jointly deployed dark midwinter lore to formulate a polemical dialogue. By the twentieth century, the dialogue had become disjointed. e e cummings, despite being no stranger to writing about the "kike,"[3] had no reason to invoke Jews in his poem about what had become a peaceful Christian holiday. The modern midwinter threat of Jewish commercialism was not calamitous to Christmas spirit like the premodern midwinter threat of Jewish devilry. Morris Rosenfeld, on the other hand, viewed the modern Christian holiday as very calamitous to Jewish culture—no less dangerous than the premodern midwinter threat of a menacing Jesus—and so he was unable to let go of the holiday's darkness. He takes the Christmas tree—botanical life that fights back midwinter death—and inverts it into bloody death itself. For Rosenfeld, Christmas is a holiday that must be situated within the realm of Christian antisemites. Whereas Yiddish Yom Kippur literature provided a modality for Jewish immigrants to promote authentic Jewish culture, Yiddish Christmas literature provided a modality to remind readers of what does not belong in Jewish culture.

Many Yiddish Christmas stories are set on the reimagined, frightening *nitl-nakht* of the Old World, which is essentially the opposite of the nostalgic Yom Kippur of the Old World. One such Yiddish Christmas story, "On the Night of *Nitl*," was published in Paris in 1969 by Polish-born Mendel Mann (1916–1975). Set one Christmas Eve in interwar Poland, the story follows the stream of consciousness of a Jewish boy who trembles in fear as he peers outside the window, watching the bright Christian celebration of "the *Yoyzl*" outside the church. The Jewish adults inside the home unnervingly play cards as they discuss the ferocious assaults that Christians committed against Jews in the past on "*nitl-nakht*." The boy worries that the Christians outside will turn violent and stone the house. He turns his ear to a rant going on inside. The adults are sounding off about how Christians stole the virgin-birth narrative from Greek mythology and Christianity is nothing more than a continuation of paganism. The tale concludes with the Jews remaining uneasy as the blare of Christian singing sweeps the street.[4] This slice-of-life story was published in a book of Yiddish stories that sentimentalize the uniqueness of Old World Jewish life. It delivers a clear message that Jews and Christians historically celebrated a very different Christmas: Christians held a gleaming outdoor celebration of Jesus's birth, and Jews hid inside their gloomy homes while rejecting the myth of Jesus's birth. The story affirms that light could only overcome darkness on Christmas for the Christians who celebrated Jesus, whereas the *nitl-nakht* for the Jews who feared *Yoyzl* was confined to a dark, somber home surrounded by ferocious Christians.

Such a message pervaded New World Yiddish literature. As early as Christmastime 1894, Ukrainian-born Jacob Gordin (1853–1909) published a Yiddish tale in New York that vividly sketched the helpless fear of Jews hiding indoors on the "*blinde nakht*."[5] The tale was routinely republished over the next three decades, both in its original Yiddish and in various English translations,[6] attesting to its popularity. Yiddish authors transformed the psychological gloom of midwinter into a trademark of the Jewish people, forming a distinctive identity that contrasted with the Christians who spend the season frolicking and rejoicing. As Gordin propounds in another Yiddish story, the national anthem of this Jewish people was "Kol Nidre."[7]

Yet there was more to gloomy Yiddish Christmas stories than their goal of promoting a sense of Jewish togetherness. Two unassuming themes from the Yiddish Christmas folklore of the Old World curiously resurged in Yiddish Christmas literature of the New World: (1) a fear of demonic forces on Christmas Eve, and (2) a fear of having sex on Christmas Eve. These themes could not have been invoked to merely remind readers of the gloominess of the Old World Jewish Christmas, since most New World Jews had come to view their old supernatural beliefs as irrational superstitions. As this chapter argues, these supernatural themes instead functioned as metaphors. Jewish immigrants were concerned about their children's assimilation into the New World, and celebrating the new Christmas was the token of this concern. The traditional Jewish fear of demonic forces on Christmas Eve became a metaphor for the new fear that Christmas evoked among Jews: the fear of a dwindling of traditional Jewish culture. The traditional Jewish abstention from sex on Christmas Eve became a metaphor for the idea that Jews can only maintain their traditional culture if they resist seduction by Christmas. In other words, while Yiddish Christmas stories often recounted the supernatural *nitl-nakht* of the Old World, they were really making a statement about the Christmas of the New World.

This chapter reviews a selection of Yiddish Christmas stories written by Jews who immigrated to North and South America in the early twentieth century. It argues that these stories resonated with Jewish immigrants afraid of Christmas seducing their children away from their heritage. We saw that Yiddish Yom Kippur stories form a literary genre analogous to the mainstream Christmas genre. This chapter makes the case that Yiddish Christmas stories, too, form a literary genre, but antithetical to the mainstream Christmas genre. Both the mainstream and the Yiddish Christmas genres are based on the theme of balancing darkness with light. However, whereas the mainstream Christmas genre stresses comfort and joy to outbalance the bleakness of midwinter, the Yiddish Christmas genre puts bleakness at the forefront by stressing the fear and abstinence associated with *nitl-nakht*.

Joseph Opatoshu's Yiddish Christmas Stories

We begin by acquainting ourselves with the master of the Yiddish Christmas story, Joseph Opatoshu. Opatoshu was among the most prolific Yiddish authors in early twentieth-century New York. His stories were well-known to Jewish immigrants across the New World, from North and South America to France to Australia.[8] Opatoshu was born on Christmas Eve 1886 in the backwoods of Congress Poland. In contrast to those from the Jew-packed *shtetl*, Opatoshu was the son of a timber merchant who mainly dealt with Christian peasants. Opatoshu thought deeply about the irony of how the boy born on Christmas in these woods was the Jew. Rather than following the trajectory of Jesus (the most famous Jew to be born on Christmas) and garnering esteem from Christians, Opatoshu's strong Jewish identity never allowed him to feel at home with his Christian neighbors. Many of his Yiddish stories are semiautobiographical, following a Jewish protagonist who grows up in the Polish woods alongside Christian peasants. A central theme of these stories is that the Jew is incapable of assimilating into the patriotic

Polish society. In his acclaimed 1921 novel *In Polish Woods*, such a Jew picks up a cross held by a slain Polish upriser and joins the Poles' revolt against the occupying Russian Empire—and the Jew is attacked by an antisemitic Polish mob.[9] Sabine Koller describes this scene as Opatoshu "ridiculing the possibility of a fusion between ideals of Polish patriotism and Jewish emancipation"[10] and disputing "the naive concept of Christian-Jewish co-messianism"[11] that was regularly invoked in the work of contemporaneous Yiddish author Sholem Asch. Opatoshu believed that a Jew, even if he shares Christ's birthday and bears Christ's cross, can never celebrate a bright Christmas in the same way as the Jew's Christian neighbors. For the Jew, there was only the dark *nitl-nakht*.

Unlike fellow Yiddish author Sholem Asch, who portrayed American Jewish engagement with Christ (and thereby Christmas) positively in his writings[12]—Asch went so far as to write his own nonpolemical story about the Nativity of Jesus[13]—Opatoshu looked down upon Jewish acculturation to non-Jewish society. He arrived in New York at age twenty and joined the Yiddish modernist movement of *Di yunge*, led by poet Mani Leib. As described earlier, Leib sought to create a distinct Yiddish literary culture that portrays Christmas as an external threat to the Jewish people. Opatoshu's earliest works to convey his pessimistic views on Jewish–Christian harmony centered on violent Eastertime antisemitism. By the mid-1920s, however, Opatoshu turned his attention to Christmas, adopting *nitl* as the Yiddish literary symbol of the darkness of Christian antisemitism. For Opatoshu, Yiddish Christmas stories provided an opportunity to convey the message that Jews can never reproduce the comfort and joy of the Christian celebration of Christmas—not because Jews don't want to, but because Christian antisemitism makes it impossible.

We get a sense of how Opatoshu viewed the idea of New York Jews celebrating Christmas by taking a look at what seems to be his earliest Christmas tale, "A Gentile in the Diaspora," published in 1922. This story is not set on the Jews' *nitl-nakht* in the Christian-dominant Old World, but rather on a Christian's Christmas in a Jewish-dominated area of New York. The story opens like a typical sentimental Christmas story, with a vivid description of a beautiful Christmas tree, decorated with colored lights and sparkling ornaments that "fill the room with joy." The adorned Christmas tree elevates the desolation of Christian protagonist Alyosha Volkov—until his Jewish wife invites her Jewish friends to play cards in front of the tree. Alyosha felt his wife's Jewish heritage to be irrelevant when they lived in a Christian area of the Russian Empire, but he becomes irritated by her Jewish identity in New York. She reunites with her Jewish cousins, speaks Yiddish on the street, and raises their children among other Jews. Alyosha can no longer suppress his antisemitism. He favors his younger blond son Petya over his older Jewish-looking son Vanya. On Christmas Eve, Alyosha explains to Petya that he is actually a Christian and that his ancestors were eminent builders of a Russian city. His ancestors would not invite Jews on Christmas Eve, but rather "real noblemen." Alyosha goes on to tell Petya about Jesus and how the Jews crucified him, not sparing any details. The story ends like a customary Christian Christmas story: Alyosha and Petya kneel in front of the beautiful Christmas tree while quietly reciting Christian hymns.[14] With this story, Opatoshu ridicules the naivete of New York Jews celebrating Christmas. It is not possible, according to Opatoshu, to strip Christmas of its Christianity—nor is it possible to strip Christmas of Christianity's inherent antisemitism.

Let us follow how Opatoshu continued to deride Christmas by turning to two of his supernatural fables, both bearing the title "On the Night of *Nitl*." The first, published a few days after Christmas 1925, begins with a virgin birth on Christmas Eve. A Jewish woman in a remote Christian area gives birth to a daughter under a constellation akin to the Star of Bethlehem. In the original Christian Christmas story, the Jewish virgin's child is born outdoors in the presence of angels, and Christians believe the father to be God. In this Yiddish Christmas story, the Jewish virgin's child is born indoors as Jews hide from evil spirits on the night of *nitl*, and Christians believe the father to be the Devil. The girl goes through a series of life events that mirror Jesus's trajectory, but unlike Jesus, Christians never come to esteem this Jewish girl. For example, the girl gets swept by an overflowing stream (alluding to the baptism of Jesus), but the blond Christians are only able to see the Jewish brunette emerging from the stream as a devil with horns.[15] Here Opatoshu inverts the Nativity story to revise the idea that Christians can ever respect a Jew. He argues that Christians will always see the Jew as an Other. In the Old World, Opatoshu reminds readers, the night of *nitl* was ruled by the Devil, and Jews hid indoors from evil spirits. In the New World, some naive Jews think that they can walk out the door and enter into the Christian Christmas. But Opatoshu insists that Christians will never welcome Jews into their holiday, because Christians will always associate Jews with the Devil.

Opatoshu's 1935 fable of the same name tells of what happens to Jews who nevertheless step outside and brave the evil spirits. Like the former fable, this tale follows a Jew who lives among Christian peasants. While this Jew is not explicitly described as having been born on Christmas, his name, Yoske, alludes to the most famous Jew to be born on Christmas, *Yoshke Pandre*. The narration recounts that "despite growing up among mountain peasants [. . .] this was not enough for Yoske to feel homey on a Christian holiday." Yoske comes home early on Christmas Eve, because on that night "it is simplest to just stay at home." He bolts the doors shut, but cold mist nonetheless seeps in. When his sons go out to provide water to the oxen, they accidentally set a fire and let out the oxen for their safety. The oxen run away, which Yoske attributes to the Devil on *nitl*. After a bleak search, the oxen are found dead at the bottom of a cliff. The dead oxen are picked at by crows, which Yoske identifies as the evil spirits of *nitl*. The narration describes how, with everything frozen in the cold, there was "no strength to drive off the evil spirits."[16] Whereas mainstream Christmas stories emphasize warmth to fight off midwinter cold, this Yiddish Christmas story could not be any colder. The oxen are a clear metaphor for traditional Jewish values: They run away from Yoske's traditional Jewish home on Christmas and wind up dead. Yoske's children did not intend to lose the oxen permanently, but the children's accidental Christmas Eve fire inflamed the evil spirits of *nitl* and caused the oxen's irreversible death. Opatoshu is sounding the alarm about Jewish children playing with fire by embracing the dangerous holiday of Christmas, which is increasingly seeping into Jewish homes.

In both of these stories, Opatoshu's portrayal of the traditional fear of evil spirits on *nitl-nakht* serves a contemporary cause. He repurposes these spirits into the source of the perceived incompatibility between celebrating Christmas and retaining a traditional Jewish identity. In the first, the Jews who hide from evil spirits on Christmas are unable to let go of their Jewish identity. In the second, the Jews who go out toward evil spirits on Christmas are unable to hold onto their Jewish identity. Jewish immigrants were afraid of their children stepping out of the metaphorical door that they traditionally hid behind on Christmas, and

Opatoshu's Yiddish Christmas stories functioned as validation of this new fear of Christmas—by reminding readers that a fear of stepping out toward Christmas is in fact justified in Yiddish tradition.

Nitl-Nakht Abstinence and Seduction by Christmas

Let us now consider the most common theme in Yiddish Christmas stories: Christmas is seductive. Yiddish Christmas stories set in the New World often follow a seducer and seducee to respectively symbolize Christmas and Jew—and if the Jew is to hang onto his traditional Jewish values, he must hang onto the traditional value of resisting sex on *nitl-nakht*.

For Opatoshu, whose stories focus on Jewish–Christian relations, these two characters are a Christian seducer and a Jewish seducee. We turn to his 1931 story "Watchmen." Set in modern America, near Opatoshu's contemporary Bronx home between the zoo and botanical garden, the story opens with a bleak depiction of a cold, snowy Christmas Eve. The frightening roars of animals and cawing of crows are once again described as evil spirits. The story follows two watchmen who guard property under construction, a Protestant named Frank and a Jew named Mendel. Frank's Catholic wife, Mary, is a personification of Christmas. She has been growing fed up with Frank because he is an alcoholic who does not care for religion, while she has been growing close with Mendel. Late on Christmas Eve, Mary visits Mendel to tell him that she is leaving Frank after he would not even attend church. There is clear sexual tension between Mendel and his seducer. In a standard American Christmas story, this would turn into a sentimental Christmas romance. Yiddish Christmas stories, however, never end with light and warmth. Mendel, recalling the frightful and supernatural "*nitl*" of the Old World, seeks Mary's warmth to ease his fear of the cawing crows. Mary responds that she cannot help Mendel unless he converts to Catholicism, because on Christmas Eve "the evil spirits only attack Jews and nonbelievers." She asks Mendel to convert to Catholicism so that they can marry, but Mendel will not comply ("I'm already a bad Jew; I'd be an even worse Catholic"). He still wants Mary to stay with him, but Mary will not stay with a nonbeliever, let alone a Jew, on Christmas Eve.[17] Hence, Mendel cannot overcome the bleakness of midwinter without replacing his

Jewish faith with Christianity. This story is yet another expression by Opatoshu that Jews are unable to both remain Jewish and participate in Christmas, no matter how strong the sexual tension.

A similar situation of a Christian woman seducing a Jewish man is found in the 1920 American Yiddish Christmas story "In the Fields of Georgia," written by Belarussian-born Baruch Glasman (1893–1945). This story follows an unnamed Jew en route to Jacksonville, Florida. He stops to spend the night at a home he stumbles upon in the fields of Georgia. This home, it turns out, belongs to a seductive Black woman who has prepared an extravagant Christmas dinner. She tells the Jew that she had hoped for her husband to return home on Christmas Eve, but alas, he did not. She invites the Jew to take her husband's place that evening, explaining that "biblical Abraham, the Jewish Father, had a Black wife, Hagar, and even had a child with her." The Jew is uncomfortable—he is hesitant to eat nonkosher food and to sleep with a nonkosher woman, especially on "*nitl-nakht.*" The Jew ultimately leaves on Christmas morning without sleeping with the woman. Both the Jew and the woman are left unsatisfied, and the reader is left to ponder whether the Jew made the right decision by adhering to his Jewish values.[18] Glasman's story does not go so far as Opatoshu's "Watchmen" in arguing that Judaism must be renounced entirely for a Jew to successfully celebrate Christmas. To Glasman, it is up to the Jew to decide if it is worth temporarily giving up traditional values and giving in to seduction by Christmas.

It is notable that Glasman uses racialization to represent the Christmas motif of contrasting darkness with light. For Glasman, the Christmas seducer is Black, contrasting with the white Jew. For another Yiddish writer, Polish-born Rosa Palatnik (1904–1981), it is the Jew who is Black, a racialized minority confronted by a seductive white Christmas. Palatnik, who immigrated to Brazil in 1936, was the South American "Opatoshu" of Yiddish Christmas stories. She had a history of critiquing the irony of Brazilian Jews celebrating Christmas.[19] Her 1961 Brazilian Yiddish Christmas tale "*Nitl* Trees" does not explicitly depict the seducer and seducee as Christian and Jew, but rather as Christmas Tree and Black Lumberjack. Being a Yiddish story, the racialized (Black) characters symbolize Jews. The narration describes the most beautiful and provocative tree in the mountains of Rio de Janeiro as both a "*nitl* tree" and an "evil-inclination tree." It is "a tall evergreen tree that had long been provoking those below, flirting with all the Black mountain climbers with its unreachable highness." Despite their best efforts, the Black lumberjacks have never been able to reach this *nitl* tree. It stands in the steepest and most dangerous part of the mountains. Nevertheless, the spoiled, rich, white young woman Senorita Magda demands this tree for Christmas. One Black lumberjack, Antonio, decides it is worth the risk of venturing through the most dangerous region of the mountains to acquire this tree, given the money he would earn to be able to pay for a graceful Christmas dinner. He wants to celebrate Christmas just like nonracialized people. Antonio does manage to reach the tree and begins cutting it down—but he ultimately slips and dies, holding onto the tree "like Jesus on a cross." The story ends with Senorita Magda receiving the tree from Antonio's fellow lumberjacks, with her only concern being the chore of washing off Antonio's blood before decorating the tree for her Christmas feast.[20]

Palatnik conveys similar sentiments about Christmas to Opatoshu. As with Opatoshu in "A Gentile in the Diaspora," Palatnik mocks the Christian celebration of Christmas as inherently bigoted. She depicts Christmas as "provocative yet unreachable" to the racialized Jewish minority. And as with Opatoshu in his 1935 "In the Night of *Nitl*," Patalnik depicts Christmas as inherently fatal to Jews who dare venture out toward it. For Palatnik, Jews will never achieve the joys of Christmas and can only die trying; and while Christians can attain the joys of Christmas, it is not attained righteously. Palatnik is also consistent with Glasman in that Jews and Christmas belong to different races. Racialization was a standard trope in Jewish stories about the Old versus New struggle. In the seminal film *The Jazz Singer*, for example, the Jewish protagonist is faced with choosing between singing "Kol Nidre" in a prayer shawl versus performing jazz in blackface. The element of seduction was likewise a standard trope. In the example of *The Jazz Singer*, the blackfaced Jew falls in love with a "*shikse*," that is, a (white) non-Jewish woman. Jessica Kirzane explains that "Yiddish writers used fictionalized sexual experiences to situate Jewish Americans in American society," with these experiences often being interracial to demonstrate "the ambivalent position of the Jew among American racial binaries."[21] Glasman and Palatnik depict such interracial sexual tension between Christmas and Jew, and the outcomes of their stories are consistent in that the tension is never relieved.

Elsewhere in South America, we find a Yiddish Christmas story where the Jewish protagonist manages to withstand seduction by Christmas. This story is the 1960 "For a Holiday," written in Argentina by Polish-born Jaime Goldzac (1910–1977). The tale follows fifty-year-old Leyb, a Jewish immigrant in Buenos Aires who finds himself in a traditional Jewish occupation, a presser at a tailor shop. Set during a suffocating heat wave, the sweatshop where Leyb works is described as *gehenem*, hell. His beautiful wife Brokhe attempts to sway her husband away from his traditional lifestyle, hoping to lure him out of *gehenem*. She resents that Leyb has not built a new life in the New World, while "all of their acquaintances had worked their way up; they drive their own coaches and have their own summer homes." Brokhe's brother, Shloyme, now going by Solomon and dressing like an Argentinian, is a former tailor who became a successful factory owner with dozens of employees. Brokhe convinces Leyb to attend a dinner party at Solomon's home to see what higher culture looks like. There Leyb gets struck by the low-cut dress and bare shoulders of Solomon's wife and flirtatious daughter. But Leyb is far from seduced. Upon laying his eyes on a decorated Christmas tree, Leyb is horrified to discover that he is attending a Christmas dinner. He recalls "*nitl*" in the Old World: All Jewish institutions were closed. Jews stayed at home with locked doors and windows. Jews were swept by fear as church bells tolled. Leyb leaves the dinner completely unashamed of his lack of upward mobility and his remaining in metaphorical *gehenem*. If upward mobility means embracing unthinkable customs like Christmas, he doesn't want it.[22] With this story, Goldzac illustrates a route for Jews to experience the light of Christmas, but like Opatoshu in "Watchmen" and Glasman in "In the Fields of Georgia," it involves the abandonment of Jewish principles.

It is clear that in the world of Yiddish literature, Jews cannot both retain their traditional culture and give in to the seductive warmth of Christmas. But this is not to say that the Yiddish literature does not offer a sexy antidote for midwinter desolation as an alternative to celebrating Christmas. Whereas Jewish couples traditionally abstained from sex on the *tume*-filled night of *nitl*, Jews were traditionally encouraged to have sex on the *kdushe*-filled night of the Sabbath, as rabbinic authorities considered sexual relations to be a "dimension of Sabbath pleasure."[23] If we are to find midwinter sex in Yiddish stories, then, we would find this sex in stories set on the Sabbath before Christmas—that is, the longest Friday night of the year, which commences following what was traditionally known in Yiddish as "*kurts frayik*" [Short Friday]. We indeed find such pleasure in the 1945 Yiddish midwinter tale "The Short Friday" by Polish-born Isaac Bashevis Singer (1903–1991). This story follows a married Jewish couple madly in love, Shmuel Leybele and Shoshe. The couple has unfortunately been unable to have children. Shmuel Leybele worries he will end up in eternal *gehenem*, since he will not have a child to recite Kaddish for him. The night before the *kurts fraytik*, a snowstorm strikes, encapsulating the couple's house in snow by Friday morning. Day passes and night arrives, at which point the snowy gloom is fought back by the cheerful Sabbath dinner in the brightly lit home. Shoshe's Sabbath cooking is described as a "taste of *ganeydn* [heaven]." The story ends with the couple engaging in passionate sex. The sex cannot result in the conception of a child to recite Kaddish, but the immense passion of the two lovers allows them to directly ascend to *ganeydn*.[24] This midwinter Sabbath story could not be any more different from the Yiddish Christmas stories that we saw. Jews cannot escape *gehenem* on Christmas because they cannot have sex on *nitl-nakht*, but they can indeed ascend to *ganeydn* if they instead have their sex on the Sabbath. For Jews who maintain their traditional culture, it is the Sabbath rather than Christmas that is the time to engage in midwinter pleasure.

Conquering *Nitl-Nakht*

We have now identified the primary driver of the Yiddish Christmas story's prevalence: Traditional themes associated with *nitl-nakht*, including Jews being vulnerable to demons and Jews refraining from sex, resonated with Jewish readers who feared their children's vulnerability to seduction by Christmas. Yet not all stories about *nitl-nakht* necessarily functioned to mirror such anxieties. The *nitl-nakht* stories we explored so far are Yiddish stories written in the Americas. A different purpose was served by two alternative types of *nitl-nakht* stories: (1) *nitl-nakht* stories written in English; and (2) *nitl-nakht* stories written in Israel.

Let us begin with the first type of alternative *nitl-nakht* story, the English type. We saw that Jewish integration into the New World is ultimately portrayed positively in Samson Raphaelson's English-language

Yom Kippur story "The Day of Atonement," in contrast to the Yom Kippur stories written in Yiddish. We find a similar trend in the English-language story "Nittel Nacht," published on the week leading up to Christmas 1901. This story was written by Martha Wolfenstein (1869–1906), who, like Raphaelson, was a second-generation immigrant in America. Wolfenstein provides a vivid portrayal of the mythical antisemitic terrors of the Old World Christmas. She describes it as "a favorite time for Jew-raids, when the people, fresh from church, where the priests had fired them with religious zeal, delighted in plundering and murdering the Jews in the name of Christ, their Lord." The story follows Jewish men who play an agitated game of cards on a frightful Christmas Eve. They tell chilling stories about the horrible things that have happened to Jews on previous Christmases. At the center of the story is Hirshl, a young boy who repeatedly expresses his desire to fight back and beat up Christians. Hirshl explains, "When I am a man I will be so good so pious that the Lord will return to [Jerusalem] where there are no wicked [Christians]." Hirshl later has a vivid dream in which he himself arrives in Jerusalem. Upon awakening, he realizes he is only at home, "but it was morning, and the terrors of the night were past."[25] In contrast to the events of many *nitl-nakht* stories written in Yiddish, the protagonist of this English story manages to make it through *nitl-nakht* unscathed. As such, Hirshl is suggestive of the Jew who has successfully overcome the plight of the Old World. This English tale reflects positively on Jews "waking up" in the New World as a form of progress, conquering the antisemitic *nitl-nakht* of the Old.

We also find a second type of Christmas story that reflects positively on Jews conquering *nitl-nakht*, namely those written in Israel, the land of Hirshl's dream. Not all Israeli fiction depicts the old *nitl-nakht* in a negative light. Hebrew author Shmuel Yosef Agnon (1887–1970), famous for inflecting his writings with references to Old World customs, makes recurrent neutral references to Jews playing cards on the night of *nitl*.[26] Nonetheless, *nitl-nakht* was a terrifying time in the broader Israeli popular memory. Such a Zionist perception of *nitl* is chiefly illustrated in the 1941 German-language play *Nittel (Blinde Nacht)* by Simon Kronberg (1891–1947), written after Kronberg fled Vienna for Palestine in 1934. The play is a dramatic commentary on the failure of Jewish assimilation into Europe. It follows an assimilated Jew named Konrad who celebrates

Christmas with his non-Jewish wife in a European village. Assimilation has given Konrad a sense of security. He insists that antisemitism is a thing of the past. But on Christmas Eve, the local Christians murder Konrad and burn down his house.[27] Here Kronberg employs the mythical terrors of *nitl-nakht* to convey the message that Zionists can only conquer antisemitism (epitomized by *nitl-nakht*) once they unveil the false security of assimilation (epitomized by celebrating Christmas).[28]

According to Israeli popular memory, Zionists officially conquered *nitl-nakht* on Christmas Eve 1945. On this night, an illegal ship of 252 Holocaust survivors arrived in the British Mandate of Palestine. The ship was named *Hannah Szenes* after the twenty-three-year-old Zionist poet (best known for the Hebrew poem "Eli, Eli") who had died fighting Nazi forces in the previous year. It chose to arrive on Christmas Eve on the premise that the British coastal guards would be less alert that evening. The *Hannah Szenes* managed to elude British patrols and evade a violent storm. Upon landing on the shore, the refugees, soaked to their skin, posted a Hebrew banner on the beach:

> This ship [. . .] has landed Jewish immigrants in their homeland and shall remain on the shores of Palestine as a tombstone commemorating our six million brothers and sisters who perished in Europe.[29]

This Christmas event transformed the depiction of *nitl-nakht* in the Yiddish Christmas stories written in Israel. Among Israel's most prominent Yiddish writers was Leyb Chain-Shimoni (1900–1974). His 1951 story "Locusts" follows the fictional journey of a Jew on the *Hannah Szenes*. The narration consistently reiterates that the last night on the ship was "*nitl-nakht*," when the protagonist was "reborn."[30] Chain-Shimoni's 1956 story "*Nitl-nakht*" also follows a ship of Jews arriving in Palestine on Christmas Eve. This story opens with British soldiers in military barracks who long for the old sentimental Christmas of their homes. While they try to have a pleasant Christmas in Palestine, they are interrupted by an unknown ship approaching the coast. Irritated, the gentiles are forced to leave their barracks and brave the stormy night. They watch as the storm nearly knocks over the incoming ship. Yet the Holocaust-surviving Jews make it through, thrilled to have reached the Land of Israel.[31] In his stories, Chain-Shimoni symbolizes Jews colonizing Palestine with a motif of Jews conquering *nitl-nakht*. The one country in which Jews are no longer a threatened minority is the one country in which Jews can attain joy in a Yiddish Christmas story. By arriving in their homeland on Christmas Eve, *nitl-nakht* is inverted from its dark place in Jewish popular memory into a night of warmth and light for Jews and cold and darkness for gentiles.

Yiddish authors in the Americas, conversely, were facing a direct threat to their minority culture and were less interested in writing about Jews overcoming the plight of their historical *nitl-nakht*. Instead, Yiddish authors in the Americas focused on writing about whether the contemporary phenomenon of Jews celebrating Christmas is any better than the historical plight of *nitl-nakht*, thereby setting the stage for the dilemma that Joshua Eli Plaut outlines in *A Kosher Christmas*.

Conclusion

Jewish immigrants wrote Yiddish Christmas stories for their fellow immigrants who were anxious about the Christmas of the New World. In the Jewish immigrant imagination, the historical Jewish *nitl-nakht* was confined to a dark, gloomy home encircled by a wild Christian celebration. Yiddish Christmas stories served as a modality to relay the conditions in which the Jewish celebration of Christmas can ever move beyond these traditional confines. In some stories, there are no conditions under which Jews can joyfully celebrate Christmas, with Christmas depicted as inherently catastrophic for Jews. In others, there are conditions under which Jews can attain the joys of Christmas, but they come at the price of abandoning core Jewish values. These Yiddish Christmas stories form a genre of Yiddish literature based on the same motif as the mainstream Christmas genre: balancing darkness and light. In Yiddish, this motif took the form of balancing old and new Jewish identities. It is hence fitting that Christmas-born Opatoshu, in rejecting the new Christmas and devoting himself to old Jewish culture, died on Yom Kippur. The Yiddish Christmas genre died together with the Yiddish Yom Kippur genre, as new identities ultimately outbalanced the old among secular Jews. And as these Jews adopted their new identities, they not only forgot about the time when evil spirits reigned on Christmas, but they came to forget that Christmas ever existed in Yiddish lore and literature at all.

Conclusion

Yiddish Christmas Today

Let us now return to the narrative that opened this book. Based on the hysterical audience reaction to Sam Broverman's Yiddish rendition of "Let It Snow,"[1] it appears that the story of Christmas in Yiddish tradition is over and forgotten. The tumultuous historical journey of *nitl-nakht* culminated with its erasure from the knowledge of the general public. Today, the idea of pairing Christmas with Yiddish comes across as an innovative comedic trope.

Yet some Jews are currently seeking to reclaim Yiddish Christmas folklore—as an antidote to the contemporary dilemma posed by Christmas.

The Hasidic Retention of *Nitl-Nakht*

Before discussing the pursued revival of Yiddish Christmas folklore, I should acknowledge that this folklore is not entirely dead. Most secular Jews eventually abandoned Yiddish, but many strictly Orthodox Jews did not. The majority of today's native Yiddish speakers come from Hasidic families who oppose modernization and assimilation. We will therefore begin by reviewing the state of Yiddish Christmas folklore among contemporary Hasidim.

On Christmas Eve 2015, Uriel Heilman published a bombshell article that appeared in five of the most prominent secular Jewish media outlets. The article was entitled "How Hasidim pointedly don't observe Christmas Eve."[2] It revealed to the secular Jewish world that Hasidic Jews engage in "counter-culture traditions" on Christmas Eve that are antithetical to celebrating. They abstain from sex and, most shockingly, do not study Torah. The article's title demonstrates how significantly the context of Christmas has changed over time: What was once a common folk vacation from religious routine on the longest night of the year is now branded as a Torah scholar's oppositional counterculture to a Christian holiday. Contemporary Hasidim retained the belief that Christmas Eve is a night reigned over by evil Christian forces, and they customarily assume that their ancestors developed their prophylactic *nitl-nakht* as a uniquely Jewish opposition to the Christian Christmas.[3] Hasidim in English-speaking lands derogatorily call this Christian Christmas *kratsmekh* [Yiddish for "scratch me"].

Nonetheless, just as *nitl-nakht* was never truly a Jewish opposition to Christmas, it is today not truly a Hasidic opposition to *kratsmekh*. Some Hasidic leaders in the New World, including the United States and especially Israel, have proclaimed that evil Christian forces are no longer active on Christmas Eve like they were back in Eastern Europe.[4] Yet many Hasidim around the world continue to adjourn their Torah study on Christmas Eve for the sake of carrying on their ancestral tradition. Yosef Rapaport, a media consultant representing New York Hasidim, reports that "Hasidic people aren't even thinking about [the Christian] Christmas" on *nitl-nakht*.[5] Instead, Hasidim view their *nitl-nakht* customs as a part of Jewish life irrespective of its putative association with Christianity. Hasidic-raised Abby Stein describes how "for most of us teenagers studying in religious school in the Catskill Mountains of New York State [in the 2000s]," *nitl-nakht* was "the most wonderful time of year."[6] Christmas Eve was and remains a singular vacation from Torah study for Hasidic boys and men. This vacation provokes opposition among the more conservative Torah scholars, just as it has for centuries. Take, for example, an article published in the Orthodox Jewish weekly *The Jewish Press* on Christmas Eve 2013 entitled "Just Say No to Nittel Nacht." The author describes how his elementary school classmates viewed *nitl-nakht* as "amazing" and a "great holiday," but in the author's opinion, "Not learning Torah on Nittel Nacht is a mistake."[7] The most conservative Hasidim refer to *nitl-nakht* as *bitl-nakht*, a reference to the concept of *bitl-toyre*—any time not spent studying Torah is a waste.[8]

Cardplaying is no longer the most common activity for occupying this Torah-less time. Some Hasidic men spend Christmas Eve partying with food and music at DreamWorks, America's (self-proclaimed) largest indoor water park.[9] Other Hasidim advocate for alternative *nitl-nakht* activities that "sharpen the mind."[10] One popular mind-sharpening activity is chess. Hasidic men around the world, from Toronto to Sydney, commonly participate in chess tournaments on Christmas Eve. As Stein says, "If that is not 'celebrating' Christmas, I don't know what is. . . ."[11] For those Hasidic men who do not party nor play chess, it is common to catch up on chores on Christmas Eve that were otherwise put off while studying Torah. These chores can include housework or managing finances, but a more popular *nitl-nakht* chore is tearing toilet paper. Jewish law does not permit the tearing of toilet paper on the Sabbath, so some Hasidim spend Christmas Eve tearing all their toilet paper for the coming year. This practice explains why Hasidic areas of Israel have seen toilet paper shortages during the Christmas season[12] (though Hasidim can now buy precut toilet paper, so this Christmas tradition is dwindling away). There are also Hasidic men who simply go to sleep early on Christmas Eve.[13]

The night of December 24 is not the only Christmas Eve in Hasidic tradition. As the Eastern Orthodox Church followed the Julian calendar, many Eastern European Jews historically observed Christmas Eve on the Gregorian date of January 6. Following mass Jewish migration, it became unclear whether *nitl-nakht* should be observed on December 24 or January 6. Based on the Jewish principle of *sfeyke d'yoyme* ["doubt about the date"]—that Jewish traditions should be observed on multiple dates if the exact date for practicing the tradition is unclear— some Hasidic sects, particularly those stemming from European towns with both Catholic and Orthodox populations, now observe *nitl-nakht* twice: from sunset to midnight on December 24, known as *kleyner nitl* [little *nitl*], and from noon to midnight on January 6, known as *groyser nitl* [big *nitl*].[14] On *groyser nitl*, Hasidic men have an entire afternoon free of study, ripe for appointments or excursions. And there is a third possible date for the Hasidic Christmas Eve. Since the exact timing of the *tkufe* [winter solstice], according to a traditional Jewish calculation system, can fall before sunset on January 6, some prudent Hasidim avoid studying Torah on the night of January 5 instead of the 6th.[15] Despite these various possible dates, it remains standard for Hasidim to adjourn their Torah study on the night of December 24. To quote Heilman's 2015 article: "At the stroke of midnight, the same time many churches hold Midnight Mass—Hasidic study halls come alive."

The Secular Rebirth of *Nitl-Nakht*

In recent years, Yiddish Christmas folklore has begun to make a comeback among secular Jews. To appreciate this phenomenon, some background is necessary.

The urban bustle of the past century saw the idealization of Christian and Jewish canonical traditions, centered on the Christmas and Yom Kippur spirits of "peace on earth, good will toward men." Yet today, people are becoming increasingly interested in rediscovering the forgotten folk traditions that were buried underneath modern romanticism. In this pursuit, as anthropologist Sabina Magliocco describes, "folklore becomes an important tool to discover the past and bring authenticity to contemporary spiritual practice."[16] Some people seek a "reenchantment" of the world by practicing folk religion and magic.[17] Others see aesthetic potential in supernatural folk horror as source material for new art.[18] Still others are interested in reclaiming past folk traditions for the present day. The most successful endeavor in this folklore revival has been the recent reclamation of Halloween. The adult Halloween that we know today began to trickle through fringe American communities in the 1970s and has since developed into one of the most popular festivals in the world.[19] More recently, the Folk Horror Revival group launched on Facebook in 2014 and has since attracted over thirty thousand members.[20] A plethora of folklore podcasts have proliferated in recent years that review ethnographic sources to retell the oral traditions of the past. Al Ridenour's *Bone and Sickle* podcast, for example, opens with the slogan "The past unburied. The books unsealed. The old celebration returning."[21]

As Halloween becomes increasingly mainstream, December is beginning to overtake October as the most exciting time of year for folk horror enthusiasts. December is the month for exploring the elaborate Christmas folklore of historical Europe: the wandering dead, Frau Holle, and any other midwinter spirits. The earliest roots of this "spooky Christmas" revival, namely the neopagan Yule revival and the slasher Santa films of the late twentieth century, were overshadowed by the proliferation of Halloween. But then, in the early twenty-first century, the spooky Christmas began to attract a bigger cult following in America. Images of the Krampus, St. Nicholas's evil helper in the Alps, began to circulate online as the perfect candidate for an alternative Santa Claus. A Christmas counterculture soon emerged—an alternative, radical way to celebrate Christmas. People around the world now hold Krampus parades and celebrations on the eve of St. Nicholas Day (December 5), which some have dubbed *"Krampusnacht."* Krampus films, books, graphic novels, videogames, T-shirts, and beers are everywhere. In the 2016 book *The Krampus and the Old, Dark Christmas: Roots and Rebirth of the Folkloric Devil*, Al Ridenour explains:

> In a secular society where the craving for the Other is more commonly satisfied through horror and fantasy than the midnight mass, this monstrous character seems custom-made to provide a thrill of holiday awe. [. . .] Somewhat myopically perceived as the "anti-Santa," he seems to express the requisite countercultural contempt. [. . .] What is significant here is the American idea of holiday horror beginning as something subversive, a knife-wielding intrusion from outside attacking the holiday ideal of domestic bliss.[22]

The Krampus is helping many secular young people satisfy their cravings for an alternative Christmas. But secular young people of Jewish heritage are left struggling, as they do not know of any "old, dark Christmas" in their own tradition to reclaim. They generally assume that the one Christmas tradition that Jewish immigrants introduced to America—going to the movies—is as far back as Jewish Christmas traditions go. Jews do have Hanukkah, which succeeded Yom Kippur as a "Jewish Christmas" in post-Yiddish culture, and some Jews have claimed *Saturday Night Live*'s "Hanukkah Harry" as their own alternative Santa Claus[23]—but Hanukkah Harry does not possess the same thrill as the Krampus. Nor do the annual Hallmark Hanukkah films that have been airing since 2019, such as the 2022 adaptation of the seminal Christmas film *The Shop Around the Corner* into *Hanukkah on Rye*, help Jews subvert midwinter sentimentality. Secular alternatives to Christmas and Hanukkah have emerged, such as the *Seinfeld*-popularized "Festivus for the rest of us"[24]—over fifteen thousand people have signed a change.org petition to "Make Festivus a National Holiday" in America[25]—but there is nothing distinctly "Jewish" about Festivus. And the secular Christmas Eve tradition of grabbing leftover trees to decorate for the New Year seems to only appeal to those Jews from the former Soviet Union, where people had awaited a visit from *Ded Moroz* [Grandfather Frost] on New Year's Eve rather than Christmas Eve.

A Christmas tradition that has become ubiquitous among North American Jews is eating Chinese food on Christmas Eve, colloquially known as "*Erev Christmas*" ("*erev*" is Hebrew for "eve"). Chinese food became a prominent part of North American Jewish folklore in the twentieth century, particularly in cities such as New York and Toronto where Jewish and Chinese immigrants lived in close proximity.[26] Scholars identify Chinese restaurants as a place where Jewish immigrants could shroud themselves in a non-Christian environment and for once not be the lowly Other; Ted Merwin argues that eating at Chinese restaurants allowed Jews to "feel culturally superior for the first time."[27] (One can get a sense of popular Jewish immigrant sentiment about Chinese culture by listening to Mickey Katz's objectionable 1951 Yiddish parody of "Chinatown, My Chinatown.")[28] For much of the twentieth century, most Jews did not associate Chinese food with Christmas. The American Jews who ate out on Christmas, if not away at a resort for the winter holidays, often made a point of doing so in an overtly Jewish environment, such as celebratory balls hosted by Jewish clubs or Eastern European–styled Jewish restaurants.[29] As the immigrant generation faded away, however, Jews increasingly chose to eat at a Chinese restaurant on Christmas, in line with the broader phenomenon of vulnerable-feeling people empowering themselves with "Otherly" foods on the long night (such as Eastern European peasants consuming garlic and "Jewish-style" fish on Christmas Eve, as we saw). The *New York Herald* reported as early as 1902 that the "oddity" of "a Christmas dinner in Chinatown" will appeal to anybody who feels isolated by the holiday's domesticity,[30] and Jews increasingly came to fit this bill.

Reports of Jews customarily eating Chinese food on Christmas began to emerge across North America in the late 1980s.[31] The custom was then codified on Christmas Eve 1993, when a thirtysomething Jewish couple published the (now oft-performed) poem "Erev Christmas" in the *Boston Globe*. The poem, a Yiddish-inflected parody of "'Twas the Night Before Christmas," follows a bored Jewish couple on Christmas Eve. The couple decides to venture out to a(n overtly nonkosher) Chinese restaurant, where they have a jubilee eating "whole fish and moo shi and shrimp chow mee foon, and General Gau's chicken and ma po tofu," and so on.[32] The poem sparked considerable controversy. One Jewish respondent wrote to the *Boston Globe* editor that the poem is "offensive" and that "no action or custom described in the poem has anything to do with being Jewish."[33] Another Jewish respondent wrote that the poem is "deeply disturbing," summing it up with: "Wallowing in self-pity and describing behavior abhorrent to Jewish values, the two authors of the poem do not represent the viewpoint of most young Jews."[34] Nevertheless, as anybody who has been to a North American Chinatown on Christmas Eve can attest, the custom of *Erev Christmas* is very prevalent. Chinese food has successfully taken off as a new Jewish "garlic" for warding off midwinter desolation. The popular folk explanation for why Jews eat at Chinese restaurants on Christmas Eve, which Chuck Schumer phrases as "No other restaurants are open,"[35] is the latest iteration of the claim that the only reason Jews played cards on Christmas Eve is that they had nothing else to do (such as in the Litvak testimony we saw).

The latest iteration of the age-old discourse about whether Jews should have sex on Christmas Eve is, in turn, the multitude of Jewish hookup parties that take place after the Chinese restaurants close for the night. First formalized by Andy Rudnick in Boston in 1987,[36] these parties are now organized under various names across North America such as the Matzo Ball, Tribal Ball, and Latkapalooza, to name a few. Emily Shire describes these late-night parties as the year's "sloppiest gathering of Jewish singles looking to get some,"[37] featuring thousands of Jews packed into clubs seeking "someone to have sex with."[38] Jenny Singer emphasizes the parties' "reputation for trashiness," noting that it can be "hard to move without knocking into people who are kissing each other."[39] I will spare further lore about what goes on at these parties, but they effectively provide an answer to the allegorical question that many first-generation Yiddish authors posed regarding whether New World Jews will be able to resist sex on Christmas Eve. Yet despite the popularity that Christmas Eve has attained in Jewish culture over the past four decades, the current customs are becoming increasingly mundane among members of the younger generation. Whereas *Krampusnacht* is a radical reclamation of a long-forgotten Christmas tradition, there is not much more to *Erev Christmas* than sex and Chinese food.

Recently, some young people of Jewish heritage have begun searching for their forgotten folk tradition—their Yiddish tradition.[40] During the 2020–2021 COVID-19 pandemic, the YIVO Institute for Jewish Research saw a tenfold increase in registered students in their Yiddish courses.[41] In April 2021, the language-learning app Duolingo launched a Yiddish course, and nearly twelve thousand people signed up immediately.[42] And by December 2021, many Jews had discovered their own authentic version of *Krampusnacht*: *nitl-nakht*. According to what these Jews discovered, it is not the Krampus who frightens people at Christmas—it is Jesus, rising from his grave of boiling excrement. Take some of the public tweets from Christmas Eve 2021:

> Gut Nittel Nacht, fellow Yids. Make sure to be extra good so that Jesus doesn't get you in the middle of the night![43]

and

> Happy nittelnacht everybody, don't forget to eat garlic and be careful of demon Jesus haunting your toilets.[44]

We are seeing a reclamation of the "old, dark Christmas" in Yiddish tradition. Akin to how young Christians see *Krampusnacht* as an antidote to the dull sentimentality of the mainstream Christmas, some young Jews see *nitl-nakht* as an antidote to being excluded from Christmas outright. The secular Yiddish culture group "Rad Yiddish," for instance, hosted a global *nitl-nakht* game night via Zoom on Christmas Eve 2021, providing Jews with something fun to do on Christmas that (unlike eating Chinese food) is deeply rooted in Jewish history.[45] In an article entitled "Have Yourself a Yiddish Little Christmas" published shortly after Christmas 2021, Yiddish-culture commentator Rokhl Kafrissen describes "the rise of 'nitl nakht' and the outsider appeal of the supernatural":

> For young people left cold by Hanukkah's uneasy position as the "Jewish Christmas," *nitl nakht* is appealing because it is entirely other: a rooted Jewish practice shaped by Christmas, but most certainly not meant to compete, or imitate. Even presented in stripped down form, the revelation of a newly discovered "holiday" makes an audacious claim to en-

larging the Jewish calendar, made all the more audacious by doing so in Yiddish. It points the reader toward Eastern Europe, not merely as a site of genocide and mass migration, but as an accessible source of nonnormative Jewish practice and folklore.[46]

The reclaimed *nitl-nakht* is popping up in various types of alternative Jewish media. An example is the 2022–2023 Jewish calendar "Ma'agal" (Hebrew for "circle"), self-described as "an effort to retrieve, excavate and reclaim the stories of our ancestors whose stories might have gotten disrupted, erased and buried over the years."[47] Ma'agal includes *nitl-nakht* as a reclaimed Jewish observance, and its calendrical marking is accompanied by an original haunting illustration of the dark night.[48] Another example is Benjy Fox-Rosen's musical composition with the namesake of the Yiddish proverb "*nitl iz a beyzer layd*" [*nitl* is a menacing affliction], featured in a 2018 alternative Christmas concert in Vienna and Jerusalem. The composition is a medley of historical Jewish Christmas texts set to chilling music. It includes Dietrich Schwab's 1616 apostate report of Jesus crawling up excrement pits, and Morris Rosenfeld's 1902 Yiddish poem "Christmas Eve Bells" proclaiming the night's darkness.[49] Other *nitl-nakht* musicals comically play up the scatology of the recovered Yiddish Christmas folklore. In December 2022, an alternative Christmas variety show at Pittsburgh's Glitter Box Theater included a musical sketch called "'Who's That Sneaking Up the Toilet'—A Nittel Nacht Carol."[50] These examples illustrate some of the ways in which people are using *nitl-nakht* to affirm the historical, pre–Chinese food role of Christmas in Jewish culture.

Other people are using *nitl-nakht* to affirm that Christmas does not in fact belong in Jewish culture, reviving the immigrant generation's terrifying reimagining of the night. Some contemporary Jews remain uneasy about celebrating Christmas. This attitude was recently mirrored on the big stage in Tom Stoppard's *Leopoldstadt*, the recipient of the 2023 Tony Award for Best Play. The play follows multiple generations of a Christmas-celebrating Jewish family in prewar Vienna that squabble over the value of assimilation. One family member suggests that "assimilation means to carry on being a Jew without insult." Yet the family is ultimately disrupted by the Holocaust, with few members surviving.[51] In accordance with the play's message, some people argue that it is naive for Jews to celebrate the Christian holiday, as it provides a false sense of security against antisemitic atrocities. This argument is made more powerful if the antisemitic atrocities are said to take place on Christmas itself, and so the dangerous *nitl-nakht* of the imagined past comes in handy. In December 2019, Vienna's TheaterArche staged Simon Kronberg's 1941 German-language play *Nittel (Blinde Nacht)*, which, we saw, essentially tells the same story as *Leopoldstadt* but with the Holocaust setting replaced by *nitl-nakht*.[52] In December 2020, A. Z. Foreman revived Mani Leib's 1952 Yiddish modernist poem about antisemitic terror, "*Nitl*," in an online reading of the original Yiddish text and a new English translation.[53] Jordan Kutzik covered Foreman's reading for the (still going) Yiddish *Forverts* on Christmas Eve 2020, writing that "the poem is a good reminder that, while Christmas for today's American Jews is a free day for going to the movies or playing chess or cards, for our ancestors in Eastern Europe it was a day of fear and terror."[54]

A 2018 article for the popular Jewish website *Aish* goes further. Yvette Alt Miller describes how, historically, "many European Jewish communities prohibited their members from going outside on Christmas, lest they be attacked" and "many Jews stayed up all night on Dec. 24, lest their homes be attacked or burned." She then proposes that "in memory of the countless Jews who came before us and feared this day [. . .] let's not forget their customs and traditions entirely. This Dec. 25, let's spare a thought for the many Jews whose lives were lost on this day."[55] The rediscovery of Yiddish Christmas traditions is thus helping Jews find meaning in December in two very different ways. For some Jews, the discovery of *nitl-nakht* is justification that celebrating Christmas is grounded in Jewish history. For other Jews, it is justification that celebrating Christmas is *not* grounded in Jewish history.

And then there are Jews like Sam Broverman who are developing a new Yiddish Christmas folklore as a counterculture to the contemporary Christmas without necessarily invoking *nitl-nakht*. This counterculture includes numerous Yiddish covers of "White Christmas," including Mandy Patinkin's "*Vaysn nitl*" [White *Nitl*],[56] Jackie Hoffman's "*Vayse kratsmekh*" [White *Kratsmekh*],[57] and Al Grand's "*Vaysn yontef*" [White Holiday],[58] all of which have become staples of contemporary Jewish Christmas concerts. These concerts, such as the New York Festival of Song's annual "A Goyishe Christmas to You!," might also include the singing of a Yiddish version of "Jingle Bells,"[59] "Rudolph, the Red-Nosed Reindeer,"[60] "Have Yourself a Merry Little Christmas,"[61] or "All I Want for Christmas Is You,"[62] or the reading of a Yiddish version of the poem "'Twas the Night Before Christmas."[63] This reclamation of Christmas in Yiddish allows Jews to engage with the sexy mainstream Christmas, as opposed to the eerie Jewish *nitl-nakht*, in a way that is indisputably "Jewish." Other examples of this growing Yiddish Christmas counterculture include the 2016 "YidLife Crisis Guide to the Holiday Classics" video that features parodic Yiddish covers of classic Christmas songs;[64] and Yossi Desser's 2021 "Yiddish Chanukah Carols" album that too features Yiddish covers of classic Christmas songs—but with the lyrics modified to pertain to Hanukkah rather than Christmas. Instead of opening with "It's beginning to look a lot like Christmas," Desser opens with "*S'haybt on oystsukikn vi khanike*" [It's beginning to look a lot like Hanukkah]. His contribution to the Yiddish collection of "White Christmas" covers is "*Vaysn khanike*" [White Hanukkah].[65]

Many people are also turning to Yiddish culture on Christmas without engaging Christmas directly. Yiddish-style klezmer concerts are becoming increasingly prevalent at Christmastime, some examples being Metropolitan Klezmer's annual *Santa Klez* show in New York (2012–2018); the Klezjammers' annual participation in London Christmas fairs (2021–2023); and Reb Yoysef and the Chanukah Goblins' Christmas Eve klezmer show at a Toronto bar (2022). Julie Benko's 2023 *Christmas With You* song album includes the classic Yiddish song "Tumbalalaika,"[66] mirroring the 1999 French Christmas film *La Bûche* that spotlights the classic Yiddish song "A Yiddishe Mama."[67] In Los Angeles, Jews have reinvented the tradition of going to the movies on Christmas into a *Fiddler on the Roof* sing-along, which in 2022 marked its fifteenth year across sixth locations—a return to the tradition's Yiddish roots of watching a film about pure *shtetl* culture.[68] In New York, Yiddish theater productions are once again premiering on Christmas.[69] Joshua Eli Plaut posits that the rise of this new Yiddish Christmas culture signals "the arrival of a new era in the Jewish response to Christmas, one in which the holiday of Christmas plays a secondary role to the interests of a thriving and self-aware Jewish community."[70] Australian cartoonist John Kron jokingly calls this phenomenon the "Yiddeltide spirit."[71] It fits that the 2017 documentary *Dreaming of a Jewish Christmas*, which features popular

Jewish-written Christmas songs performed at a Toronto Chinese restaurant, concludes with a grand Yiddish cover of "Winter Wonderland," symbolic of this new era.[72]

Most notably, since 2015, a major annual Yiddish culture festival has been held in New York on the week of Christmas. In the opening skit for the 2021 festival, a dispirited Jew (Pete Rushefsky) melancholily eats Chinese food on his porch while lamenting about his midwinter desolation ("Oy vey, I'm so lonely"). Suddenly, the world's top Yiddish klezmer musicians show up at his door. They execute a boisterous Yiddish musical performance on the street, bringing great joy to the Jew.[73] In a 2015 article entitled "How to have yourself a very Yiddishe Christmas in NY," Suzanne Selengut introduces this "Yiddish New York" festival:

> The dance party and other fun activities are a far cry from the tense, solemn way Eastern European Jews marked *Nittel Nacht* (Yiddish for "Christmas Eve") a few generations ago, when annual pogroms ravaged Jewish communities. They are also a departure from the more recent American Jewish custom of going out for Chinese food and a movie on Christmas day. But for a diverse group of New York Jews and their friends, it seems that increasingly 'tis the season to revel in Ashkenazi culture.[74]

Yiddish is hence becoming a quintessential language of the modern Christmas counterculture. Whether it is through a Yiddish-language opening scene to a Christmas-themed television episode (as in *The West Wing* and *Crazy Ex-Girlfriend*),[75] a fiction-book scene about American Jews spending Christmas Eve eating stereotypical *shtetl* foods (as in *You Should Have Known*),[76] or Santa's elves uttering Yiddish in a Christmas adventure film (as in *The Polar Express*),[77] Yiddish is the one language in which Christmas is inherently subverted. And due to high fertility rates in Hasidic communities alongside relatively high intermarriage rates among secular Jews, the majority of future Jewry may be descendants of today's Yiddish-speaking Hasidim,[78] boding well for the prospect of the future development of a Yiddish Christmas culture. Eli Benedict estimates that over seventy-five thousand Yiddish-speaking Jews in Israel alone will leave their strictly Orthodox communities between 2017 and 2067, and that nearly half of them will raise their children with Yiddish, suggesting that the rebound in secular Yiddish will continue to rise.[79]

Given the recent rise of alternative Christmas horror films featuring the Krampus, as well as a new resurgence of Yiddish-inflected films based on Yiddish folk horror (such as the 2019 *The Vigil* and the 2023 *The Offering*), it may soon be time for a Yiddish Christmas horror flick about *nitl-nakht*.

Conclusion

What's a Jew to do on Christmas? The Jew can search the rabbinic literature to confirm that there is no Christmas in the canonical Jewish tradition. But it turns out that there is a Christmas in Yiddish tradition. The Jewish observance of Christmas managed to stay out of most rabbis' Hebrew texts, but it flourished in the mouths of Yiddish-speaking women and men over the course of many centuries. The contemporary dilemma facing Jews on Christmas is hence not due to Jews lacking an ethnohistorical connection to Christmas, but is rather the product of a modern reimagining of dichotomous Jewish and Christian pasts. Rediscovering Yiddish Christmas folklore completely redefines the dilemma. Whether it is through celebrating *nitl-nakht* with games (as per the Old World tradition), using *nitl-nakht* to justify *not* celebrating (as per the early New World tradition), or creating brand-new Yiddish Christmas traditions—Yiddish language and culture open a new avenue for contemporary Jews to engage with Christmas. Joshua Eli Plaut's *A Kosher Christmas* tells the story of how some Jews chose to engage with Christmas after abandoning Yiddish, but that story is just one chapter of a larger saga about the intersection between Jews and Christmas. It is not the final chapter. And it may end up being the only chapter that does not play out in Yiddish. How exactly the saga plays out will depend on how the entangled circumstances of Jews and non-Jews continue to unfold.

ACKNOWLEDGMENTS

Writing this book took me back to December 2006, when a special episode of *One Tree Hill* filled me with awe. Being the sentimental twelve-year-old that I was, I was stunned by how an hour of television could be so filled with Christmas spirit without any overt reference to the holiday itself. This mindset apparently stuck with me during my extracurricular studies in Yiddish literature a decade later, as I argued to my classmates that David Pinski's 1895 Yiddish story "Yom Kippur Eve" is a quintessential Christmas story. I consequently realize that a multitude of unassuming developments in my life have influenced aspects of this book. I cannot possibly enumerate them all here.

I do, nevertheless, wish to gratefully acknowledge a few individuals who directly contributed to the development of this book. Elisabeth Maselli was instrumental in helping me transform a first draft into a substantive manuscript. Taylor Baruchel and Miriam Borden kindly helped me navigate the Aramaic literature, and Miriam was an especially supportive colleague and friend throughout the preparation of this book. I am grateful to Itzik Gottesman, Andrey Shlyakhter, and Catherine Szkop for lending me their ethnographic eyes as we discussed the world of Christmas folklore. I also thank Kalman Weiser for our fruitful discussions that benefited this book. For helping me obtain access to various materials, I thank Ruby Landau-Pincus and Hallel Yadin from the YIVO Institute for Jewish Research; Lisa and Sharon Rivo from the National Center for Jewish Film; Pete Rushefsky from Yiddish New York; and Caleb Sher from the Yiddish Book Centre.

It was such a pleasure working with NYU Press. I am ever amazed at the dedication and conscientiousness of my acquisitions editor, Jennifer Hammer, as well as at the enthusiasm of her assistant, Brianna Jean. I am beholden to my copyeditor, David Hornik, for graciously accommodating my unconventional stylistic practices. I also thank the many marketing and production staff who worked on this book, including Lia Hagen, Charles Hames, Rachel Perkins, and Valerie Zaborski.

Finally, I must single out two individuals without whom I would have never thought to write a book like this. Anna Shternshis wondrously drew me into Yiddish Studies back when I was an undergraduate physics student, and she remained a loyal mentor to me as I went on to moonlight as an ethnographer of Ashkenazic Jewry. Her continual guidance was invaluable for bringing the current project to fruition. Robert Brym, in turn, has shown endless support for all of my academic endeavors and has been a driving influence on my interpretation of Jewish social history. I am ever so grateful that he handed me his phone at the 2015 University of Toronto Hanukkah party to film his costumed Yiddish performance of "Home on the Range" (in a duet with none other than Sam Broverman), as the friendship that we have since formed ultimately spawned much of my inspiration for writing this book.

GLOSSARY

BESMEDRESH (בית-מדרש)
Jewish study hall

BITL-TOYRE (ביטול-תורה)
Something other than studying Torah; i.e. a waste of time

BLINDE NAKHT (בלינדע נאַכט)
Blind Night; a Ukrainian Yiddish term for Christmas Eve

CHRISTNACHT
Christ Night; i.e. Christmas Eve

DIES IRAE
"The Day of Wrath"; a Christian liturgical poem

DREIDEL (דריידל)
Spinning top used for gambling at midwinter

GANEYDN (גן־עדן)
Garden of Eden; i.e. heaven

GEHENEM (גיהנום)
Valley of Hinnom; i.e. hell or purgatory

HASIDIM (חסידים)
Hasidic Jews; pious adherents of Jewish mysticism

KADDISH (קדיש)
Jewish praise of God recited for the dead

KDUSHE (קדושה)
Holiness; the opposite of *tume*

KEY(T)SEKH (קצח / קסח)
Easter

KHANUKRISMES (חנוכריסמס)
Hanukkah–Christmas hybrid in modern Israel

KHEYDER (חדר)
Physical room for traditional schooling of Jewish children

KINDERFRESSER
Child Gobbler; a type of *Kinderschreck* figure

KINDERSCHRECK
Disciplinary style of instilling fear in children

KOL NIDRE (כל נדרי)
Central declaration recited on the eve of Yom Kippur

LITVAK (ליטוואַק)
Jew who is stereotypically intellectual rather than mystical

MASKILIM (משׂכילים)
Enlightened Jews

MAYSE TOLE (מעשׂה תלוי)
Name of the Jewish version of the story of Jesus

MISNAGDIM (מתנגדים)
Opponents of Hasidic Jews

MITZVAH (מצווה)
Obligatory Jewish custom (lit: divine commandment)

NATALIS
Birthday

NITL(-NAKHT) ((ניטל-(נאַכט))
Nothing Night; a Yiddish epithet for Christmas Eve

OLEYNU (עלינו)
"It is our duty [to praise God]"; a Jewish prayer

OYSE HO'ISH (אותו האיש)
That Man; i.e. Jesus

REBE (רבי)
Teacher at *kheyder*

SEYFER (סֿפר)
Religious Jewish book

SHTETL (שטעטל)
Town with a Jewish population

SILVESTER(-NAKHT) (סילבסטר(-נאַכט))
New Year's Eve

TE DEUM
"Thee God [we praise]"; a Christian prayer

TEYVES (טבת)
Month of winter solstice in Jewish calendar

TIKN (תּיקון)
A spiritual rectification to make a soul fit for *ganeydn*

TKUFE (תּקופה)
Quarterly period; i.e. a solstice or equinox

TOLE (תּלוי)
Hanged One; i.e. Jesus

TUME (טומאה)
Uncleanliness; the opposite of kdushe

UNSANE TOYKEF (ונתנה תוקף)
Central poem in Yom Kippur liturgy

WEIHNACHT
Holy Night; i.e. Christmas Eve

YESHIVE (ישיבה)
Jewish institute for higher learning

YISHU (ישו)
Jesus (formal Hebrew name)

YOMIM NEROIM (ימים נוראים)
Days of Fear leading up to Yom Kippur

YOSHKE PANDRE (יאָשקע פּאַנדרע)
Jesus

YOSL PANDREK (יוסל פּאַנדרעק)
Jesus

YOYZL (יויזל / יוזל)
Jesus

NOTES

PREFACE

1 David, "A Very Larry David Christmas."
2 Collins Dictionary, "Christmas."
3 Collins Dictionary, "Yiddish."
4 Shandler, *Yiddish*, 6–16.

INTRODUCTION

1 I thank Sam Broverman for permitting me to disclose this information about his show.
2 Plaut, *A Kosher Christmas*.
3 Plaut, *A Kosher Christmas*, 29–30.
4 Plaut, *A Kosher Christmas*, 8.
5 Plaut, *A Kosher Christmas*, 29–35.
6 Goldzac, "*Af a yontef*," 85.
7 Shandler, *Jews, God, and Videotape*, 185–229.
8 Shandler, *Jews, God, and Videotape*, 189–90.
9 Opatoshu, "*Vekhter*."
10 Plaut, *A Kosher Christmas*, 30–31.
11 Goldberg, "*Kristmes*."
12 Klier, *Imperial Russia's Jewish Question*, 68–69; Klier, *Russians, Jews, and the Pogroms*, 24–33, 44–47, 66–68, 92; Nirenberg, "The Two Faces of Sacred Violence"; Penkower, "The Kishinev Pogrom"; Person, "The 1940 'Easter Pogrom'"; Roth, "The Eastertide Stoning of the Jews."
13 Neither of the two most cited anti-Jewish incidents that occurred near Christmas, namely the 1235 Fulda blood libel and the 1881 Warsaw pogrom, took place on Christmas Eve. These incidents both had definitive non-Christmas-related causes (Dubnow, *History of the Jews*, 280–83; Langmuir, *Toward a Definition*, 276–81). Note also that the legend that the Christians of Judenburg wiped out the local Jews on Christmas Eve 1312 has been shown to be historically implausible (Göth, "Das Herzogthum Steiermark," 486).
14 Mark, "*Nitl*," 184.
15 Shapiro, "Torah Study on Christmas Eve."
16 Scharbach, "The Ghost in the Privy," 340–41.
17 Rivkind, "*Nitl*."

18 Quoted by Rivkind, *Der kamf*, 54.

19 Grayzel, *The Church and the Jews*, 309, 317, 333; Nirenberg, "The Two Faces of Sacred Violence."

20 Rivkind, "*Nitl*," 840.

21 Yuval, *Two Nations*, 29.

22 Carlebach and Schacter, *New Perspectives*; Cohen and Rosman, *Rethinking European Jewish History*; Elukin, *Living Together*; Marcus, *Jewish Culture and Society*; Schainker, *Confessions of the Shtetl*.

23 Flanders, *Christmas*; Frodsham, *From Stonehenge to Santa*; Jerman, *Santa Claus Worldwide*; Miller, *Unwrapping Christmas*; Ridenour, *The Krampus*.

24 Flanders, *Christmas*, 2–3.

CHAPTER 1. GHOSTS OF CHRISTMAS PAST

1 For a review, see Shapiro, "Torah Study on Christmas Eve."

2 Shandler, *Jews, God, and Videotape*, 189.

3 These details are described by Shapiro, "Torah Study on Christmas Eve."

4 Shapiro, "Torah Study on Christmas Eve," 322. In Western Christianity, Christmas traditionally began with a midnight Eucharist, known to Catholics and many Protestants as Midnight Mass. In Eastern Christianity, the sole Eucharist of Christmas was traditionally celebrated on Christmas morning, but it was usually preceded by an all-night vigil from midnight. On the historical variability of Christmas Eve worship across denominations, see Larsen, *The Oxford Handbook of Christmas*, 113–82.

5 Scharbach, "The Ghost in the Privy."

6 Scharbach, "The Ghost in the Privy," 357.

7 Scharbach, "The Ghost in the Privy," 342.

8 Scharbach, "The Ghost in the Privy," 371–72.

9 Scharbach, "The Ghost in the Privy," 372.

10 Kohler, *Martin Luther*, 71–72.

11 Tille, *Die Geschichte*, 129.

12 Pfefferkorn, *Handt Spiegel*, 12 [page not explicitly numbered].

13 Hess, *Flagellum Iudeorum*, 45; Brenz, *Jüdischer abgestreiffter*, 13–14; Schwab, *Detectum velum*, 7.

14 Hutton, *The Stations of the Sun*, 1–8.

15 Baumgarten, *Biblical Women*, 169; Carlebach, *Palaces of Time*, 166–67.

16 Baumgarten, *Biblical Women*, 161; Carlebach, *Palaces of Time*, 163, 169–70.

17 Lecouteux, *Phantom Armies*, 43, 194; Geiler von Kaysersberg, *Die Emeis*, 37; Rumpf, *Perchten*, 29.

18 Baumgarten, *Biblical Women*, 169; Carlebach, *Palaces of Time*, 163–64.

19 Ridenour, *The Krampus*, 3.

20 Baring-Gould, *The Book of Were-wolves*, 53–58, 108, 116; Senn, "Romanian Werewolves."

21 Magnus, *Historia de gentibus septentrionalibus*, 642; translated by Baring-Gould, *The Book of Were-wolves*, 53–54.

22 Miles, *Christmas in Ritual*, 244–47; Senn, "Romanian Werewolves."

23 Lawson, *Modern Greek Folklore*, 194.

24 Geiler von Kaysersberg, *Die Emeis*, 37.

25 Simek, *Dictionary of Northern Mythology*, 379–80.

26 Le Goff, *The Birth of Purgatory*.

27 Hutton, "The Wild Hunt," 165–71.

28 Schmitt, *Ghosts in the Middle Ages*, 174–75.

29 Vitalis, *The Ecclesiastical History*, 512.

30 Weissman, *Final Judgement*.

31 Weissman, *Final Judgement*, 223–29.

32 Ben-Samuel, *Seyfer khsidim*, 48.

33 Weissman, *Final Judgement*, 243.

34 Lasker, "Jewish Knowledge of Christianity," 109.

35 Baumgarten, *Introduction to Old Yiddish*, 155–62.

36 Baumgarten, "Shared and Contested Time," 264, 276. On the exact timing of the *tkufe*, see Shapiro, "Torah Study on Christmas Eve," 326, n. 7.

37 Hutton, "The Wild Hunt," 168.

38 Map, *De nugis curialium*, 206–7.

39 Othloni, *Opera omnia*, 367.

40 Goldberg, "*Kristmes*," 135–36; Shapira, *Seyfer regel yeshoro*, 116; Sutzkever and Kaczerginski, "Customs for Nitl," 2; Khes, "*Refleksn*."

41 Bar-Moses, *Seyfer or zorua II*, 61; Ben-Judah, *Perushey sidur*, 602–3; Ben-Samuel, *Makhzer Vitri*, 112–13.

42 Ben-Samuel, *Makhzer Vitri*, 113.

43 Hess, *Flagellum Iudeorum*, 45.

44 Adrian, *Send und Warnungs-Brieff*, 29.

45 Cf. Scharbach, "The Ghost in the Privy," 362, who makes a similar argument.

46 Fogel, *Beliefs and Superstitions*, 262–63; Heller, *Christmas*, 14; Holberg, *The Fussy Man*, 6; Riser, "Volksbrauch und Volksglauben," 65.

47 Miles, *Christmas in Ritual*, 246.

48 Miles, *Christmas in Ritual*, 245.

49 Allatius, *De templis*, 142.

50 Brundage, *Law, Sex, and Christian Society*, 158.

51 Senn, "Romanian Werewolves," 206.

52 Opatoshu, "*In der nakht fun 'nitul.'*"

53 Palachi, *Seyfer yimtso Khayim*, 73a; based on Shore, *Baal Shem Tov*, 28:1.

54 Forbes, *America's Favorite Holidays*, 15.

55 Simek, *Dictionary of Northern Mythology*, 379–80; Sommer, "The Pre-Christian Jól."

56 Livius, *The History of Rome*, ch. 1.

57 Macrobius, *Saturnalia*, 135 [11.49].

58 Hutton, *The Stations of the Sun*, 2–3.

59 Benovitz, *Hordus v'khanuka*.

60 Shapiro, "Torah Study and Christmas Eve," 347.

61 Frodsham, *From Stonehenge to Santa*, 229.

62 Cf. Scharbach, "The Ghost in the Privy," 363–65, who argues that both Christians and Jews were afraid that "religious sparks are diverted to feed the power of evil" on Christmas Eve.

63 Carus, "The Nativity," 728. This sermon has been attributed to both Ambrose (Ambrose, *Sancti Ambrosii*, 10) and Maximus (Maximus, *S. Maximi*, 403).

64 Babylonian Talmud Avodo Zoro 8a:8.

65 Divjak and Wischmeyer, *Das Kalenderhandbuch*, 329–30. Note that the pagan term "*natalis solis invictus*" for December 25 may have arisen in response to Christianization rather than vice versa (Hijmans, *Sol*, 1008–27).

66 Robertson, *Requiem*, 16–17; Senn, *Introduction to Christian Liturgy*, 116.

67 On other potential factors involved in the Christianization of December 25, see Nothaft, "The Origins of the Christmas Date."

68 Hutton, *The Stations of the Sun*, 123.

69 Welsford, *The Fool*, 197–217.

70 Welsford, *The Fool*, 200.

71 Greene, "The Song of the Ass," 534.

72 Busch, "Die Zauberpflanzen," 493; von Perger, *Deutsche Pflanzensagen*, 211–12; Wuttke, *Der deutsche Volksaberglaube*, 94–95.

73 Lenhoff, "Chronological Error," 155. See also Manaev, "Russian Svyatki."

74 McClelland, *Slayers and Their Vampires*, 57–58.

75 Hutton, "The Wild Hunt," 165–71.

76 Hugues de Mans, "*Actus Pontificum*," 326; translated by Lecouteux, *Phantom Armies*, 34–35.

77 Hilscher, *De exercitu furioso*, S. 2.

78 McGowan, "Roman Catholicism," 117.

79 Schuldes, *Die Teufelsszenen*, 110–14; Young, *The Drama of the Medieval Church*, 9.

80 Ben-Samuel, *Makhzer Vitri*, 113.

81 Scharbach Wollenberg, *The Closed Book*.

82 Fishman, *Becoming the People*; Scharbach Wollenberg, *The Closed Book*, 221–45.

83 Heller, "Notes de folk-lore," 308–12. More generally, whereas Christians believed that charity, Christian prayer, and Mass offerings can alleviate the dead's suffering (Le Groff, *The Birth of Purgatory*), Jews believed that charity, Jewish prayer, and Torah study can do so (Weissman, *Final Judgement*).

84 Adrian, *Send und Warnungs-Brieff*, 29. Adrian describes this folklore as pertaining to "*Himmelfahrtstag*," which translates to Ascension Day, but he presumably meant Christmas. See the commentary in Eisenmenger, *Entdecktes Judenthum*, 563; Shapiro, "Torah Study on Christmas Eve," 336.

85 Frid, "*Rov Khayim*," 484.

86 Cassel, *Weihnachten*, 275–76.

87 Miles, *Christmas in Ritual*, 233–34; Ridenour, *The Krampus*, 167–69.

88 King, *Liturgy of the Roman Church*, 187. For context, see Petri venerabilis, *Opera omnia*, 880; Saurette, "Making Space."

89 The term "Devil's Knell" is used today for the Midnight Mass church bells in Dewsbury, England.

90 Tille, *Die Geschichte*, 22; Tille, *Yule and Christmas*, 147–56.

91 Kletke, "Die heilige Nacht."

92 Krainz, "Sitten, Bräuche und Meinungen," 244.

93 Brenz, *Jüdischer abgestreiffter*, 14. My translation is influenced by Hirsch, *Yudisher Theriak*, 63.

94 Schwab, *Detectum velum*, 7.

95 Cassel, *Weihnachten*, 285–86; Chambers, *The Book of Days*, 778; Chatto, *Facts and Speculations*, 97–98; Horr, "Legal Notes on Card-Playing"; Frankl-Grün, *Geschichte der Juden*, 46; Scharbach, "The Ghost in the Privy," 361.

96 Neal, *The History of the Puritans*, 133.

97 Rivkind, "Nitl," 841.

98 Cf. Shapiro, "Torah Study on Christmas Eve," 322–23, on rabbis urging Jews to resist sex for the entire night.

CHAPTER 2. CHRIST IN YIDDISH TRADITION

1 Scharbach, "The Ghost in the Privy," 371–72.

2 Alleson-Gerberg, "Nittel Nacht."

3 Barbu, "Feeling Jewish," 197.

4 Diemling, "Navigating Christian Space," 404.

5 Schäfer, Meerson, and Deutsch, *Toledot Yeshu*; Barbu and Deutsch, *Toledot Yeshu in Context*.

6 Crossan, *Jesus*, 145.

7 Berger, "Captive at the Gate."

8 Lauterbach, "Jesus in the Talmud," 482; cf. Flusser, *The Sage from Galilee*, 6.

9 Eisenmenger, *Entdecktes Judenthum*, 67; Huldreich, *Seyfer Toldes Yeshue*.

10 Origen, *Contra Celsum*, I:28.

11 Nitzsch, "Über eine Reihe," 116.

12 Babylonian Talmud Shabbos 104b:5 and Sanhedrin 67a:15.

13 For further details on the birth of Jesus in Jewish folklore, see Schäfer, *Toledot Yeshu*.

14 Origen, *Contra Celsum* I:28.

15 Schäfer, "Toledot Yeshu as a Tool," 10.

16 Limor and Yuval, "Judas Iscariot."

17 Gager, "Simon Peter."

18 Babylonian Talmud Sanhedrin 43a:20.

19 Schäfer, *Jesus in the Talmud*, 74.

20 Marcus, *How the West*, 87–107.

21 Babylonian Talmud Gittin 57a:4.

22 Brenz, *Jüdischer abgestreiffter*, 4–5.

23 Otto, *Gali Razia*, 177 [page not explicitly numbered].

24 Huldreich, *Seyfer Toldes Yeshue*.

25 Schäfer, *Jesus in the Talmud*, 113.

26 This English translation is derived from Sacks, "Lucky Packet," 39.

27 Biale, "Counter-History"; Goldstein, "A Polemical Tale."

28 Mead, *Did Jesus Live 100 B.C.?*

29 Schäfer, *Jesus in the Talmud*, 37. The legend is recorded in Babylonian Talmud Sanhedrin 107b:12–14 and Soto 47a:12–14.

30 Note that some *Mayse Tole* iterations are instead set a hundred years *after* the time of the New Testament (Rosenzweig, "When Jesus Spoke Yiddish"), based on an extrapolation of Babylonian Talmud Berokhos 61b:6.

31 Bastomski, *Baym kval: materialn*, 39; Gnozovits, "*Miskhakim*," 209.

32 Lerner, "*Ma'ase ha'tana v'ha'met*"; Kushelevsky, "*Ha'tana v'ha'met ha'noded*" (2004).

33 Friedmann, "*Pirke derekh erets*," 22–23.

34 Lehnardt, "Christian Influences"; Weissman, *Final Judgement*, 301–4.

35 Bar-Moses, *Seyfer or zorua II*, 61; Ben-Judah, *Perushey sidur*, 602–3; Ben-Samuel, *Makhzer Vitri*, 112–13.

36 Heller, "Notes de folk-lore," 308–12; cf. Kushelevsky, "*Ha'tana v'ha'met ha'noded*" (1994).

37 Shinan, *Oto ha'ish*. In modern Yiddish, Jesus was referred to as "the" *oyse ho'ish* (*der oyse ho'ish*), which means "'the' that man." I use this same convention.

38 Ben-Samuel, *Makhzer Vitri*, 112–13.

39 Ben-Samuel, *Makhzer Vitri*, 113.

40 Ben-Samuel, *Makhzer Vitri*, 113.

41 Shyovitz, "You Have Saved Me," 62; cf. Kushelevsky, *Sigufim u'fituyim*, 262–68.

42 Biale, *Power and Powerlessness*, 60–69.

43 Trachtenberg, *The Devil and the Jews*.

44 For other potential reasons that Christians may have been thinking about Jews at Christmas, see Fabre-Vassas, *The Singular Beast*, 62–63, 83, 176–91, 271–72.

45 Lee, "Augustine vs. Archisynagogus"

46 Schuldes, *Die Teufelsszenen*, 110–14.

47 Trachtenberg, *The Devil and the Jews*, 23.

48 Anderson, *The Legend of the Wandering Jew*.

49 Müllenhoff, *Sagen*, 547–48.

50 Blind, "Wodan, the Wild Huntsman."

51 Klintberg, "The Swedish Wanderings," 117.

52 Dundes, *Life Is Like*, 119–41.

53 Marcus, *How the West*, 4.

54 Yuval, *Two Nations*, 68–77.

55 Klier, *Imperial Russia's Jewish Question*, 68–69; Klier, *Russians, Jews, and the Pogroms*, 24–33, 44–47, 66–68, 92; Nirenberg, "The Two Faces of Sacred Violence";

Penkower, "The Kishinev Pogrom"; Person, "The 1940 'Easter Pogrom'"; Roth, "The Eastertide Stoning of the Jews."

56 Horowitz, *Reckless Rites*.
57 Gribetz, "Hanged and Crucified."
58 Horowitz, *Reckless Rites*, 84–87.
59 Tokarska-Bakir, "The Hanging of Judas," 399.
60 Cala, *The Image of the Jew*, 81.
61 Tokarska-Bakir, "The Hanging of Judas."
62 Roth, "The Feast of Purim."
63 Yuval, *Two Nations*, 164–68.
64 Voß, *Sons of Saviors*, 63–67. Jews reclaimed the redness trope based on 1 Samuel 16:12, which states that King David was "ruddy."
65 Marcus, *Rituals of Childhood*, 102–28.
66 Hilton, *Bar Mitzvah*, 216–19.
67 Gaster, *Festivals of the Jewish Year*, 71–79; Hilton, *The Christian Effect*, 47–59.
68 Töyrylä, *Abraham Bar Hiyya*, 276.
69 Leiman, "The Scroll of Fasts," 182–83.
70 Leiman, "The Scroll of Fasts," 185–92.
71 Bader, *Unzere gaystike rizen*, 415.
72 Inhat, "The Middle Ages," 16; Williams, *The Organ*, 93.
73 Tyrnau, *Seyfer ha'minhogim*, 13.
74 Hoffman, "The Image of the Other."
75 Yuval, *Two Nations*, 199–202.
76 Prisha, *Orekh khayim*, 238:1.
77 Frid, "*Rov Khayim*," 484; Sofer, *Igros Sofrim*, 121–22 [sec. 2, no. 2].
78 Strawn, "Moses' Shining."
79 Thornton, "The Crucifixion of Haman."

CHAPTER 3. *NIDELNACHT* AND *NITL-NAKHT*
1 I thank the participants of the debate for permitting me to write about it here.
2 Yiddish Translator, "*A gut nitl*."
3 Yiddish Translator, "*Ikh meyn*."
4 Viswanath, "*Vertshpiln*."
5 Viswanath, "👍."
6 Viswanath, "Yeah that's what's odd."
7 Kenotic Neutral, "But it's just wrong"; Viswanath, "1. Nidelnacht." These earliest references to *nitl* spell it ניתל (a pun with the Hebrew "hanged") instead of the modern ניטל (a pun with the Yiddish "not").
8 Viswanath, "I'm not sure."
9 Viswanath, "These three factors."
10 Bernstein, *Yudishe shprikhverter*, 179; Cassel, *Weihnachten*, 129; Harkavy, "*Di opshtamung*"; Rubin, *Geschichte des Aberglaubens*, 153; Weill, "Le Yidisch alsacien-lorrain," 74.

11 Grunwald, "Fünfundzwanzig Jahre," 14.

12 Grunwald cites Stutz, "Nidelnacht."

13 Weinreich's notes in Lunski, "*Iserlin's yidish*," 297–98.

14 Grimm and Grimm, *Deutsches Wörterbuch*, 7:742, based on Birlinger, *Wörter-büchlein zum Volksthümlichen*, 71.

15 Weinreich, *Geshikhte fun der yidisher shrapkh*, 3:204, citing Fischer, *Schwäbisches Wörterbuch*, 4:2029.

16 Weinreich, *Geshikhte fun der yidisher shrapkh*, 3:204.

17 Beider, "Romance Elements," 81–82; Pietruszka, *Yidishe folks-entsiklopedye*, 384; Rivkind, "*Nitl*," 840.

18 Beider, *Origins of Yiddish Dialects*, 402, n. 155.

19 Eidelberg, "*Tsror hearot*," 647; Ta-Shma, "*Yemey eydeyhem*," 201–2.

20 Carlebach, *Palaces of Time*, 115–40.

21 Shapiro, "Torah Study on Christmas Eve," 338.

22 Chatto, *Facts and Speculations*, 60–91.

23 Ridenour, *The Krampus*, 167–69.

24 For a brief review, see Hoffmann-Krayer and Bächtold-Stäubli, "Nidelnächte."

25 Birlinger, *Volksthümliches aus Schwaben*, 501.

26 Birlinger, *Volksthümliches aus Schwaben*, 501, based on Birlinger, *Volksthümliches aus Schwaben*, 47, no. 60, which is linked to wandering revenants via Crusius, *Annales Suevici*, 653–54.

27 Grünenwald, "Pfälzischer Bauernkalender," 104.

28 Birlinger, *Wörterbüchlein zum Volksthümlichen*, 71, which is linked to wandering revenants via Lecouteux, *Phantom Armies*, 193.

29 Rochholz, *Drei Gaugöttinnen*, 47.

30 Gugitz, *Fest- und Brauchtumskalender*, 153; Höfler, *Das Jahr*, 44. To appreciate these sources, see Wuttke, *Der deutsche Volksaberglaube*, 94–95.

31 Höfler, *Das Jahr*, 44, which has no citation for a fourteenth-century source that includes the word *Nidelnacht*.

32 Höfler, "Gebäcke in der Zeit," 16.

33 Hutton, *Queens of the Wild*, 122–23.

34 Hutton, "The Wild Hunt."

35 On the history of Holle, see Hutton, *Queens of the Wild*, 110–142; Timm and Beckmann, *Frau Holle*.

36 Lecouteux, *Phantom Armies*, 19.

37 Sommer, "The Pre-Christian Jól."

38 Lecouteux, *Phantom Armies*, 17–18.

39 Klapper, "Deutscher Volksglaube," 36.

40 Waschnitius, *Perth*, 62.

41 Hutton, *Queens of the Wild*, 122–23.

42 Haiding, "Berchtenbräuche"; Motz, "The Winter Goddess"; Rumpf, *Perchten*; Waschnitius, *Perth*.

43 Hoffmann-Krayer and Bächtold-Stäubli, "Weihnachtsgebäck, Weihnachtsbrot."

44 Fischer, *Schwäbisches Wörterbuch*, 4:2029; Rumpf, *Perchten*, 49.

45 Grimm, *Deutsche Mythologie I*, 262.

46 Wuttke, *Der deutsche Volksaberglaube*, 26; Höfler, "Das Haaropfer in Teigform."

47 Haiding, "Berchtenbräuche."

48 Smith, "Perchta the Belly-Slitter."

49 Hutton, *Queens of the Wild*, 142.

50 Hutton, *Queens of the Wild*, 117.

51 Perles, "Die Berner Handschrift," 24. On the dating of this Yiddish glossing, see
    Timm and Beckmann, *Frau Holle*, 17–19.

52 *"Got mit der gotekhe hobn zikh geshlogn un tseflikt s'betgevant"* (discussed by
    Sadan, *"Marat Hole"*).

53 For a review, see Hammer, "Holle's Cry"; cf. Matveyev, *"Di yidn."*

54 Mayer, *Das Judenthum*, 226–29.

55 Golinkin, "Hanukkah Exotica," 45–46.

56 Wexler, *The Ashkenazic Jews*, 115–17.

57 Bar-Moses, *Seyfer or zorua I*, 97.

58 Suslin HaKohen, *Seyfer ha'agudo* 72b; quoted in clearer font by Güdemann, *Ge-
    schichte des Erziehungswesens*, 215, n7.

59 cf. Kohlbach, "Das Zopfgebäck," who argues that Jews embraced this braided
    bread in the context of medieval Jewish women sacrificing braids of hair to a
    pagan goddess.

60 Hutton, *The Witch*, 130–43; Lecouteux, *Phantom Armies*, 8–23.

61 Waschnitius, *Perth*, 60.

62 John of Salisbury, *Policraticus II*, 87.

63 Landau, "Holekreisch"; Waschnitius, *Perth*, 18, 49, 55.

64 Baumgarten, *Mothers and Children*, 93–99.

65 Mintz, *Shayles u'tshuves*, 62, no. 19.

66 Weinreich, "Holekrash"; cf. Baumgarten, *Mothers and Children*, 98–99, who
    argues (without evidence) that Jews believed Holle to kidnap babies à la Lilith.

67 Patai, *The Hebrew Goddess*, 244–45.

68 Cooper, *Eat and Be Satisfied*, 175.

69 Lunski, *"Iserlin's yidish,"* 289. On the content of Isserlein's text, see Carlebach,
    Palaces of Time, 115.

70 Tyrnau, *Seyfer ha'minhogim*, 13.

71 cf. the Judaization of the cookie *montash* [poppy pocket] as *ho'montash* [Haman
    pocket] in a poke at Haman, an alias for Jesus. Such a Purimization responded to
    the Easter cookie *Judasohr* [Judas ear] poking at Judas, an alias for Jews (Lewin-
    sky, *Sefer ha'moadim*, 154).

72 Baumgarten, *Introduction to Old Yiddish*, 364–65; Hilton, *The Christian Effect*,
    24–29.

73 Yuval, *Two Nations*, 124.

74 On the history of St. Nicholas, see Mezger, *Sankt Nikolaus*.

75 a Sancta Clara, "Um Fest."

76 a Sancta Clara, "Um Fest," 197.

77 a Sancta Clara, "Um Fest," 196–97.

78 Hägrad. *Ein ächter Beitrag*, 19–20. The dating of this text to the eighteenth century is based on *Provinzialnachrichten*, 14.

79 For illustrations of the *Kinderfresser*, see Ridenour, *The Krampus*, 23–24.

80 Lewis, *Infanticide and Abortion*, 94; cf. Ridenour, *The Krampus*, 24–27.

81 Tarleton, "The Devil's in the Details."

82 M., *Curiöser Bericht*, 6.

83 On scaring children with stories of the wandering dead on Christmas Eve, see Fischer, *Das Buch vom Aberglauben*, 329–30. On Holle's conflation with the wandering dead, see Hutton, "The Wild Hunt."

84 The phrasing "ritual transaction with the dead" is from Ridenour, *The Krampus*, 140.

85 Meisen, *Die Sagen*, 111–20.

86 Reproduced in Ridenour, *The Krampus*, 27.

87 Rumpf, *Perchten*.

88 Klintberg, "The Swedish Wanderings," 117.

89 This description is based on Müllenhoff, *Sagen*, 547–48, which is quoted in chapter 2 of the current book.

90 Ebendorfer, *Das jüdische Leben*, 36; Hutton, *Queens of the Wild*, 122.

91 Pfefferkorn, *Handt Spiegel*, 12 [page not explicitly numbered].

92 Hess, *Flagellum Iudeorum*, 45.

93 Barbu, "Feeling Jewish," 197.

94 It is also at this point in time (or shortly thereafter) that rabbis begin ascribing a custom of not studying Torah to the eve of a Christian holiday (Bachrach, *Shulkhn orekh*, 256, *kitser halokhes* section).

95 As noted by Shapiro, "Torah Study on Christmas Eve," 336, a slightly earlier report by apostate Johann Adrian (from 1609) describes this same Jewish tradition of refraining from Torah study to withhold rest from Jesus who must "crawl through nasty latrines." However, Adrian describes this event as taking place on "*Himmelfahrtstag*," which translates to Ascension Day. He presumably meant Christmas. He describes that the Jews tell their children who go out to the latrines at this time to "see that the *Tole* does not pull you in" (Adrian, *Send und Warnungs-Brieff*, 29).

96 Brenz, *Jüdischer abgestreiffter*, 3.

97 Brenz, *Jüdischer abgestreiffter*, 13–14.

98 Brenz, *Jüdischer abgestreiffter*, 14. My translation is influenced by Hirsch, *Yudisher Theriak*, 63.

99 Schwab, *Detectum velum*, 7.

100 Ebendorfer, *Das jüdische Leben*, 58; Schäfer, "Toledot Yeshu as a Tool," 10–12.

101 Krauss, *Das Leben Jesu*, 43.

102 Carlebach, *Palaces of Time*, 125.

103 Eisenmenger, *Entdecktes Judenthum*, 560; Shapira, *Seyfer regel yeshoro*, 116.

104 Böhme, *Deutsches Kinderlied*, 643.

105 The dreidel is specifically associated with Hanukkah today, but historically it was
intertwined with broader midwinter merriment. See Bachrach, *Khavos Yair*, 126;
Ungar, "*Khanike minhogim*"; and chapter 4 of the current book.

106 Bernshteyn, "*Likhtlekh*"; Golinkin, "Hanukkah Exotica," 41–42. At the turn of the
twentieth century, Eastern European Jews popularly understood the four letters
n/g/h/sh as an acronym for *Note Ganef hakt shleser* [Nota the Thief breaks locks]
(Rivkind, *Der Kamf*, 52).

107 List, "Frau Holda"; Kohler, *Martin Luther*, 71–72.

108 Christmann, "Weihnachten," 47.

109 Tille, *Yule and Christmas*, 116–17.

110 Frank, *System*, 516.

111 Hasche, *Diplomatische Geschichte*, 383.

112 M., *Curiöser Bericht*, 5–6.

113 Shapiro, "Torah Study on Christmas Eve," 343.

114 Hirsch, *Yudisher Tiryak*, 29–30; translated with modifications by Morris Faierstein
(Hirsch, *Yudisher Theriak*, 63).

115 Wülfer, *Theriaca Judaica*, 91.

116 Fried, *Neupolierter und wohlgeschliffener*, 31.

117 Fried, *Neupolierter und wohlgeschliffener*, 31.

118 Schudt, *Jüdische Merkwürdigkeiten*, 318.

119 Würfel, *Historische Nachricht*, 70.

120 Eisenmenger, *Entdecktes Judenthum*, 563–64.

121 Eckstein, *Geschichte der Juden*, 111.

122 Friedenheim, *Die Hoffnung Israel*, 379.

123 Friedenheim, *Die Hoffnung Israel*, 313.

CHAPTER 4. AN EASTERN EUROPEAN JEWISH CHRISTMAS

1 Sofer, *Igros Sofrim*, 121–22 [sec. 2, no. 2]. In Sofer's setting, the date of Christmas
Eve followed the Gregorian Calendar, thus falling nearly two weeks before the
traditional Julian-based Jewish dating of the *tkufe*.

2 Shapiro, "Torah Study on Christmas Eve," 332 n. 49, 350–53; cf. Bachrach, *Yair
nesiv*, 75/84: "A famous rabbi said that women should not purify themselves [i.e.
prepare for sex] on the night of *nitl*."

3 Implied in Sofer, *Igros Sofrim*, 121–22 [sec. 2, no. 2].

4 Sofer, *Igros Sofrim*, 121–22 [sec. 2, no. 2].

5 Sofer, *Igros Sofrim*, 122–23 [sec. 2, no. 3].

6 Stampfer, "Settling Down."

7 Shapiro, "Torah Study on Christmas Eve," especially p. 328.

8 Shapiro, "Torah Study on Christmas Eve," 336.

9 For a cursory analysis of these materials, see Gottesman, "Old World Jewish
Christmas"; Shandler, *Jews, God and Videotape*, 185–229.

10 Bogatyrev, *Vampires in the Carpathians*, 37–58.

11 Oişteanu, *Inventing the Jew*, 347–53.

12 Bogatyrev, *Vampires in the Carpathians*, 54–55.

13 Fudem, "Gizela Fudem"; Heller, *Strange and Unexpected Love*, 32; Sandberg-Mesner, *Light From the Shadows*, 30; Schoenfeld, *Shtetl Memoirs*, 116; Sher with Rosenberg Stenge, "Olga's Story"; Shnayderman, *Ven di Visl*, 74.

14 Oişteanu, *Inventing the Jew*, 353–56.

15 Kotula, *Tamten Rzeszów*. 390–91.

16 Abramowicz, *Farshvundene geshtaltn*, 421.

17 The dish has been better known as *karp po żydowsku* [Jewish-style carp] ever since Hilary Minc (1905–1974), the Jewish minister of industry and commerce in postwar Poland, called for there to be "carp on every Christmas Eve table in Poland" (Kruszyńska, "Karp na każdym").

18 Pall Mall Gazette, "Christmas Customs in Russia"; Polish Review, "Christmas in Poland."

19 Senn, "Romanian Werewolves," 211.

20 Senn, "Romanian Werewolves," 206–10.

21 Oişteanu, *Inventing the Jew*, 54, 242–43.

22 Rosenfeld, *Eyner aleyn*, 183.

23 Fuchs, "*Di blinde nakht*," 581; Metzker, *Afn zeydns felder*, 351; Rus, *Der Dnyester roysht*, 153. Of these three examples, only Metzker depicts a Jew joining the Christian carolers.

24 Gutman, *Mayn shtetl Yedinets*, 124; Katz, *A rayze in mayn lebn*, 30; Słomka, *Pamiętniki włościanina*, 139; Spector, "*Vos ikh gedenk*," 94.

25 Bialik, "*Ha'khatsotsra nitbaysha*," 151; Goldberg, "*Kristmes*," 136; Joffe and Mark, *Groyser verterbukh*, 773; Spector, "*Vos ikh gedenk*," 94.

26 Whereas *ryba po żydowsku* retains a strong association with Christmas across Poland, many Polish people now associate *chałka* with Easter rather than Christmas.

27 Landmann, *Erinnerungen an Galizien*, 69–70.

28 Rechtman, *Yidishe etnografye*, 63.

29 Based on Babylonian Talmud Berokhos 31b:10 and Sanhedrin 90b:10.

30 Simon, "*Yidishe vortslen*."

31 Pomerancblum, "*Azoy hot oysgezen Stashev*," 254.

32 Burshteyn, "*Di 'blinde nakht*"; Der Idisher Zhurnal, "*Di nakht fun 'nitl*"; Naymark, "*Haynt iz nitel-nakht*," 4; Oguz, "*B'layle ha'hu*"; Tsvien, "*Yidishe interesen*."

33 Lipetz, *Seyfer matamim*, 82.

34 Rivkind, "*Nitl*," 841.

35 *Literarishe Bleter*, "*Yedies*," 112.

36 Sutzkever and Kaczerginski, "Customs for Nitl," 8.

37 Sutzkever and Kaczerginski, "Customs for Nitl," 4.

38 Karras, "The Aerial Battle."

39 Tsvien, "*Yidishe interesen*."

40 Sutzkever and Kaczerginski, "Customs for Nitl," 8.

41 Sutzkever and Kaczerginski, "Customs for Nitl," 10.

42 Sutzkever and Kaczerginski, "Customs for Nitl," 8.

43 Grabowicz, "'Dumy' as Performance." On folk etymologies for *blinde nakht*, see Ungar, "*Yidn shraybn*"; Ungar, "*Nokh mayses*"; Ungar, "*Der opshtam*."

44 Goldberg, "*Kristmes*," 134.

45 Mark, "*Di shprakh*," 79.

46 Frimer, "*Bamerkungen fun a podolier*," 47.

47 *South Park*, "Mr. Hankey."

48 Frimer, "*Bamerkungen fun a podolier*," 47.

49 Trachtenberg, *Jewish Magic*, 258.

50 Sutzkever and Kaczerginski, "Customs for Nitl," 2.

51 Fuchs, "*Di blinde nakht*," 580.

52 Bashevis, "The Last Demon"; Bashevis, "*Mayse Tishevits*."

53 Resneck, "Let Others Share," 799.

54 Sambatyon, *Khayey Sambation*, 104.

55 Sadan, "*Di blinde nakht*"; Sadan, *Mi'mekhoz ha'yaldut*, 244.

56 Eliscu, "Itzig's Party," 2. In addition to contaminating food and drink, Jesus's blood could also strike an open *seyfer* (Burshteyn, "*Di 'blinde nakht*"; Oguz, "*B'layle ha'hu*").

57 Sutzkever and Kaczerginski, "Customs for Nitl," 6.

58 Wilkansky, *B'Kheder*, 179–80.

59 Grunwald, "Aus Hausapotheke," 217; Mayer, *Das Judenthum*, 226–29.

60 *Hayntike Nayes*, "*Vi azoy*."

61 Miles, *Christmas in Ritual*, 234; White, *The Frank C. Brown*, 203, no. 6017.

62 Grimm, *Deutsche Mythologie III*, 454, no. 589; Lee, "Saint John's Wort."

63 Trachtenberg, *Jewish Magic*, 257–58; Baumgarten, *Biblical Women*, 161–62.

64 Bastomski, *Baym kval: Yidishe shprikhverter*, 110; Finkelshteyn, "*Vegn Sholem Ashs*," 181; Goldberg, "*Kristmes*," 136.

65 Ansky, "*Di tseylm frage*," 55.

66 Rivkind, *Der kamf*, 54.

67 Rivkind, "*Nitl*," 841.

68 Rotenberg, "*Unzere kinder-yorn*," 288.

69 Kahan, "*Ver un vi azoy*," 118.

70 Kotik, *Mayne zikhroynes*, 208.

71 Gross, "*Mayselekh un mesholim*."

72 Frimer, "*Bamerkungen fun a podolier*," 47.

73 Cohen, *Shpole*, 160.

74 Naymark, "*Haynt iz nitel-nakht*," 4.

75 Frischmann, "*Shrago*," 55–56.

76 Erdberg, "*In der ortodoksisher velt*."

77 Kotler, "*Khanike in goles*."

78 Katz, "*Altvarg*"; Leivick, "*Dray khanike-likhtelekh*"; Litvin, "*Khanike in dem alten kheyder*"; Saphire, "*Yene gliklikhe kinder-yoren*"; Zayfert, "*Khane mit ire 7 zin*."

79 Mikaela, "*Beys Shamay*."

80 Isaacs, "*An umglaykhe shutfes*."

81 Milch, "*Papirosen*"; Naymark, "*Haynt iz nitel-nakht*"; Sidroni, "*Pirke zikhroynes*," 286–87.
82 Burshteyn, "*Di 'blinde nakht.*"
83 Nayman, "*Mayn zeyde R' Gdalye*," 444.
84 Krauss, "Aus der jüdischen Volksküche," 17. See also Treyster, "*Der shuldiker.*"
85 *Kol Mevaser felieton*, "*Nitl oder vaynakhtn.*"
86 Nachmani and Chinitz, "*Pinkes Slutsk*, 351.
87 Shneour, *Noyekh Pandre*, 71.
88 Mark, "*Nitl*," 184.
89 Shapiro, "Torah Study on Christmas Eve," 322–23.
90 Gutman, *Mayn shtetl Yedinets*, 124.
91 Gutman, *Mayn shtetl Yedinets*, 123.
92 Gocz, "Żydzi z Zyndranowej," 89.
93 Schoenfeld, *Shtetl Memoirs*, 116.
94 Schoenfeld, *Shtetl Memoirs*, 104.
95 Bernstein, "*Gedanken vegn der blinder nakht.*"
96 Blond, *Tolmitsh*, 317.
97 *Forverts*, "*Di blinde nakht.*"
98 Avromtshik, "*Unzere melamdim*," 120.
99 Kanar, *Ikh un Lemekh*, 103.
100 Tsvien, "*Yidishe interesen.*"
101 *Emanu-el*, "Correspondence," 8.
102 Alekseev, *Besedy pravoslavnago*, 90.
103 Tsvien, "*Yidishe interesen.*"
104 Zhitlowsky, "*Di kristenthum-shayle*," 628–29.
105 Shapiro, "Torah Study on Christmas Eve," 322.
106 Babylonian Talmud Megilo 25b:17.
107 Berkowitz, *Kinder-yorn*, 192.
108 Berkowitz, *Kinder-yorn*, 195.
109 Marmor, *Mayn lebns-geshikhte*, 91–92.
110 Passy, "Christmas & Chopsticks."
111 Burshteyn, "*Di 'blinde nakht*"; Gottesman, "*Nitl in der alter heym*"; Kohn, "When All the World"; Lewinsky, "*Al ha'folklor*"; Lifschultz, "Yesterday and Today," 14; Rivkind, "*Nitl*," 840; Ungar, "*Vegn opshtam.*"
112 Naymark, "*Haynt iz nitel-nakht*," 5; Rappaport, "Nittel."
113 *Kol Mevaser felieton*, "*Nitl oder vaynakhtn.*"
114 Eastern European Jews generally included *nitl* in lists of Jewish holidays (e.g. *Kol Mevaser*, "*Di mode*," 2; *Kol Mevaser*, "*Fun dem tsaytgayst*," 5; Zinger, "*Di literatur*," 115).
115 Herzog, *The Language and Culture Atlas*, 294; Gold and Prager, "Replies to Queries," 246–49.
116 Bernstein, *Yudishe shprikhverter*, 179; Stutchkoff, *Der oyster*, 729.
117 Tendlau, *Sprichwörter und Redensarten*, 340.

118 Lewinsky, *Seyfer Zembrove*, 364.
119 *Unzer ekspres*, "*'Karbones' fun der nitl-nakht.*"
120 Mishna Pirke Ovos 1:2.
121 Aschkenasy, *Oytsres fun idishn humor*, 24, no. 53; El Melekh, "*Vos iz 'nitl'?*";
    Engelsher, *Der yudisher oytser*, 369, no. 1394; Horowitz, *Khsides un etik*, 32; Judäus,
    "Wie Rabbi Israel Salant," 446; Kirshenbaum, *Fun unzer gaystiker khrifes*, 108;
    Rawnitzki, *Yudishe vitsn*, 260, no. 46; Yushzon, *Fun unzer altn oyster.*
122 Menes, "*Der krizis*"; Naymark, "*Haynt iz nitel-nakht,*" 5.
123 Cahan, *Yidisher folklor*, 181–82 [no. 101]; cf. Bohdanowicz, "Demonologia ludowa,"
    54, 58; Kmietowicz, *Slavic Mythical Beliefs*, 158.
124 Rechtman, *Yidishe etnografye*, 63–65; Rubin, *Hantbukh far idishe geshikhte*, 14–15.
125 Elzer, "*Mi'minhagey yisrael,*" 350; cf. Alter, "*Al isur.*"
126 Kafka, *Tagebüch 1910–23*, 490. Steinberg, "*In der 'nitel-nakht,*'" adds that Christmas
    Eve was the one night when ardent Hasidim would reportedly play games at the
    besmedresh without fear of punishment.
127 Shapiro, "Torah Study on Christmas Eve," 323–24.
128 Sadan, "*Di blinde nakht.*"
129 Isaacs, "*Di nisht glaykhe shutfes.*"
130 Klausner, "*'Nitl' b'mishnat khabad.*"
131 Veltz, *Shayles u'tshuves*, 28, no. 21.
132 Bornstein, *Seyfer shem mi'Shmuel*, 202–3.
133 Shore, *Baal Shem Tov*, 28:1.
134 Linetzky, *Dos poylishe yingl*, 18.

CHAPTER 5. THE REINVENTION OF *NITL-NAKHT*
1 *Detroit Jewish News*, "The Saga of an Eminent Family."
2 Goldberg, "*Kristmes,*" 132–33.
3 Goldberg, "*Kristmes,*" 134–35.
4 Goldberg, "*Kristmes,*" 135–36.
5 The malicious woman in Goldberg's description is akin to European Christmas
  witches such as Gryla, Berchta, La Befana, and Baba Yaga—the latter of whom
  was widely known in Ukraine, Goldberg's place of birth.
6 Golomb, *Umvegn un oysveg*, 47.
7 Golomb, "*Tsu shpet,*" 137.
8 Charney, *Afn shvel*, 162.
9 Weber, *Wissenschaft als Beruf*, 16.
10 Hoffman, *From Rebel to Rabbi.*
11 Hoffman, *From Rebel to Rabbi*, 21–23.
12 Hertz, *How Jews Became Germans.*
13 My phrasing here is influenced by Magid, *Hasidism Incarnate*, 114.
14 Hoffman, *From Rebel to Rabbi*, 34–51.
15 Biale, "A Journey Between Worlds"; cf. Nathans, *Beyond the Pale*; Petrovsky-
   Shtern, *Jews in the Russian Army.*

16 Zhitlowsky, *"Di kristenthum-shayle,"* 629–31.

17 Isaacs, *"An umglaykhe shutfes."*

18 Hoffman, *From Rebel to Rabbi*, 117–69.

19 On Asch: Norich, "Sholem Asch and the Christian Question"; Hoffman, "Sholem Asch's True Christians." On Opatoshu: Koller, "The Two Souls of Mordkhe"; and chapter 7 of the current book.

20 Asch, *"In a karnival nakht."*

21 Opatoshu, *"Der mishpet."*

22 Goldshteyn, *"Unzer khanike-kibetsarnye."*

23 Man, *"Nitl."*

24 Starkman, *"Baym dernentern zikh."*

25 Kaplan, *"Di nitl-nakht."*

26 On Argentina: Himitian, "Cómo fue la Navidad"; Svarch, "'Don Jacobo en la Argentina,'" 126–27. On Australia: *Australian Jewish News*, "Christmas for non-Christian Australians"; Rutland, "Reflections on 'Culture Mavens,'" 307–8. On Brazil: Viera, "Outsiders and Insiders"; Khes, *"Refleksn."* On Canada: Maynard, "Jewish Christmas"; S. G. B., "Menorah or Christmas Tree?." On England: Duschinsky, *The Rabbinate*, 12, 15–16; Vice, "Christmas Trees," 242–46. On France: Bokobza, *Jewish Identity*, 146–47; Vigée, *Moisson de Canaan*, 109–11. On Germany: Embacher, "Weihnukka"; Perry, *Christmas in Germany*, 68–76. On Israel: Ahituv and Glazer, *"Khag ha'molad asli"*; Elia-Shalev, "For a growing number." On post-war Poland: Ilicki, "Changing Identity," 270–71.

27 Herzl, *Theodor Herzls Tagebücher*, 328.

28 Ilan, *"Al ha'khasidim."*

29 Khes, *"Refleksn."*

30 The German term *Weihnukka* has been used since at least the 1920s (Rosenzweig, *Der Mensch*, 1009), although it did not become popular until the 1980s and 1990s. The Hebrew term *khanukrismes* likewise became popular in the 1980s and 1990s (Avigal, *"Lo la'inyan"*; Sharaby, *"M'khag ha'khanuka"*; Ungar, *"L'vade bitsua"*). The English term Chrismukkah was popularized in December 2003 by *The O.C.* (O.C., "The Best Chrismukkah Ever"), although this term had already been on the rise for some years prior (Adamski, "Couple's engagement"; Brownstein, "Jew-bilee"; Lydon, "Reflections"; Rzepka, "It's beginning"). The term "Hanukkah bush" is much older, dating back to the nineteenth century (Plaut, *A Kosher Christmas*, 43), and popularized when the American Hanukkah proliferated in the 1950s.

31 Scholem, *Von Berlin*, 42.

32 Jerman, *Santa Claus Worldwide*, demonstrates that Santa is descended from the German figures rather than the Dutch *Sinterklaas* (see especially pp. 156–57). However, on Jerman's unlikely argument that Santa is ultimately descended from the Germanic god Odin, see Lecouteux, *Phantom Armies*, 202–8.

33 Deitch, *Inm land fun di Yenkis*, 52–63; Tsesler, *Feygl in der luftn*, 115–20; Tsesler, *Fun gantsn hartsn*, 86–87.

34 Brand, "*Santa Kloz*"; Lieberman, *Dos problem*, 33; Reisen, "*Afn farher*," 47; Zolf, *Af fremder erd*, 515.

35 Khes, "*Refleksn.*"

36 Shandler, *Jews, God and Videotape*, 193–95.

37 Friedman, "*Santa Kloz hot gekhalesht.*"

38 Planter, "*Arunter di maskes.*"

39 Liessin, "*Santa Klooz.*"

40 Biron, "Strictly Confidential"; *Ployne v'Koyen*, "*Santa Klouz.*"

41 Friedman, "*Der farmaskirter 'Santa Klauz.*'"

42 Sheyn, "*Humor fun amerikaner.*"

43 Shneyman, "*Bilder un stsenes*"; Wigoder, "Chanukah and all the glitter."

44 *Forverts*, "*Afile Santa Klouz.*"

45 Schreig, "From Everywhere."

46 *New York Tribune*, "Jews Keep Christmas."

47 *Forverts* Reporter, "*Der kristmes-yarid.*"

48 S. G. B., "Menorah or Christmas Tree?"

49 Charney, "*Der traditsioneler yidisher yontef.*"

50 *Der Tog-Morgn Zhurnal*, "*Kristmas iz take.*"

51 Rosenfeld, "*Erev kristmas.*"

52 Ashton, *Hanukkah in America*, 105–37. See also chapter 6 of the current book.

53 Rosenfeld, "*Vaynakhts-glokn.*" Originally published as Rosenfeld, "*Kristmes.*"

54 Stanislawski, "A Preliminary Study," 85.

55 *Kol Mevaser felieton*, "*Nitl oder vaynakhtn*," 5.

56 Yushzon, "*Fun unzer alten oyster*"; cf. Zweifel, *Likutey Tsvi*, 34.

57 Observer, "To the Editor."

58 Dorson, *Folklore and Fakelore*, 5.

59 Herzog, *The Yiddish Language*, 38–42; Lown, *Memories of My Life*, 24; Newall, "Easter Eggs," 268–69; Schoenfeld, *Shtetl Memoirs*, 116; Ungar, "*A modner mineg.*"

60 Roskies, *The Jewish Search*. See also Estraikh and Krutikov, *The Shtetl*; Katz, *The Shtetl*; Krah, *American Jewry*; Shandler, *Shtetl*; Zipperstein, *Imagining Russian Jewry*.

61 Roskies, *A Bridge of Longing*, 7.

62 Roskies, "The Shtetl," 7.

63 Miron, "The Literary Image," 2, 5.

64 Roskies, *A Bridge of Longing*, 10.

65 Back in Europe, the expansion "*nes godl hoye shom*" was considered a secondary (rather than the primary) explanation of the four letters (*Deborah*, "Noch einmal Chanukka," 10).

66 Aleichem, "*Khanike-geld*," 2.

67 Stern, *From Jester to Gesture*.

68 Isaacs, *What Every Jewish Woman*, 54.

69 Leyb, "*Nitl.*"

70 Young, "*Der sholem-prints.*"

184 | NOTES

Auerbach, "*Af der vogshol.*"

Bilis, "*Nekhtn.*"

Bilis, "*Nekhtn.*"

74 Biale, *Power and Powerlessness.*

75 Weinfeld, "Antisemitism in Canada," 51.

76 Bernstein, "*Di shvartse, finstere, blinde nakht.*"

77 Bernstein, "*Di shvartse, finstere, blinde nakht.*"

78 Giladi, "*M'nitl ad silvester*"; Klinov, "*Silvester un 'nitel*'"; Neudorfer, "*Kitsur toldot ha'silvester*"; Sylvetsky, "Sylvester Night"; cf. Shneour, *Noyekh Pandre*, 71.

79 Siegler, *Tife vortslen*, 274–77.

80 Goldhar, "*Zikhroynes un batrakhtungen*," 283.

81 Ben-Yishai, "*Leyl ha'nitl.*"

CHAPTER 6. PEACE ON EARTH, GOOD WILL TO MEN

1 *Forverts* Reporter, "*S'iz erev kristmas.*"

2 *Forverts*, "*Kristmes-diburim*"; *Forverts*, "*Kristmes un yonkiper*"; *Forverts*, "*Shoyn der tsveyter*"; *Forverts* Reporter, "*S'iz erev kristmas.*"

3 *Forverts*, "*Kristmes-diburim.*"

4 *Forverts*, "*Kristmes un yonkiper*"; *Forverts*, "*Shoyn der tsveyter.*"

5 Hutton, *The Stations of the Sun*, 123.

6 Hutton, *The Stations of the Sun*, 29.

7 Brown, *Scotland Before 1700*, 349; Grant, *History of the Burgh*, 184.

8 Hutton, *The Stations of the Sun*, 25–33; Nissenbaum, *The Battle for Christmas*, 3–48.

9 Massachusetts, *The Charters and General Laws*, 119.

10 Irving, "Christmas."

11 *Troy Sentinel*, "Account of a Visit."

12 Perry, *Christmas in Germany*, 26.

13 Perry, *Christmas in Germany*, 17, 39.

14 Miller, "A Theory of Christmas."

15 Standiford, *The Man Who Invented Christmas.*

16 Dickens, *A Christmas Carol.* On English Christmas ghost stories, see Briggs, *Night Visitors*, 40–42.

17 On whether Scrooge is Jewish, see Grossman, "The Absent Jew."

18 Dickens, *A Christmas Carol*, 49.

19 Dickens, *A Christmas Carol*, 118.

20 Dickens, *A Christmas Carol*, 35.

21 Carpenter, "The Little Tear-Gatherer," 742.

22 Coolidge, "Born in Us a Savior."

23 Morton, *Trick or Treat.*

24 Irving, "Christmas," 31.

25 Shandler, *Jews, God and Videotape*, 188.

26 Coles, "The Spirit of Christmas."

27 Barnett, *The American Christmas*, 136.
28 Babylonian Talmud Rosh Hashono 16b:12.
29 The term *yomim neroim* is first documented by the Maharil (1360–1427) (Steiman, *Custom and Survival*, 87).
30 Bernstein, *Yudishe shprikhverter*, 31.
31 Werner, *The Sacred Bridge*, 252–55; Yuval, "Gedichte und Geschichte."
32 Sable, "The Day of Atonement."
33 Trachtenberg, *Jewish Magic*, 165; Tuszewicki, *A Frog Under the Tongue*, 184–86.
34 Weissman Joselit, *The Wonders of America*, 247.
35 HaCohen and Tarsi, "The Moment and Momentum."
36 Kligman, "The Music of Kol Nidre."
37 Zahavy, "A Pragmatic Study of *Kol Nidre*."
38 Miller, "'Hark! The Herald Angels Sing.'"
39 Storey, "The Invention of the English Christmas," 145.
40 Boeckler, "The Magic of the Moment," 39, 40, 66.
41 Hoffman, *The Art of Public Prayer*, 192.
42 Rosewarne, *Analyzing Christmas in Film*, 11.
43 Rosewarne, *Analyzing Christmas in Film*, 11.
44 Rosewarne, *Analyzing Christmas in Film*, 35.
45 Rich, "Paying for Praying."
46 Weissman Joselit, "Holiday Cheer," 11.
47 Freedman, "The Change."
48 Epsteen, "Order of B'nai B'rith."
49 Shmulewitz, "*Di yomim neroim*," 6.
50 Malkes, "*Vi azoy men pravet.*"
51 Thissen, "Something Special."
52 Malkes, "*Vi azoy men pravet.*"
53 Emanu-el, "S. F. Jewry."
54 *Der Tog*, "Chanukah and the Christmas Spirit."
55 See, "The Christmas Story."
56 Electric Christmas lights were introduced by Albert Sadacca (1901–1980). Aluminum Christmas trees were introduced by Si Spiegel (1924–2024). The most influential retailer of merchandise from Santa Claus was Robert L. May (1905–1976), who invented the character of Rudolph, the Red Nosed Reindeer in a shopping pamphlet.
57 Melendez, *A Charlie Brown Christmas*.
58 Dickens, *Vaynakht*.
59 Hoffmann, *Knaknisl un moyznkeyser*.
60 Diamant, "*Far di khagoes.*"
61 Miller, "*Men farshprayt proklomatsyes*," 220–21.
62 H., "Some Stray Thoughts."
63 Rosenfeld, "*Ha'neyres halole.*"
64 I thank Binyumen Schaechter for collecting these six melodies.

65 Ben-Aaron, "*A dreydl*" (on Gelbart's authorship, see Cahan-Simon, "Gelbart/ dreydl"); Rivesman, "*A khanike-lid.*" For an extended discussion, see Ashton, *Hanukkah in America*; Plaut, *A Kosher Christmas*, 41–64.

66 Idelsohn, *Jewish Music*, 171.

67 Gay, *Unfinished People*, 246.

68 Ashton, *Hanukkah in America*, 129.

69 Ashton, *Hanukkah in America*, 131.

70 Ashton, *Hanukkah in America*, 106.

71 Gailing, "*Khanike un kristmas.*" See also Hofman-Sheyn, "*Yidn un nisht-yidn,*" 265–66.

72 Weissman Joselit, *The Wonders of America*, 242–43.

73 Bonesho, "Foreign Holidays," 130–40; Yuval, "Was das Judentum," 176–77.

74 *Yidishe Velt*, "*Kunst geshmak.*"

75 *Der Morgen Zhurnal*, "*Shulzinger kontsert*"; *Der Tog*, "*Khazn Shulzinger's.*"

76 Some Yiddish Hanukkah stories do bear similarity to sentimental Christmas stories (e.g. Bashevis, "*An erev-khanike*"), but Yiddish Hanukkah stories are not as a rule more sentimental than Yiddish stories set on other Jewish holidays (see e.g. Aleichem, *Fun peysekh biz peysekh*; Peretz, *Ertseylungen IV*; Sforim, *Ale Verk IX*).

77 Jacobson, *Special Sorrows*, 105–6.

78 Peretz, "*Oyb nisht nokh hekher!*"

79 Margolis, "A Tempest in Three Teapots," 48.

80 Pinski, "*Erev yonkiper.*"

81 Goldin, *Mizrekh un Mayrev*.

82 Jacobson, *Special Sorrows*, 101.

83 Palatnik, "*Oysgeloshn s'yonkiper likht.*"

84 Raphaelson, "The Day of Atonement."

85 HaCohen, "Vocal Communities."

86 Rosewarne, *Analyzing Christmas in Film*, 175.

87 Crosland, *The Jazz Singer*.

88 Hoberman, *Bridge of Light*, 257–73; Shandler, *Jews, God and Videotape*, 13–55.

89 Stern, "The Idealized Mother."

90 Lynn, *Hayntike Mames*.

91 American Film Institute, "AFI's 100 Years . . . 100 Cheers."

92 American Jewish World, "At Homewood Theater"; *Forverts*, "*Teater anonsen.*"

93 Capra, *It's A Wonderful Life*; Seiden, *Kol Nidre*.

94 Loeffler, "Promising Harmonies."

95 Nosseck, *Der Vilner Shtot Khazn*.

96 Abeliovich, "Kol Nidre," 15.

97 Green, *A Brivele der Mamen*.

98 Irving, "Christmas," 31.

99 *Di Varhayt*, "David Kessler"; *Forverts*, "*Pablik teater*"; Forverts, "*Thalia Theater*"; Plaut, *A Kosher Christmas*, 38.

100 *Der Morgen Zhurnal*, "Irving Place Theatre," 11 Dec. 1919. The production was ultimately canceled in favor of an encore performance of *Di tentserin* [*The Dancer*] (*Der Morgen Zhurnal*, "Irving Place Theatre," 23 Dec. 1919).

101 *Forverts*, "*Tevye der milkhiker*" (21 Dec. 1939; 24 Dec. 1939).

102 American Israelite, "Talkie at Forest"; American Jewish World, "At Homewood Theater"; *Forverts*, "Kol Nidre" (19 Dec. 1939; 24 Dec. 1939).

103 *Forverts*, "*Mamele.*"

104 *Forverts*, "*Dem khazn's zundel.*"

105 Goldin and Motyleff, *Dem Khazns Zundl.*

106 Slobin, *Global Soundtracks*, 71.

107 Jameson, "Postmodernism and Consumer Society," 116–18.

108 Libin, "*Vos hert zikh.*"

109 The American Film Institute lists *The Shop Around the Corner* as #28 on their list of "The 100 Greatest Love Stories Of All Time" (American Film Institute, "AFI's 100 Years . . . 100 Passions").

110 Earlier films that were incidentally set on Christmas, such as *Love Finds Andy Hardy* (1938), are not considered "Christmas films."

111 Reporter, "*Irving Berlin.*"

112 On this song, see Koskoff, "Is 'White Christmas' a Piece of Jewish Music?"

113 Plaut, *A Kosher Christmas*, 88–91.

114 Daniels, "Have I Got a Christmas."

115 American Jewish World, "Jews' Benevolence."

116 *Marvelous Mrs. Maisel*, "Strike Up the Band."

117 *Northern Exposure*, "Shofar So Good."

118 Plaut, *A Kosher Christmas*, 4.

CHAPTER 7. THE YIDDISH CHRISTMAS LITERARY GENRE

1 cummings, "little tree."

2 Rosenfeld, "*Der kristmes tri.*"

3 Miller, "Jews and Anti-Semitism."

4 Mann, "*In der nakht fun nitl.*"

5 Gordin, "*Di blinde nakht*" (1895); cf. Fuchs, "*Di blinde nakht*"; Horovits, "*Di blinde nakht*"; Young, "*In blinder nakht*"; Zeltzer, "*Di blinde nakht.*"

6 Gordin, "*Di blinde nakht*" (1905); Gordin, "*Di blinde nakht*" (1908); Gordin, "The Blind Night"; Gordin, "Die Blinde Nacht (The Blind Night)."

7 Gordin, "*Vos zingt der Yid?*"

8 On Opatoshu's legacy, see Koller, *Joseph Opatoshu.*

9 Opatoshu, *In poylishe velder*, 299.

10 Koller, "The Two Souls of Mordkhe," 75.

11 Koller, "The Two Souls of Mordkhe," 81.

12 Lieberman, "*Sholem Ash's Kristmes.*"

13 Asch, *Nativity.*

14 Opatoshu, "*A goy in goles.*"

15 Opatoshu, "*In der nakht fun 'nitul.*'"

16 Opatoshu, "*In der nakht fun nitul.*"

17 Opatoshu, "*Vekhter.*"

18 Glasman, "*Af di felder.*"

19 In one of Palatnik's Yiddish stories, she describes a young Jewish family in Brazil celebrating *Natal* [Christmas] with "a tree, lights, confetti . . . no different than their Christian neighbors . . . including even a '*Yoysef Pandre*' with a white beard in a red robe" (Palatnik, "*Af dervayl*," 129). See also Palatnik, "*Gebrakht.*"

20 Palatnik, "*Nitl beymer.*"

21 Kirzane, "What Kind of a Man," 195–97.

22 Goldzac, "*Af a yontef.*"

23 Maimonides, *Mishne toyre,* 30:14. See also Biale, *Eros and the Jews,* 54, 81–82, 105, 110–15; Horowitz, "Sabbath Delights," 137–43; Patai, *The Hebrew Goddess,* 255–76.

24 Bashevis, "*Der kurtser fraytik.*"

25 Wolfenstein, "Nittel Nacht."

26 Agnon, *Hakhnasat kala,* 172–73; Agnon, "*Ketaim,*" 384; Agnon, "*Mazal dagim,*" 608.

27 Kronberg, "Nittel (Blinde Nacht)."

28 On Kronberg's ideology, see Wallas, "Kibbuznik."

29 Kimche, "*Eykh buts'a*"; translated by *Palestine,* "Notes on the Palestine Situation," 11.

30 Chain, "*Heysherik.*"

31 Chain-Shimoni, "*Nitl-nakht.*"

CONCLUSION

1 This Yiddish version of "Let It Snow" was composed in 1999 by Hindy Abelson for Theresa Tova.

2 This is the title used by *The Times of Israel.* Heilman, "Hasidic 'Silent Night'"; Heilman, "How Hasidic Jews"; Heilman, "How Hasidim pointedly"; Heilman, "Silent night: How the Hasidim"; Heilman, "What Hasidic Jews."

3 See Heilman's article for contemporary Hasidic opinions on the origin of the customs. A plethora of Hasidic lectures on the topic (in Yiddish) can be found at https://koltorahonline.com.

4 Shapiro, "Torah Study on Christmas Eve," 323–24.

5 Quoted by Heilman.

6 Stein, "'The Most Wonderful Night.'"

7 JoeSettler, "Just Say No to Nittel Nacht."

8 Plaut, *A Kosher Christmas,* 35.

9 Hellinger, "What Are You Doing."

10 Greisman, "Brief Themes," section "Nittel."

11 Stein, "'The Most Wonderful Night.'"

12 Shapiro, "Torah Study and Christmas Eve," 322.

13 For a nonrepresentative Yiddish poll and discussion of what contemporary Hasidim (who use internet forums) do on Christmas Eve, see *Idishe Velt Forums*, "*Leyl nitl.*"

14 In interwar Poland, *kleyner nitl* and *groyser nitl* were respectively known as "*nitl bney Royme*" [Roman Catholic *nitl*] and "*nitl bney Yovn*" [Greek Orthodox *nitl*] (*Nayer Morgn*, "*Nitl bney Yovn*").

15 Shapiro, "Torah Study on Christmas Eve," 326. For further details on contemporary Hasidic Christmas practices, see Tzion, *Hilkhes nitl nakht*.

16 Magliocco, *Witching Culture*, 4.

17 Partridge, *The Re-enchantment of the West*; Hutton, *The Triumph of the Moon*; Magliocco, *Witching Culture*.

18 Scovell, *Folk Horror*.

19 Morton, *Trick or Treat*.

20 *Facebook*, "Folk Horror Revival."

21 https://www.boneandsickle.com/.

22 Ridenour, *The Krampus*, 2.

23 Plaut, *A Kosher Christmas*, 104–8.

24 Plaut, *A Kosher Christmas*, 156–60.

25 Seinfeld TV, "Make Festivus a National Holiday."

26 Leung, "The history."

27 Berman, "The secret history." On Jews and Chinese food, see Liu, "Kung Pao Kosher"; Merwin, *Pastrami on Rye*, 131–35; Miller, "Identity Takeout"; Plaut, *A Kosher Christmas*, 65–86; Tuchman and Levine, "New York Jews."

28 Katz, "Chiny Town."

29 Among many other examples: *Di Varhayt*, "*Kontsert un ball*"; *Forverts*, "*Bielsker bol*"; *Forverts*, "Katz's Delicatessen"; *Forverts*, "*Nayes fun Nuark*"; *Forverts*, "Russian Palace Restaurant"; Kaufman, "Unaccustomed guests," 13; Syfy, "Cafay"; Ward Biederman, "Jews Celebrate Dec. 25."

30 *New York Herald*, "Chinese Cuisine," 11.

31 Early reports of Jews eating Chinese food on Christmas come from states such as Ohio (Simon, "Jews volunteer"), Michigan (Neuser, "Lending a hand," 18), and California (Freestone, "Jews invited").

32 Marcus and Factor, "Erev Christmas."

33 Scharf, "'Jewish style.'"

34 Spector, "'Erev Christmas.'"

35 Graham, "Senator Graham," 18:40.

36 Kirchick, "Matzoball Memories."

37 Shire, "Finding Love."

38 Shire, "The Craziest Date Night."

39 Singer, "Three Hours."

40 Margolis, "Forays into a Digital Yiddishland"; Shandler, *Adventures in Yiddishland*.

41 Weiser, "Are We in the Midst."

42 *Duolingo*, "Yiddish for English Speakers."

43 Spatola, "Gut Nittel Nacht."

44 Izenson, "Happy nittelnacht."

45 Biskowitz, gertsovski, and Brunet-Jailly, "Rad Yiddish."

46 Kafrissen, "Have Yourself a Yiddish Little Christmas."

47 Ma'agal, "Our Ma'agal Manifesto."

48 Nicholls, "detail of some work."

49 Ensemble Wiener Collage, "Okataven des Lichts."

50 Devorah, "Who's That Sneaking."

51 Stoppard, *Leopoldstadt*.

52 TV21 Austria, "Blinde Nacht."

53 Leyb, "Christmas" (2020); cf. Leyb, "Christmas" (1987).

54 Kutzik, "*Der pakhed bay yidn.*"

55 Miller, "Black Christmas."

56 Patinkin, "Der Alter Tzigayner."

57 Hoffman, "White Christmas."

58 Grand, "Irving Berlin's White Xmas."

59 Klezmonauts, "Jingle Bells."

60 Kugelplex, "Yiddish Rudolph."

61 Shapiro, "*Mazl-brokhe.*"

62 Cohen, "*Oy ikh vil.*"

63 Jaffe, "Erev Krismes."

64 YidLife Crisis, "The YidLife Crisis Guide."

65 Desser, *Yiddish Chanukah Carols*.

66 Benko, *Christmas With You*.

67 Thompson, *La Bûche*.

68 Deglise Moore, "FIDDLER is back!"

69 A production of *Got fun nekome* [*God of Vengeance*] premiered on Christmas 2016; a production of *Di kishefmakherin* [*The Sorceress*] premiered on Christmas 2019; and *Di psure loyt khaim* [*The Gospel According to Chaim*] premiered on Christmas 2023.

70 Plaut, *A Kosher Christmas*, 85.

71 *Australian Jewish News*, "Kosher at Christmas."

72 Weinstein, *Dreaming of a Jewish Christmas*.

73 *Yiddish New York*, "Would You Like."

74 Selengut, "How to have."

75 *Crazy Ex-Girlfriend*, "My Mom"; *West Wing*, "Holy Night."

76 Korelitz, *You Should Have Known*, 300–319.

77 Zemeckis, *The Polar Express*.

78 According to the findings of Staetsky, "Haredi Jews," nearly a quarter of world Jewry will be strictly Orthodox as soon as 2040 (in 2020, only 14% of world Jewry was strictly Orthodox).

79 Benedict, "Yiddish among Former Haredim."

REFERENCES

Abeliovich, Ruthie. "Kol Nidre and the Making of the Jewish Theatre Audience." *In geveb: A Journal of Yiddish Studies.* April 2023, https://bit.ly/3FqLSgI.

Abramowicz, Hirsz. *Farshvundene geshtaltn.* Tsentral-Farband fun Poylishe Yidn in Argentine, 1958.

Adamsky, Mary. "Couple's engagement brings twist of faiths." *Honolulu Star-Bulletin,* March 27, 1999, 4.

Adrian, Johann. *Send und Warnungs-Brieff.* Johann Gorman, 1609.

Agnon, Shmuel Yosef. *Hakhnasat kala.* Schocken, 1950 [1931].

——. "*Ketaim.*" In *Ir u'meloa,* 377–93. Schocken, 1973.

——. "*Mazal dagim.*" In *Ir u'meloa,* 602–31. Schocken, 1973.

Ahituv, Netta and Hilo Glazer. "*Khag ha'molad asli: Eykh nira krismes etsel ha'mishpakhot b'Yisrael?*" *Haaretz,* December 24, 2015, https://bit.ly/414v1rc.

Aleichem, Sholem. *Fun peysekh biz peysekh.* Sholem Aleichem's Folksfond, 1920.

——. "*Khanike-geld: A mayse far yudishe kinder.*" *Der Yud,* December 13, 1900, 2–14.

Alekseev, Alexander. *Besedy pravoslavnogo khristianina iz yevreyev.* Tipografiya Ministerstva Vnutrennikh Del, 1872.

Allatius, Leo. *De templis Graecorum recentioribus.* Jodocus Kalcovius, 1645.

Alleson-Gerberg, Shai. "Nittel Nacht: An Inverted Christmas with Toledot Yeshu." *TheTorah.com,* 2016, https://bit.ly/2Xqhwld.

Alter, Meir. "*Al isur limud tora b'nitl.*" *Haaretz,* January 3, 1936, 6.

Ambrose. *Sancti Ambrosii mediolanensis episcopi.* Ex typographia Dominici Basae, 1585.

American Film Institute. "AFI's 100 Years . . . 100 Cheers." https://bit.ly/4f1zb8G.

——. "AFI's 100 Years . . . 100 Passions." https://bit.ly/4eUd6ZK.

American Israelite, The. "Talkie at Forest Dec. 12th-13th." *The American Israelite,* December 7, 1939, 11.

American Jewish World, The. "At Homewood Theater." *The American Jewish World,* December 15, 1939, 11.

——. "Jews' Benevolence Provides Holiday." *The American Jewish World,* January 1, 1965, 11.

Anderson, George Kumler. *The Legend of the Wandering Jew.* University Press of New England, 1991 [1965].

Ansky, S. "*Di tseylm frage.*" *Dos Naye Lebn* 1, no. 10 (1909): 610–17.

a Sancta Clara, Abraham. "Um Fest des heil. Bischofs und Beichtigers Nikolai." In *Sämtliche Werke XI,* 182–201. Friedrich Winkler, 1837.

Asch, Sholem. "*In a karnival nakht.*" *Dos Naye Lebn* 1, no. 7 (1909): 382–90.

———. *Nativity: Sholem Asch's Story of the Birth of Jesus,* narrated by Pete Seeger. Folkway Records, 1963.

Aschkenasy, Isaac. *Oytsres fun idishn humor.* Farlag "Tel Aviv," 1929.

Ashton, Dianne. *Hanukkah in America: A History.* New York University Press, 2013.

Auerbach, Ephraim. "*Af der vogshol.*" *Der Tog—Morgn Zhurnal,* December 26, 1955, 4.

Australian Jewish News. "Christmas for non-Christian Australians." *Australian Jewish News, Sydney Edition,* December 18, 1992, 3.

———. "Kosher at Christmas." *Australian Jewish News, Sydney Edition,* January 8, 1999, 2.

Avigal, Shosh. "*Lo la'inyan.*" *Hadashot,* November 4, 1988, 2.

Avromtshik, Yehoyshue. "*Unzere melamdim un lerer.*" In *Pultusk: Seyfer zikorn,* Yitzkhok Ivri ed., 119–20. Yotse Pultusk b'Yisrael, 1971.

Bachrach, Yair Chaim. *Khavos Yair.* Uri Zev Wolf Salat, 1896 [1699].

———. *Shulkhn orekh, orekh khayim: Im peyrush mekor khayim II.* Machon Yerushalayim, 1984 [c. 1675].

———. *Yair nesiv.* The National Library of Israel, NNL_ALEPH71206011760005171.

Bader, Gershom. *Unzere gaystike rizen.* Moyneshter, 1934.

Banasiewicz-Ossowska, Ewa. *Między dwoma światami: Żydzi w polskiej kulturze ludowej.* Wydawnictwo, 2007.

Barbu, Daniel. "Feeling Jewish." In *Feeling Exclusion: Religious Conflict, Exile and Emotions in Early Modern Europe,* Giovannia Tarantino and Charles Zika ed., 185–206. Routledge, 2019.

Barbu, Daniel and Yaacov Deutsch (eds.). *Toledot Yeshu in Context.* Mohr Siebeck, 2020.

Baring-Gould, Sabine. *The Book of Were-wolves: Being an Account of a Terrible Superstition.* Smith, Elder & Co., 1865.

Bar-Moses, Isaac of Vienna. *Seyfer or zorua I.* Shapira, 1862 [c. 1260].

———. *Seyfer or zorua II.* Shapira, 1862 [c. 1260].

Barnett, James H. *The American Christmas.* Arno Press, 1976.

Bashevis, Isaac. "*An erev-khanike in Varshe.*" *Di Goldene Keyt* 132 (1991): 26–29.

———. "*Der kurtser fraytik.*" *Di Tsukunft* 50, no. 1 (1945): 19–23.

———. "*Mayse Tishevits.*" *Forverts,* March 29, 1959, 6.

Bashevis Singer, Isaac. "The Last Demon," trans. Elaine Gottlieb and Cecil Hemley. *Prism* 1 (1962): 7–17.

Bastomski, Shloyme. *Baym kval: Materialn tsum yidishn folklor, yidishe folkslider.* Naye Yidishe Folkshul, 1923.

———. *Baym kval: Yidishe shprikhverter, vertlekh, glaykhvertlekh, rednsartn, farglaykhenishn, brokhes, vintshenishn, kloles, khromes, simonim, zgules, zababones, a. a.* Brider Rozental, 1920.

Baumgarten, Elisheva. *Biblical Women and Jewish Daily Life in the Middle Ages.* University of Pennsylvania Press, 2022.

———. *Mothers and Children: Jewish Family Life in Medieval Europe.* Princeton University Press, 2004.

———. "Shared and Contested Time: Jews and the Christian Ritual Calendar in the Late Thirteenth Century." *Viator* 46, no. 2 (2015): 253–76.

Baumgarten, Jean. *Introduction to Old Yiddish Literature*, trans. Jerold C. Frakes. Oxford University Press, 2005 [1993].

Beider, Alexander. *Origins of Yiddish Dialects*. Oxford University Press, 2015.

———. "Romance Elements in Yiddish." *Revue des Études Juives* 173, no. 1–2 (2014): 41–96.

Ben-Aaron. "*A dreydl.*" In *Gezang bukh far der elementar-shul*, Mikhl Gelbart ed., no. 44. Arbeter Ring, undated.

Benedict, Eliyahu. "Yiddish among Former Haredim." *Journal of Jewish Languages* 10, no. 2 (2022): 224–66.

Ben-Judah, Eleazar of Worms. *Perushey sidur ha'tefilo la'rokeyekh*. Hershler, 1992 [c. 1200].

Benko, Julie. *Christmas With You*. Club 44 Records, 2023.

Benovitz, Moshe. "*Hordus v'khanuka.*" *Zion* 68, no. 1 (2003): 5–40.

Ben-Samuel, Judah. *Seyfer khsidim*. Judah Wistinetzky, 1891 [c. 1200].

Ben-Samuel, Simhah of Vitry, *Makhzer Vitri*. Alef, 1963 [c. 1100].

Ben-Yishai, Aharon Zeev. "*Leyl ha'nitl.*" In *Ir ha'plaot*, Aharon Wardi ed., 52. L'Maan ha'Sefer, 1929.

Berger, Abraham. "Captive at the Gate of Rome: The Story of a Messianic Motif." *Proceedings of the American Academy for Jewish Research* 44 (1977): 1–17.

Berkowitz, Y. D. *Kinder-yorn*. Farlag "Sholem Aleichem" and "I. L. Peretz," 1970.

Berman, Jesse. "The secret history of Jews and Chinese food." *Baltimore Jewish Times*, December 22, 2021, https://bit.ly/3JODYNu.

Bernshteyn, Mortkhe V. "*Likhtlekh, dreydlekh un latkes.*" *Forverts*, December 11, 1963, 2.

Bernstein, Herman. "*Di shvartse, finstere, blinde nakht.*" *Der Tog*, December 24, 1915, 8.

———. "*Gedanken vegn der blinder nakht.*" *Der Tog*, December 25, 1917, 8.

Bernstein, Ignatz. *Yudishe shprikhverter un rednsartn*. Ha-Tsfira, 1908.

Biale, David. "A Journey Between Worlds: East European Jewish Culture from the Partitions of Poland to the Holocaust." In *Cultures of the Jews: A New History*, David Biale ed., 799–860. Schocken, 2002.

———. *Blood and Belief: The Circulation of a Symbol Between Jews and Christians*. University of California Press, 2007.

———. "Counter-History and Jewish Polemics Against Christianity: The *Sefer toldot yeshu* and the *Sefer zerubavel.*" *Jewish Social Studies* 6, no. 1 (1999): 130–45.

———. *Eros and the Jews: From Biblical Israel to Contemporary America*. University of California Press, 1997.

———. *Power and Powerlessness in Jewish History*. Schocken, 1986.

Bialik, Hayim Nahman. "*Ha'khatsotsra nitbaysha.*" In *Kneset*, H. N. Bialik ed., 145–66. Moriah, 1917.

Bilis, A. "*Nekhtn.*" *Der Morgen Zhurnal*, December 25, 1928, 6.

Birlinger, Anton. *Volksthümliches aus Schwaben*. Herder, 1862.

———. *Wörterbüchlein zum Volksthümlichen aus Schwaben*. Herder, 1862.

Biron, Phineas J. "Strictly Confidential." *The Sentinel*, January 2, 1941, 14.

Biskowitz, Sarah, freygl gertsovski, and Asa Brunet-Jailly. "Rad Yiddish Presents: Nitl Nakht!" *Facebook*, December 24, 2021, https://bit.ly/4b8DBtA.

Blind, Karl. "Wodan, the Wild Huntsman, and the Wandering Jew." *The Gentleman's Magazine* 2449 (1880): 32–48.

Blond, Shloyme (ed.). *Tolmitsh: Seyfer eydes v'zikorn*. Yotse Tolmitsh b'Yisrael, 1976.

Boeckler, Annette M. "The Magic of the Moment: Kol Nidre in Progressive Judaism." In *All These Vows*, Lawrence A. Hoffman ed., 39–66. Jewish Lights, 2011.

Bogatyrev, Petr. *Vampires in the Carpathians: Magical Acts, Rites, and Beliefs in Subcarpathian Rus'*, trans. Stephen Reynolds and Patricia Ann Krafcik. East European Monographs, 1998 [1929].

Bohdanowicz, J. "Demonologia ludowa: Relikty wierzeń w strzygonie i zmory." *Literatura Ludowa* 38, no. 2 (1994): 43–62.

Böhme, Franz Magnus. *Deutsches Kinderlied und Kinderspiel*. Breitkopf & Härtel, 1897.

Bokobza, Serge. *Jewish Identity in French Cinema (1950–2010)*. Cambridge Scholars, 2016.

Bonesho, Catherine E. "Foreign Holidays and Festivals as Representative of Identity in Rabbinic Literature." PhD diss., University of Wisconsin-Madison, 2018.

Bornstein, Shmuel. *Seyfer shem mi'Shmuel*. Keren ha'Tsdaka shel Mishpakhat Parshan, 1974 [1927].

Brand, Bernard. *"Santa Kloz, der Elyenove fun di amerikaner kinder."* *Forverts*, December 13, 1925, 17.

Brenz, Samuel Friederich. *Jüdischer abgestreiffter Schlangenbalg*. Balthasar Scherffen, 1614.

Briggs, Julia. *Night Visitors: The Rise and Fall of the English Ghost Story*. Faber, 1977.

Brown, P. Hume. *Scotland Before 1700*. David Douglas, 1893.

Brownstein, Bill. "Jew-bilee fills void on Christmas Eve." *The Gazette*, December 23, 2001, A4.

Brundage, James A. *Law, Sex, and Christian Society in Medieval Europe*. University of Chicago Press, 2009.

Burshteyn, L. *"Di 'blinde nakht' oder di 'tkufe."* *Der Tog*, December 25, 1917, 5.

Busch, Moriß. "Die Zauberpflanzen im Volksglauben." *Die Grenzboten: Zeitschrift für Politik, Literatur und Kunst* 35 (1876): 481–94.

Cahan, Y. L. *Yidisher folklor*. YIVO, 1938.

Cahan-Simon, Lori. "Gelbart/dreydl." *Chazzanut Online*, https://bit.ly/3UB40Jj.

Cala, Alina. *The Image of the Jew in Polish Folk Culture*. Magnes Press, 1995 [1987].

Capra, Frank (dir.). *It's a Wonderful Life*. RKO Radio Pictures, 1946.

Carlebach, Elisheva. *Palaces of Time*. Harvard University Press, 2011.

Carlebach, Elisheva and Jacob J. Schacter (eds.). *New Perspectives on Jewish-Christian Relations*. Brill, 2012.

Carpenter, Millie W. "The Little Tear-Gatherer." *The American Magazine* 28 (1889): 739–44.

Carus, Paul. "The Nativity: Similarities in Religious Art." *The Open Court* 13, no. 12 (1899): 710–30.

Cassel, Paulus. *Weihnachten: Ursprünge, Bräuche und Aberglauben*. L. Rauh, 1862.

Chain, Leib. "*Heysherik*." In *Barg aroyf*, 51–67. Tsvisho, 1951.

Chain-Shimoni, Leib. "*Nitl-nakht*." In *Untervegs*, 41–47. Tsveyter Sholem Aleykhem-Shul in Argentine, 1956.

Chambers, Robert. *The Book of Days: A Miscellany of Popular Antiquities in Connection with the Calendar*. W. & R. Chambers, 1881.

Charney, Daniel. *Afn shvel fun eyner velt*. Marstin Press, 1947.

Charney, Shmuel. "*Der traditsioneler yidisher yontef—'kristmes.'*" *Dos Naye Lebn* 1, no. 5 (1923): 53–55.

Chatto, William Andrew. *Facts and Speculations on the Origin and History of Playing Cards*. John Russell Smith, 1848.

Christmann, Ernst. "Weihnachten." *Oberdeutsche Zeitschrift für Volkskunde* 17, no. 1–3 (1943): 40–47.

Cohen, Annie. "*Oy ikh vil nit keyn zakh af nitl*." *YouTube*, February 5, 2024, https://bit.ly/3yTnqB8.

Cohen, David. *Shpole: Masekhet khayey yehudim b'ayara*. Yotse Shpole b'Yisrael, 1965.

Cohen, Jeremy and Moshe Rosman (eds.). *Rethinking European Jewish History*. Littman Library of Jewish Civilization, 2009.

Collins Dictionary. "Christmas." https://bit.ly/4dK4ELt.

———. "Yiddish." https://bit.ly/4dKqKgH.

Coolidge, Calvin. "Born in Us a Savior." *Miami Daily News*, December 25, 1927, 1.

Cooper, John. *Eat and Be Satisfied: A Social History of Jewish Food*. Jason Aronson, 1993.

Crazy Ex-Girlfriend. Season 1, episode 8: "My Mom, Greg's Mom and Josh's Sweet Dance Moves!" Directed by Steven Tsuchida. Aired November 30, 2015, on The CW.

Crosland, Alan (dir.). *The Jazz Singer*. Warner Bros. Pictures, 1927.

Crossan, John Dominic. *Jesus: A Revolutionary Biography*. Harper, 1994.

Crusius, Martin. *Annales suevici*. Nicolai Bassaei, 1596.

cummings, e e. "little tree." *The Dial* 68, no. 1 (1920): 22.

Daniels, Marc (dir.). "Have I Got a Christmas for You." *Hallmark Hall of Fame*, December 16, 1977.

David, Larry. "A Very Larry David Christmas." *Air Mail*, December 18, 2021, https://bit.ly/3AwIQp2.

Deborah. "Noch einmal Chanukkah." *Deborah*, January 1, 1866, 9–10.

Deglise Moore, Jordan. "FIDDLER is back!" *Laemmle Theatres Blog*, December 7, 2022, https://bit.ly/3JRq8d4.

Deitch, Mattes. *Inm land fun di Yenkis*. Brikn, 1935.

Der Idisher Zhurnal. "Di nakht fun 'nitl' bay yidn." *Der Idisher Zhurnal*, December 29, 1905, 4.

Der Morgen Zhurnal. "Irving Place Theatre." *Der Morgen Zhurnal*, December 11, 1919, 8.

———. "Irving Place Theatre." *Der Morgen Zhurnal*, December 23, 1919, 2.

———. "*Shulzinger kontsert.*" *Der Morgen Zhurnal*, December 4, 1922, 10.

Der Tog. "Chanukah and the Christmas Spirit." *Der Tog*, December 25, 1927, Eng. section, 1.

———. "*Khazn Shulzinger's kontsert in taun hol.*" *Der Tog*, December 30, 1922, 3.

Der Tog—Morgn Zhurnal. "*Kristmas iz take nit keyn yidisher yontef, ober dint far a fayner vakatsye far yedn.*" *Der Tog—Morgn Zhurnal*, December 19, 1957, 8.

Desser, Yossi. *Yiddish Chanukah Carols.* MRM Music, 2021.

Detroit Jewish News, The. "The Saga of an Eminent Family: Ab., Sarah Goldberg in Chapter of American Zionist History." *Detroit Jewish News*, April 28, 1978.

Diamant, Zaynvl. "*Far di khagoes.*" *Di Tsukunft* 55 (1950): 144–48.

Dickens, Charles. *A Christmas Carol.* Robert O. Law, 1920 [1843].

———. *Vaynakht*, trans. Esther Kreitman. Helios, 1929 [1843].

Devorah, Olivia. "'Who's That Sneaking Up the Toilet'—A Nittel Nacht Carol." *Facebook*, December 12, 2022, https://bit.ly/3vAyL4o.

Diemling, Maria. "Navigating Christian Space: Jews and Christian Images in Early Modern German Lands." *Jewish Culture and History* 12, no. 3 (2012): 397–410.

Di Varhayt. "David Kessler Second Ave Theatre." *Di Varhayt*, December 24, 1911, 3.

———. "*Kontsert un ball.*" *Di Varhayt*, December 24, 1914, 3.

Divjak, Johannes and Wolfgang Wischmeyer. *Das Kalenderhandbuch von 354: Der Chronograph des Filocalus I.* Holzhausen, 2014.

Dorson, Richard M. *Folklore and Fakelore: Essays Toward a Discipline of Folk Studies.* Harvard University Press, 1976.

Dubnow, Simon. *History of the Jews in Russia and Poland II*, trans. Israel Friedlaender. Jewish Publication Society of America, 1913.

Dundes, Alan. *Life Is Like a Chicken Coop Ladder: A Portrait of German Culture Through Folklore.* Columbia University Press, 1984.

Duolingo, "Yiddish for English Speakers." *Duolingo*, https://bit.ly/3YnmoI2.

Duschinsky, Charles. *The Rabbinate of the Great Synagogue, London from 1756–1842.* Oxford University Press, 1921.

Ebendorfer, Thomas. *Das jüdische Leben Jesu, Toldot Jeschu*, trans. Brigitta Callsen. R. Oldenbourg, 2003 [1463].

Eckstein, Adolf. *Geschichte der Juden im ehemaligen Fürstbistum Bamberg.* Handels-Druckerei, 1898.

Eidelberg, Shlomo. "*Tsror hearot.*" *Tarbiz* 52, no. 4 (1982): 647–50.

Eisenmenger, Johann Andreas. *Entdecktes Judenthum.* Frankfurt: n.p., 1700.

Elia-Shalev, Asaf. "For a growing number of Jews in Israel, it's beginning to look a lot like Christmas." *Jewish Telegraphic Agency*, December 23, 2021, https://bit.ly/41N39bd.

Eliscu, Edward. "Itzig's Party." *The Hebrew Standard* 50, no. 24 (1917): 1–2.

El Melekh, Y. "*Vos iz 'nitl'?*" *Haynt* (Riga), December 25, 1934, 3.

Elukin, Jonathan. *Living Together, Living Apart: Rethinking Jewish-Christian Relations in the Middle Ages.* Princeton University Press, 2009.

Elzer, Judah. "*Mi'minhagey yisrael.*" *Reshumot* 1 (1918): 335–77.

Emanu-el. "Correspondence." *Emanu-el*, March 16, 1900, 7–8.

Emanu-el and the Jewish Journal. "S. F. Jewry Ready to Observe High Holy Days." *Emanu-el and the Jewish Journal*, September 7, 1934, 22.

Embacher, Helga. "Weihnukka." In *Politische Weihnacht in Antike und Moderne*, Richard Faber and Esther Gajek ed., 287–306. Konigshausen & Neumann, 1997.

Engelsher, Avrom. *Der yudisher oytser.* Sinai Offset Co., undated.

Ensemble Wiener Collage. "Oktaven des Lichts. Konzert zu Weihnachten und Chanukka." *YouTube*, October 19, 2020, https://bit.ly/3Z1ZC73.

Epsteen, Elliot M. "Order of B'nai B'rith." *Emanu-el*, August 7, 1914, 5.

Erdberg, Sh. "*In der ortodoksisher velt.*" *Der Tog*, December 20, 1935, 7.

Estraikh, Gennady and Mikhail Krutikov (eds.). *The Shtetl: Image and Reality.* Routledge, 2017.

Fabre-Vassas, Claudine. *The Singular Beast: Jews, Christians, and the Pig*, trans. Carol Volk. Columbia University Press, 1997 [1994].

Facebook. "Folk Horror Revival." *Facebook*, https://bit.ly/3U4cRDh.

Finkelshteyn, Leo. "*Vegn Sholem Ashs pro-kristlekhe verk.*" In *Loshn yidish un yidisher kiyem*, 172–212. La Sociedad Pro Cultura Y Ayuda, 1954.

Fischer, Heinrich Ludwig. *Das Buch vom Aberglauben I.* Schwickert, 1791.

Fischer, Hermann. *Schwäbisches Wörterbuch.* Lauppschen Buchhandlung, 1904.

Fishman, Talya. *Becoming the People of the Talmud: Oral Torah as Written Tradition in Medieval Jewish Cultures.* University of Pennsylvania Press, 2011.

Flanders, Judith. *Christmas: A Biography.* St. Martin's, 2017.

Flusser, David. *The Sage from Galilee: Rediscovering Jesus' Genius.* William B. Eerdmans, 2007.

Fogel, Edwin Miller. *Beliefs and Superstitions of the Pennsylvania Germans.* American Germanica Press, 1915.

Forbes, Bruce David. *America's Favorite Holidays: Candid Histories.* University of California Press, 2015.

Forverts. "*Afile Santa Klouz.*" *Forverts*, December 25, 1924, 6.

———. "*Bielsker bol.*" *Forverts*, December 9, 1939, 2.

———. "*Dem khazn's zundel.*" *Forverts*, December 25, 1937, 11.

———. "*Di blinde nakht.*" *Forverts*, December 24, 1902, 1.

———. "Katz's Delicatessen." *Forverts*, December 22, 1963, 9.

———. "*Kol Nidre.*" *Forverts*, December 19, 1939, 9.

———. "*Kol Nidre.*" *Forverts*, December 24, 1939, sec. 2, 8.

———. "*Kristmes-diburim.*" *Forverts*, December 26, 1900, 4.

———. "*Kristmes un yonkiper: Fantazie un virklikhkayt.*" *Forverts*, December 26, 1910, 4.

———. "*Mamele.*" *Forverts*, December 24, 1938, 10.

———. "*Nayes fun Nuark.*" *Forverts*, December 23, 1940, 9.

———. "*Pablik teater.*" *Forverts*, December 19, 1938, 9.

———. "Russian Palace Restaurant." *Forverts*, December 24, 1926, 6.

———. "*Shoyn der tsveyter blutiker kristmas.*" *Forverts*, December 25, 1915, 6.

———. "*Teater anonsen.*" *Forverts*, February 28, 1943, 2.

———. *"Tevye der milkhiker."* Forverts, December 21, 1939, 8.

———. *"Tevye der milkhiker."* Forverts, December 24, 1939, sec. 2, 8.

———. *"Thalia Theater."* Forverts, December 23, 1899, 3.

Forverts Reporter, A. *"Der kristmes-yarid af di yidishe gasn fun Nyu-York."* Forverts, December 25, 1922, 5.

———. *"S'iz erev kristmas af di gasn."* Forverts, December 23, 1922, 3.

Frank, Johann Peter. *System einer vollständigen medizinischen Polizey.* Schwan, 1779.

Frankl-Grün, Adolf. *Geschichte der Juden in Kremsier III.* J. Kauffmann, 1901.

Freedman, D. F. "The Change." *Australian Jewish Herald*, September 10, 1925, 9.

Freestone, Julie. "Jews invited to explore identity issues on Dec. 25." *Jewish News of Northern California*, December 17, 1993, 24.

Frid, Feygl. *"Rov Khayim der radner shamesh."* Di Tsukunft 62, no. 10 (1957): 483–85.

Fried, Lothar Franz. *Neupolierter und wohlgeschliffener Juden-Spiegel.* Fried, 1715.

Friedenheim, Caspar Joseph. *Die Hoffnung Israel auf die Erlösung durch den Meßias ist kommen und vorhanden in Jesu von Nazareth.* Friedenheim, 1770.

Friedman, Bezalel. *"Santa Kloz hot gekhalesht."* In *Mayn bukh: Lernbukh farn tsveytn yor*, 62–63. Internatstionaler Arbeter Ordn, 1939.

Friedmann, Meir (ed.). *"Pirke derekh erets."* In *Nispokhim l'seyder Eliyohu Zuto.* Achiasaf, 1908.

Frimer, Pesakhye. *"Bamerkungen fun a Podolier tsu der shprakh fun der 'genarter velt.'"* Yidishe Shprakh 4, no. 2 (1944): 44–49.

Frischmann, David. *"Shrago."* In *Ale verk fun Dovid Frishman V*, 53–60. Tsentral, 1914.

Frodsham, Paul. *From Stonehenge to Santa Claus: The Evolution of Christmas.* History Press, 2008.

Fuchs, Avrom Moyshe. *"Di blinde nakht."* Di Tsukunft 29 (1924): 578–82.

Fudem, Gizela, interview by Jakub Rajchman. *Centropa*, December 2004, https://bit.ly/4f2qGdl.

Gager, John. "Simon Peter, Founder of Christianity or Saviour of Israel?" In *Toledot Yeshu ("The Life Story of Jesus") Revisited*, Peter Schäfer, Yaacov Deutsch, and Michael Meerson ed., 221–46. Mohr Siebeck, 2011.

Gailing, Ben. *"Khanike un kristmas."* In *Git a shmeykhl: A bukh fun laykhtn humor un satire far ale teg fun a gants yor*, 105–6. Zikh Aleyn, 1949.

Gaster, Theodor. *Festivals of the Jewish Year.* William Sloane Associates, 1953.

Gay, Ruth. *Unfinished People: Eastern European Jews Encounter America.* W. W. Norton, 1996.

Geiler von Kaysersberg, Johannes. *Die Emeis.* Johannes Grüninger, 1516.

Giladi, David. *"M'nitl ad silvester."* Maariv, January 2, 1973, 5.

Glasman, Baruch. *"Af di felder fun Dzhordzhia."* Shriften 6 (Winter–Spring 1920): 3–12.

Gnozovits, Yitskhok. *"Miskhakim shel yaldey ha'yehudim b'Lide."* In *Seyfer Lide*, Alexander Manor, Yitskhok Gnozovits, and Aba Lando ed., 203–10. Yotse Lide b'Yisrael, 1970.

Gocz, Teodor. *"Żydzi z Zyndranowej."* Płaj: Zeszyt krajoznawczy Towarzystwa Karpackiego 5 (1991): 89–92.

Gold, David L. and Leonard Prager (eds.). "Replies to Queries in JLR 1–5." *Jewish Language Review* 6 (1986): 242–365.

Goldberg, Ab. "*Kristmes.*" In *Grenetsen*, 131–37. Progress, 1924.

Goldhar, Pinchas. "*Zikhroynes un batrakhtungen.*" In *Seyfer Stashev*, Elkhonen Erlich ed., 274–86. Yotse Stashev b'Yisrael, 1962.

Goldin, Sidney M. (dir.). *Mizrekh un Mayvrev.* Listo/Picon Films, 1923.

Goldin, Sidney and Ilya Motyleff (dirs.). *Dem Khazns Zundl.* Eron Pictures, 1937.

Goldshteyn, Yoysef-Shimen. "*Unzer khanike-kibetsarnye.*" *Forverts*, December 11, 1955, 6.

Goldstein, Miriam. "A Polemical Tale and its Function in the Jewish Communities of the Mediterranean and the Near East." *Intellectual History of the Islamicate World* 7, no. 1 (2019): 192–227.

Goldzac, Chaim. "*Af a yontef.*" In *Ale viln lebn*, 79–86. Hojas Literarias Ilustradas, 1960.

Golinkin, David. "Hanukkah Exotica: On the Origin and Development of Some Hanukkah Customs." *Conservative Judaism* 53, no. 2 (2001): 41–50.

Golomb, Abraham. "*Tsu shpet.*" In *Geklibene shriftn V*, 135–45. A. Golomb, 1945.

———. *Umvegn un oysveg: A pruv tsu formulirn a yidishn velt-banem.* A. Golomb, 1942.

Gordin, Jacob. "*Di blinde nakht.*" *Der Teglikher Herald*, January 6, 1895, 2.

———. "*Di blinde nakht.*" *Di Varhayt*, December 25, 1905, 5.

———. "*Di blinde nakht.*" In *Yankev Gordins ertseylungen*, 96–99. A. M. Evalensko, 1908.

———. "Die Blinde Nacht (The Blind Night)," trans. A Freed. *Hebrew Union College Monthly* 8, no. 1 (1921): 79–81.

———. "The Blind Night," trans. Barnet Brickner. *The Maccabæan* 21, no. 7 (1912): 192–93.

———. "*Vos zingt der Yid?*" *Di Varhayt*, November 25, 1905, 5.

Göth, Georg. "Das Herzogthum Steiermark." *Österreichische Blätter für Literatur und Kunst* 2, no. 62 (May 24, 1845): 484–87.

Gottesman, Itzik. "A Very Jewish Christmas: Old World Jewish Christmas Traditions." *YIVO Institute for Jewish Research* (lecture, December 23, 2019).

———. "*Nitl in der alter heym.*" *Forverts*, December 17, 2019, https://bit.ly/3SEN5U7.

Grabowicz, Oksana I. "'Dumy' as Performance." *Harvard Ukrainian Studies* 32/33, no. 1 (2011): 291–313.

Graham, Lindsey. "Senator Graham Questions Supreme Court Nominee Elena Kagan." *YouTube*, June 29, 2010, https://bit.ly/3pNvrDw.

Grand, Al. "Irving Berlin's White Xmas af yidish." *Der Bay* 14, no. 2 (2004): 2.

Grant, James. *History of the Burgh and Parish Schools of Scotland.* William Collins, Sons & Co., 1876.

Grayzel, Solomon. *The Church and the Jews in the XIIIth Century.* Hermon Press, 1966.

Green, Joseph (dir.). *A Brivele der Mamen.* Sphinx Films Corp., 1939.

Greene, Henry Copley. "The Song of the Ass." *Speculum* 6 (1931): 534–49.

Greisman, Nechoma. "Brief Themes: Random Thoughts Extracted from Shiurim." *Chabad.org*, https://bit.ly/3PT6C1Q.

Gribetz, Sarit Kattan. "Hanged and Crucified: The Book of Esther and Toledot Yeshu." In *Toledot Yeshu ("The Life Story of Jesus") Revisited*, Peter Schäfer, Michael Meerson, and Yaacov Deutsch ed., 159–80. *Mohr Siebeck*, 2011.

Grimm, Jacob. *Deutsche Mythologie I*. Dieterich, 1835.

———. *Deutsche Mythologie III*. C. Bertelsmann, 1877.

Grimm, Jacob and Wilhelm Grimm. *Deutsches Wörterbuch*. S. Hirzel, 1889.

Gross, Naftoli. "*Mayselekh un mesholim*." *Forverts*, November 30, 1955, 5.

Grossman, Jonathan H. "The Absent Jew in Dickens: Narrators in 'Oliver Twist,' Our Mutual Friend,' and 'A Christmas Carol.'" *Dickens Studies Annual* 24 (1996): 37–57.

Grünenwald, Lukas. "Pfälzischer Bauernkalender." *Der Urquell* 1 (1897): 103–6.

Grunwald, Max. "Aus Hausapotheke und Hexenküche III." *Mitteilungen zur jüdischen Volkskunde* 25 (1923): 178–226.

———. "Fünfundzwanzig Jahre jüdische Volkskunde." *Jahrbuch für Jüdische Volkskunde* 25 (1923): 1–22.

Güdemann, Moritz. *Geschichte des Erziehungswesens und der Cultur der abendländischen Juden I*. Alfred Hölder, 1880.

Gugitz, Gustav. *Fest- und Brauchtumskalender für Österreich, Süddeutschland und die Schweiz*. Hollinek, 1981.

Gutman (Krimer), Golde. *Mayn shtetl Yedinets*. Buenos Aires: n.p., 1943.

H. "Some Stray Thoughts on 'Nittel Night' and what a Future Historian will have to say about it!" *The Reform Advocate*, December 30, 1893, 319.

HaCohen, Ruth. "Vocal Communities in the Twilight: Kol Nidre Before Total Darkness." *Kol Nidre: Audio-Visual Dramaturgies Conference* 4 (lecture, December 15, 2021).

HaCohen, Ruth and Boaz Tarsi. "The Moment and Momentum of Kol Nidre: A Multi-Layered Analysis of Yom Kippur's Grand Overture." *Kol Nidre: Audio-Visual Dramaturgies Conference* 2 (lecture, October 10, 2021).

Hägrad. *Ein ächter Beitrag zur Schilderung Wiens*. Vienna and Prague: n.p. [1782].

Haiding, Karl. "Berchtenbräuche im steirischen Ennsbereich." *Mitteilungen der anthropologischen Gesellschaft in Wien*, 95 (1965): 322–38.

Hammer, Jill. "Holle's Cry: Unearthing a Birth Goddess in a German Jewish Naming Ceremony." *Nashim: A Journal of Jewish Women's Studies & Gender Issues* 9 (2005): 62–87.

Harkavy, Alexander. "*Di opshtamung fun eynike yidishe verter*." *Minikes Yontef Bleter*, April 1, 1924, 59.

Hasche, Johann Christian. *Diplomatische Geschichte Dresdens von seiner Entstehung bis auf unsere Tage I*. Johann Christian Hasche, 1816.

Hayntike Nayes. "*Vi azoy R' Shloyme Leyb Lentshner hot gehat gile-Elye in der nitelnakht*." *Hayntike Nayes*, December 24, 1933, 3.

Heilman, Uriel. "Hasidic 'Silent Night': No Torah and No Sex." *Haaretz*, December 22, 2015, https://bit.ly/3YQpBOB.

———. "How Hasidic Jews in the diaspora observe Christmas." *Jerusalem Post*, December 23, 2015, https://bit.ly/3GkT8IO.

———. "How Hasidim pointedly don't observe Christmas Eve." *The Times of Israel,* December 24, 2015, https://bit.ly/3fEdFO8.

———. "Silent night: How the Hasidim observe Christmas Eve." *Jewish Telegraphic Agency,* December 22, 2015, https://bit.ly/3FZzJfa.

———. "What Hasidic Jews Do—and Don't Do—on Christmas Eve." *Forward,* December 22, 2015, https://bit.ly/3GlTcZ5.

Heller, Bernard. "Notes de folk-lore Juif." *Revue des Études Juives* 82 (1926): 308–12.

Heller, Fanya Gottesfeld. *Strange and Unexpected Love: A Teenage Girl's Holocaust Memoirs.* KTAV, 1993.

Heller, Ruth. *Christmas: Its Carols, Customs & Legends.* Schmidt, Hall & McCreary, 1948.

Hellinger, Rabbi Shimon. "What Are You Doing This Nittel Nacht?" *Anash,* December 24, 2020, https://bit.ly/3JeamZV.

Hertz, Deborah. *How Jews Became Germans: The History of Conversion and Assimilation in Berlin.* Yale University Press, 2008.

Herzl, Theodor. *Theodor Herzls Tagebücher I.* Jüdischer Verlag, 1922.

Herzog, Marvin (ed.). *The Language and Culture Atlas of Ashkenazic Jewry III: The Eastern Yiddish-Western Yiddish Continuum.* Max Niemeyer Verlag, 2000.

———. *The Yiddish Language in Northern Poland: Its Geography and History.* Indiana University, 1965.

Hess, Ernst Ferdinand. *Flagellum Iudeorum, Juden Geissel.* Hess, 1598.

Hijmans, Steven E. *Sol: Image and Meaning of the Sun in Roman Art and Religion II.* Brill, 2024.

Hilscher, Paul Christian. *De exercitu furioso, vulgo wütenden Heer.* Johann Georgl, 1688.

Hilton, Michael. *Bar Mitzvah: A History.* University of Nebraska Press, 2014.

———. *The Christian Effect on Jewish Life.* SCM Press, 1994.

Himitian, Evangelina. "Cómo fue la Navidad de los que no festejaron." *La Nación,* December 22, 2017, https://bit.ly/43DUmuP.

Hirsch, Solomon Zebi. *Yudisher Theriak: An Early Modern Yiddish Defense of Judaism,* trans. Morris M. Faierstein. Wayne State University Press, 2016.

———. *Yudisher Tiryak.* Hirsch, 1615.

Hoberman, J. *Bridge of Light: Yiddish Film Between Two Worlds.* Schocken, 1991.

Hoffman, Jackie. "White Christmas." *YouTube,* December 25, 2013, https://bit.ly/3NAi5CA.

Hoffman, Jeffrey. "The Image of The Other in Jewish Interpretations of Alenu." *Studies in Christian-Jewish Relations* 10, no. 1 (2015): 1–41.

Hoffman, Lawrence A. *The Art of Public Prayer: Not for Clergy Only.* SkyLight Paths, 1999 [1983].

Hoffman, Matthew. *From Rebel to Rabbi: Reclaiming Jesus and the Making of Modern Jewish Culture.* Stanford University Press, 2007.

———. "Sholem Asch's True Christians." In *Sholem Asch Reconsidered,* Nanette Stahl ed., 279–88. Beinecke Rare Book and Manuscript Library, 2004.

Hoffmann, E. T. A. *Knaknisl un moyznkeyser*, trans. Lipe Reznik. Kultur-Lige, 1922 [1816].

Hoffmann-Krayer, Eduard and Hanns Bächtold-Stäubli. "Nidelnächte." In *Handwörterbuch des deutschen Aberglaubens VI*, 1071. Walter de Gruyter, 1935.

———. "Weihnachtsgebäck, Weihnachtsbrot." In *Handwörterbuch des deutschen Aberglaubens IX*, 256–83. Walter de Gruyter, 1941.

Höfler, Max. "Das Haaropfer in Teigform." *Archiv für Anthropologie* 32 (1906): 130–48.

———. *Das Jahr im oberbayerischen volksbeben*. Friedrich Bassermann, 1899.

———. "Gebäcke in der Zeit der sogenannten Rauchnächte." *Zeitschrift für österreichische Volkskunde* IX (1903): 15–22.

Hofman-Sheyn, Nekhe. "*Yidn un nisht-yidn in Serafinits*." In *Seyfer Horodenke*, Shimshon Meltzer ed., 265–67. Yotse Horodenke, 1963.

Holberg, Ludvig. *The Fussy Man*, trans. Henry Alexander. In *Four Plays by Holberg*, 1–62. Princeton University Press, 1946 [1731].

Horovits, Ber. "*Di blinde nakht*." *Kritik* 5 (November 10, 1920): 18–19.

Horowitz, Elliott. *Reckless Rites: Purim and the Legacy of Jewish Violence*. Princeton University Press, 2006.

———. "Sabbath Delights: Toward a Social History." In *Sabbath: Idea, History, Reality*, Gerald J. Blidstein ed., 131–59. Ben-Gurion University Press, 2004.

Horowitz, Naftali. *Khsides un etik*. Um, 1965.

Horr, Norton T. "Legal Notes on Card-Playing." *The Green Bag* 3 (1891): 399–400.

Hugues de Mans. "*Actus Pontificum Cenomannis in urbe degentium* (chap. XXXVII: *Gesta Hugonis*)." In *Vetera analecta*, Jean Mabillon ed., 324–27. Paris: Montalant, 1723.

Huldreich, Johann Jacob (ed.). *Seyfer toldes Yeshue ha'noytsri. Wikisource*, https://bit.ly/3U88aZg.

Hutton, Ronald. *Queens of the Wild: Pagan Goddesses in Christian Europe: An Investigation*. Yale University Press, 2022.

———. *The Stations of the Sun: A History of the Ritual Year in Britain*. Oxford University Press, 1996.

———. *The Triumph of the Moon: A History of Modern Pagan Witchcraft*. Oxford University Press, 1999.

———. "The Wild Hunt and the Witches' Sabbath." *Folklore* 125, no. 2 (2014): 161–78.

———. *The Witch: A History of Fear, from Ancient Times to the Present*. Yale University Press, 2017.

Idelsohn, Abraham Z. *Jewish Music: Its Historical Development*. Dover, 1992.

Idishe Velt Forums. "*Leyl nitl—vos tut ir?*" https://bit.ly/4eExSNd.

Ilan, Shahar. "*Al ha'khasidim v'leyl ha'nitl*." *Haaretz*, December 24, 2004, https://bit.ly/4hOjFik.

Ilicki, Julian. "Changing Identity Among Younger Polish Jews in Sweden After 1968." In *Poles and Jews: Perceptions and Misconceptions*, Wladyslaw T. Bartoszewski ed., 269–80. Littman Library of Jewish Civilization, 2004.

Inhat, Kati. "The Middle Ages." In *The Oxford Handbook of Christmas*, Timothy Larsen ed., 15–26. Oxford University Press, 2020.

Irving, Washington. "Christmas." In *The Sketch Book of Geoffrey Crayon, Gent II*, 27–40. John Murray, 1820.

Isaacs, Miriam. *What Every Jewish Woman Should Know: A Guide for Jewish Women.* Jewish Book Club, 1941.

Isaacs, Tuvia. "*An umglaykhe shutfes.*" *Der Tog—Morgn Zhurnal*, December 25, 1964, 16.

———. "*Di nisht glaykhe shutfes.*" *Der Tog—Morgn Zhurnal*, December 22, 1967, 16.

Izenson, Andy (@AndyEyeballs). "Happy nittelnacht everybody." *Twitter*, December 24, 2021, https://bit.ly/4eHGanc.

Jacobson, Matthew Frye. *Special Sorrows: The Diasporic Imagination of Irish, Polish, and Jewish Immigrants in the United States.* University of California Press, 2002.

Jaffe, Marie B. "Erev Krismes." In *Gut Yuntif, Gut Yohr*, 12–15. Citadel Press, 1969.

Jameson, Fredric. "Postmodernism and Consumer Society." In *The Anti-Aesthetic: Essays on Postmodern Culture*, Hal Foster ed., 111–25. Bay Press, 1983.

Jerman, Tom A. *Santa Claus Worldwide.* McFarland, 2020.

JoeSettler, "Just Say No to Nittel Nacht." *The Jewish Press*, December 24, 2013, https://bit.ly/3WOLRqn.

Joffe, Judah A. and Yudl Mark. *Groyser verterbukh fun der yidisher shprakh II.* Yiddish Dictionary Committee, 1966.

John of Salisbury. *Policraticus II*, trans. Joseph B. Pike. University of Minnesota Press, 1938 [1159].

Judäus. "Wie Rabbi Israel Salant zu einer Uhr kam." In *Eine ungekannte Welt II: Zwischen Rhein und Wolga*, 439–58. Sänger und Friedberg, 1913 [1907].

Kafka, Franz. *Tagebüch 1910–23.* Schocken, 1946.

Kafrissen, Rokhl. "Have Yourself a Yiddish Little Christmas." *Tablet*, January 18, 2022, https://bit.ly/3IAaTDU.

Kahan, Berl. "*Ver un vi azoy men hot gelernt in Ratne.*" In *Yizker-bukh Ratne*, Jacob Botoshansky and Itzhak Yanosowicz ed., 118–24. Ratner Landslayt, 1954.

Kanar, Zvi. *Ikh un Lemekh.* Yisorel Bukh, 1994.

Kaplan, Pesach. "*Di nitl-nakht in Amerike.*" *Dos Naye Lebn*, January 18, 1929, 3.

Karras, Ruth Mazo. "The Aerial Battle in the Toledot Yeshu and Sodomy in the Late Middle Ages." *Medieval Encounters* 19, no. 5 (2013): 493–533.

Katz, Mickey. "Chiny Town." Capitol Records (1951): F1419.

Katz, Mortkhe. "*Altvarg.*" *Di Idishe Gazeten*, November 12, 1920, 5.

Katz, Pinye. *A rayze in mayn lebn.* In *Geklibene shriftn I.* YKUF, 1946.

Katz, Stephen T. (ed.). *The Shtetl: New Evaluations.* New York University Press, 2007.

Kaufman, Jonathan. "Unaccustomed guests enjoy a free stay on hotel's VIP floor." *Boston Globe*, December 26, 1984, 1, 13.

Kenotic Neutral (@OrNistar). "But it's just wrong." *Twitter*, December 24, 2020, https://bit.ly/3U9eT51.

Khes, A. "*Refleksn.*" *Der Nayer Moment*, December 20, 1968, 4.

Kimche, Jon. "*Eykh buts'a alit 250 ha'maapilim.*" *Haaretz*, December 28, 1945, 1.

King, Archdale Arthur. *Liturgy of the Roman Church*. Bruce, 1957.

Kirchick, James. "Matzoball Memories." *Tablet*, December 22, 2014, https://bit.ly/3NpBnuN.

Kirshenbaum, David. *Fun unzer gaystiker khrifes II*. Pardes, 1937.

Kirzane, Jessica. "'What Kind of a Man Are You?' Interethnic Sexual Encounter in Yiddish American Narratives." In *The Sacred Encounter: Jewish Perspectives on Sexuality*, Rabbi Lisa J. Grushcow ed., 195–208. CCAR Press, 2014.

Klapper, Joseph. "Deutscher Volksglaube in Schlesien in ältester Zeit." *Mitteilungen der Schlesischen Gesellschaft für Volkskunde* 17, no. 1 (1915): 19–57.

Klausner, Issachar Dov. "'Nitl' b'mishnat khabad." In *Kovets ha'moadim*, Yosef Buksboim ed., 233–34. Moriah, 2001.

Kletke, Hermann. "Die heilige Nacht." *Der Bazar* 11, no. 48 (1865): 419.

Klezmonauts, The. "Jingle Bells." Track #8 on *Oy to the World! A Klezmer Christmas*. Satire Records, 1998.

Klier, John D. *Imperial Russia's Jewish Question, 1855–1881*. Cambridge University Press, 2005.

———. *Russians, Jews and the Pogroms of 1881–1882*. Cambridge University Press, 2011.

Kligman, Mark. "The Music of Kol Nidre." In *All These Vows*, Lawrence A. Hoffman ed., 67–70. Jewish Lights, 2011.

Klinov, Shaye. "*Silvester un 'nitel' in Tel-Aviv.*" *Haynt*, January 8, 1935, 4.

Klintberg, Bengt Af. "The Swedish Wanderings of the Eternal Jew." *Proceedings of the World Congress of Jewish Studies* 4, no. 2 (1965): 115–19.

Kmietowicz, Frank A. *Slavic Mythical Beliefs*. F. Kmietowicz, 1982.

Kohlbach, Berthold. "Das Zopfgebäck im jüdischen Ritus." *Zeitschrift des Vereins für Volkskunde* 24 (1914): 265–71.

Kohler, Erika. *Martin Luther und der Festbrauch*. Böhlau, 1959.

Kohn, Moshe. "When All the World Rejoices." *Jerusalem Post*, December 28, 1988, 5.

Koller, Sabine (ed.). *Joseph Opatoshu: A Yiddish Writer between Europe and America*. Routledge, 2017.

———. "The Two Souls of Mordkhe: *In poylishe velder*." In *Joseph Opatoshu: A Yiddish Writer between Europe and America*, Sabine Koller ed., 68–85. Routledge, 2017.

Kol Mevaser. "*Di mode.*" *Kol Mevaser*, February 15, 1866, 1–2.

———. "*Fun dem tsaytgayst.*" *Kol Mevaser*, May 12, 1864, 4–5.

Kol Mevaser felieton. "*Nitl oder vaynakhtn.*" *Kol Mevaser*, January 17, 1867, 2–5.

Korelitz, Jean Hanff. *You Should Have Known*. Grand Central, 2014.

Koskoff, Ellen. "Is 'White Christmas' a Piece of Jewish Music?" In *Mazal Tov, Amigos! Jews and Popular Music in the Americas*, Amalia Ran and Moshe Morad ed., 11–24. Brill, 2016.

Kotik, Yekhezkl. *Mayne zikhroynes*. Klal, 1922.

Kotler, Z. "*Khanike in goles un in erets-yisroel.*" *Voliner Leben*, December 7, 1928, 2.

Kotula, Franciszek. *Tamten Rzeszów: Czyli wędrówka po zakątkach i historii miasta*. Krajowa Agencja Wydawnicza, 1985.

Krah, Markus. *American Jewry and the Re-Invention of the East European Jewish Past.* De Gruyter, 2017.

Krainz, Johann. "Sitten, Bräuche und Meinungen des deutschen Volkes in Steiermark." *Zeitschrift für österreichische Volkskunde* 1, no. 8/9 (1895): 243–52.

Krauss, Samuel. "Aus der jüdischen Volksküche." *Mitteilungen zur jüdischen Volkskunde* 53 (1915): 1–40.

———. *Das Leben Jesu nach jüdischen Quellen.* S. Calvary, 1902.

Kronberg, Simon. "Nittel (Blinde Nacht)." In *Werke II*, 165–202. Boer, 1993.

Kruszyńska, Anna. "Karp na każdym wigilijnym stole, czyli jak to z tą tradycją było." *Polska Agencja Prasowa*, December 22, 2018, https://bit.ly/43jjO8Q.

Kugelplex. "Yiddish Rudolph." *YouTube*, December 15, 2007, https://bit.ly/3prihfA.

Kushelevsky, Rella. *"Ha'tana v'ha'met ha'noded."* In *Entsiklopedya shel ha'sipur ha'yehudi I*, Yoav Elstein, Avidov Lipsker, and Rella Kushelevsky ed., 281–96. Bar-Ilan University Press, 2004.

———. *"Ha'tana v'ha'met ha'noded: Ha'omnam agada lo yehudit?"* *Bikoret u'farshanut* 30 (1994): 41–63.

———. *Sigufim u'fituyim: Ha'sipur ha'ivri b'Ashkenaz.* Y. L. Magnes, 2010.

Kutzik, Jordan. *"Der pakhed bay yidn um nitl."* *Forverts*, December 24, 2020, https://bit.ly/41vfUXi.

Landau, Alfred. "Holekreisch." *Zeitschrift des Vereins für Volkskunde* 9 (1899): 72–77.

Landmann, Salcia. *Erinnerungen an Galizien.* Knaur, 1983.

Langmuir, Gavin I. *Toward a Definition of Antisemitism.* University of California Press, 1990.

Larsen, Timothy (ed.). *The Oxford Handbook of Christmas.* Oxford University Press, 2020.

Lasker, Daniel J. "Jewish Knowledge of Christianity in the Twelfth and Thirteenth Centuries." In *Studies in Medieval Jewish Intellectual and Social History*, David Engel, Lawrence H. Schiffman, and Elliot R. Wolfson ed., 97–109. Brill, 2012.

Lauterbach, Jacob Zallel. "Jesus in the Talmud." In *Rabbinic Essays*, 473–570. Hebrew Union College Press, 1951.

Lawson, John Cuthbert. *Modern Greek Folklore and Ancient Greek Religion: A Study in Survivals.* Cambridge University Press, 1910.

Lecouteux, Claude. *Phantom Armies of the Night: The Wild Hunt and the Ghostly Processions of the Undead*, trans. Jon E. Graham. Inner Traditions, 2011 [1999].

Lee, Christopher A. "Augustine vs. Archisynagogus: Competing Modes of Christian Instruction in the Benediktbeuern *Ludus de nativitate.*" *Florilegium* 23, no. 2 (2006): 81–97.

Lee, M. R. "Saint John's Wort (*Hypericum perforatum*). A Balm for Hurt Minds?" *Proceedings of the Royal College and Physicians of Edinburgh* 29 (1999): 253–57.

Le Goff, Jacques. *The Birth of Purgatory*, trans. Arthur Goldhammer. University of Chicago Press, 1984 [1981].

Lehnardt, Andreas. "Christian Influences on the *Yahrzeit Qaddish.*" In *Death in Jewish Life: Burial and Mourning Customs Among Jews of Europe and Nearby Communi-*

ties, Stefan C. Reif, Andreas Lehnardt, and Avriel Bar-Levav ed., 65–78. De Gruyter, 2014.

Leiman, Sid Z. "The Scroll of Fasts: The Ninth of Tebeth." *Jewish Quarerly Review* 74, no. 2 (1983): 174–95.

Leivick, H. "*Dray khanike-likhtelekh.*" *Der Nayer Moment*, December 9, 1966, 5.

Lenhoff, Gail. "Chronological Error and Irony in Bulgakov's *Days of the Turbins.*" In *Russian Literature and American Critics*, 144–60. University of Michigan Press, 1984.

Lerner, Myron Bialik. "*Ma'ase ha'tana v'ha'met: Gilgulav ha'sifrutim v'ha'hilkhatiyim.*" *Asufot* 2 (1988): 29–69.

Leung, Marlene. "The history of Jewish families eating Chinese food on Christmas." *CTV News*, December 25, 2019, https://bit.ly/3r2QQJp.

Lewinsky, Yom Tov. "*Al ha'folklor b'leyl ha'nitl.*" *Davar*, December 28, 1934, 12.

———. *Sefer ha'moadim*. Oneg Shabbat, 1959.

———(ed.). *Seyfer Zembrove*. Ha'Irgunim shel Yotse ha'Ir b'Artsot ha'Brit, 1963.

Lewis, Margaret Brannan. *Infanticide and Abortion in Early Modern Germany*. Taylor & Francis, 2016.

Leyb, Mani. "Christmas," trans. A. Z. Foreman. *YouTube*, November 21, 2020, https://bit.ly/3CKOMbp.

———. "Christmas," trans. John Hollander. In *The Penguin Book of Modern Yiddish Verse*, Irving Howe, Ruth R. Wisse, and Kohne Shmeruk ed., 140. Viking, 1987.

———. "*Nitl.*" *Forverts*, September 14, 1952, sec. 2, 5.

Libin, Z. "*Vos hert zikh un vos zeht zikh in di muvis?*" *Forverts*, January 30, 1940, 5.

Lieberman, Chaim. *Dos problem fun der idisher ertsiung*. Jewish National Workers' Alliance, 1912.

———. "*Sholem Ash's kristmes.*" *Forverts*, December 19, 1945, 2.

Liessin, Abraham. "*Santa Klooz.*" *Forverts*, December 25, 1897, 1.

Lifschultz, Burton B. "Yesterday and Today." *The Reform Advocate*, May 21, 1937, 13–14.

Limor, Ora and Israel Jacob Yuval. "Judas Iscariot: Revealer of the Hidden Truth." In *Toledot Yeshu ("The Life Story of Jesus") Revisited*, Peter Schäfer, Michael Meerson, and Yaacov Deutsch ed., 197–220. Mohr Siebeck, 2011.

Linetzky, Isaac Joel. *Dos poylishe yingl*. Der Kval, 1921.

Lipetz, Isaac. *Seyfer matamim*. Warsaw: n.p., 1887.

List, Edgar A. "Frau Holda as the Personification of Reason." *Philological Quarterly* 32 (1953): 446–48.

Literarishe Bleter. "*Yedies fun yidishn visnshaftlekhn institut.*" *Literarishe Bleter*, February 12, 1926, 111–13.

Litvin, A. "*Khanike in dem alten kheyder.*" *Der Morgen Zhurnal*, December 25, 1932, 6.

Liu, Haiming. "Kung Pao Kosher: Jewish Americans and Chinese Restaurants in New York." *Journal of Chinese Overseas* 6, no. 1 (2010): 80–101.

Livius, Titus. *The History of Rome XXI*, trans. Benjamin Oliver Foster. Harvard University Press, 1929 [c. 0 BCE].

Loeffler, James. "Promising Harmonies: The Aural Politics of Polish-Jewish Relations in the Russian Empire." *Jewish Social Studies* 20, no. 3 (2014): 1–36.

Lown, Bella. *Memories of My Life: A Personal History of a Lithuanian Shtetl.* Joseph Simon/Pangloss Press, 1991.

Lunski, Khaykl. "*Iserlin's yidish.*" *Yidishe Filologye* 4–6 (1924): 288–302.

Lydon, Susan. "Reflections, regrets from vanishing year." *Oakland Tribune*, December 23, 2001, 2.

M., M. *Curiöser Bericht wegen der schändlichen Weynacht—Larven so man insgemein Heiligen Christ nennet.* Johann Christoph Miethen, 1702 [1677].

Ma'agal. "Our Ma'agal Manifesto." https://bit.ly/4dKQqdh.

Macrobius. *Saturnalia*, trans. Robert A. Kaster. Harvard University Press, 2011 [c. 430].

Magid, Shaul. *Hasidism Incarnate: Hasidism, Christianity, and the Construction of Modern Judaism.* Stanford University Press, 2014.

Magliocco, Sabina. *Witching Culture: Folklore and Neo-Paganism in America.* University of Pennsylvania Press, 2010.

Magnus, Olaus. *Historia de gentibus septentrionalibus.* Johannes Maria de Viottis, 1555.

Maimonides. *Mishne toyre: Hilkhes shabes. Sefaria*, https://bit.ly/3YjchE5.

Malkes, L. "*Vi azoy men pravet di yomim neroim af 'amerikaner stail.*'" *Forverts*, September 20, 1930, 7.

Man, Y. "*Nitl.*" *Yidishes Tageblat*, December 24, 1920, 5.

Manaev, Georgy. "Russian Svyatki: The Most Unholy Time of Year." *Russian Beyond*, December 23, 2017, https://bit.ly/3qEpLMx.

Mann, Mendel. "*In der nakht fun nitl.*" In *Der shvartser demb*, 142–47. Unzer Kiyem, 1969.

Map, Walter. *De nugis curialium*, trans. Montague R. James. Cymmrodorion Record Series, 1923 [c. 1200].

Marcus, Bruce and Lori Factor. "Erev Christmas." *Boston Globe*, December 24, 1993, 9.

Marcus, Ivan G. *How the West Became Antisemitic: Jews and the Formation of Europe, 800–1500.* Princeton University Press, 2024.

———. *Jewish Culture and Society in Medieval France and Germany.* Ashgate, 2014.

———. *Rituals of Childhood: Jewish Acculturation in Medieval Europe.* Yale University Press, 2008.

Margolis, Rebecca E. "A Tempest in Three Teapots: Yom Kippur Balls in London, New York and Montreal." *Canadian Jewish Studies* 9 (2001): 38–84.

———. "Forays into a Digital Yiddishland: Secular Yiddish in the Early Stages of the Coronavirus Pandemic." *Contemporary Jewry* 41 (2021): 71–98.

Mark, Yudl. "*Di shprakh fun der komedye 'di genarte velt.*'" *Yidishe Shprakh* 3, no. 3 (1943): 68–86.

Mark, Z. "*Nitl.*" In *Agev-urkhe*, 183–85. Israelite Press, 1948.

Marmor, Kalman. *Mayn lebns-geshikhte.* YKUF, 1959.

Marvelous Mrs. Maisel, The. Season 3, episode 1: "Strike Up the Band." Directed by Amy Sherman-Palladino. Released December 6, 2019, on Amazon Prime.

Massachusetts. *The Charters and General Laws of the Colony and Province of Massa-chusetts Bay.* T. B. Wait, 1814.

Matveyev, Yoel. "*Di yidn un di Santa-Klauste.*" *Forward*, December 20, 2021, https://bit.ly/40kCB1Y.

Maximus. *Sancti Maximi episcopi Taurinensis.* Rome: Typis Sac. Congr. de Propaganda Fide, 1784.

Mayer, Bonaventura. *Das Judenthum in seinen Gebeten, Gebräuchen, Gesetzen und Ceremonien.* G. Joseph Manz, 1843.

Maynard, Fredell Bruser. "Jewish Christmas." In *Raisins and Almonds*, 19–29. Penguin Books Canada, 1985.

McClelland, Bruce A. *Slayers and their Vampires: A Cultural History of Killing the Dead.* University of Michigan Press, 2006.

McGowan, Anne. "Roman Catholicism." In *The Oxford Handbook of Christmas*, Timothy Larsen ed., 113–25. Oxford University Press, 2020.

Mead, G. R. S. *Did Jesus Live 100 B.C.?* Theosophical Publishing Society, 1903.

Meisen, Karl. *Die Sagen vom Wütenden Heer und wilden Jäger.* Aschendor, 1935.

Melendez, Bill (dir.). *A Charlie Brown Christmas.* Lee Mendelson Film Productions, 1965.

Menes, Avrom. "*Der krizis in unzere yidishe kultur-organizatsies.*" *Forverts*, May 28, 1949, 2.

Merwin, Ted. *Pastrami on Rye: An Overstuffed History of the Jewish Deli.* New York University Press, 2018.

Metzker, Isaac. *Afn zeydns felder.* Matones, 1953.

Mezger, Werner. *Sankt Nikolaus: Zwischen Kult und Klamauk.* Schwabenverlag, 1993.

Mikaela. "*Beys Shamay.*" *Unzer Leben*, December 20, 1916, 3.

Milch, Jacob. "*Papirosn.*" In *Oytobiografishe skitsn*, 110–16. YKUF, 1946.

Miles, Clement A. *Christmas in Ritual and Tradition.* T. Fisher Unwin, 1912.

Miller, Cait. "'Hark! The Herald Angels Sing': An Illustrated History." *The Library of Congress*, December 20, 2016, https://bit.ly/3E7q05v.

Miller, Daniel. "A Theory of Christmas," In *Unwrapping Christmas*, Daniel Miller ed., 3–37. Oxford University Press, 1993.

——— (ed.). *Unwrapping Christmas.* Oxford University Press, 1993.

Miller, Esther. "*Men farshprayt proklomatsyes.*" In *Fun Telekhan keyn Amerike*, 217–24. YKUF, 1956.

Miller, Hanna. "Identity Takeout: How American Jews Made Chinese Food Their Ethnic Cuisine." *Journal of Popular Culture* 39, no. 3 (2006): 430–65.

Miller, Marc. "Jews and Anti-Semitism in the Poetry of E. E. Cummings." *New Series* 7 (1998): 13–22.

Miller, Yvette Alt. "Black Christmas: December 25 in Jewish History." *Aish*, December 23, 2018, https://bit.ly/3prjpj1.

Mintz, Moses. *Shayles u'tshuves ha'Rov Moyshe Mints.* Krakow: n.p., 1617 [c. 1500].

Miron, Dan. "The Literary Image of the Shtetl." *Jewish Social Studies* 1, no. 3 (1995): 1–43.

Morton, Lisa. *Trick or Treat: A History of Halloween*. University of Chicago Press, 2012.

Motz, Lotte. "The Winter Goddess: Percht, Holda, and Related Figures." *Folklore* 95, no. 2 (1984): 151–66.

Müllenhoff, Karl. *Sagen, Märchen und Lieder der herzogthümer Schleswig, Holstein und Lauenburg*. Schwerssche Buchhandlung, 1845.

Nachmani, Shimshon and Nachum Chinitz (eds.). *Pinkes Slutsk u'venoyseye*. Ahdut, 1962.

Nathans, Benjamin. *Beyond the Pale: The Jewish Encounter with Late Imperial Russia*. University of California Press, 2002.

Nayer Morgn. "Nitl bney Yovn, nitl bney Royme." *Nayer Morgn*, January 7, 1938, 3.

Nayman, Khane. "*Mayn zeyde R' Gdalye.*" In *Yizker bukh Gonyondz*, M. Sh. Ben Meir and A. L. Payans ed., 443–52. Yotse Gonyondz, 1960.

Naymark, D. "*Haynt iz nitel-nakht, ven yidn lernen nisht keyn toyre.*" *Forverts*, December 24, 1953, 4–5.

Neal, Daniel. *The History of the Puritans III*. Printed for Brice Edmond, 1755.

Neudorfer, Rami. "*Kitsur toldot ha'silvester.*" *Oneg Shabbat*, January 1, 2014, https://bit.ly/3X15yeB.

Neuser, Noam M. M. "Lending a Hand on the Holidays." *Detroit Jewish News*, December 20, 1991, 18–19.

Newall, Venetia. "Easter Eggs." *Folklore* 79, no. 4 (1968): 257-78.

New York Herald. "Chinese Cuisine a Christmas Dinner Oddity." *New York Herald*, December 14, 1902, sec. 5, 11–12.

New York Tribune. "Jews Keep Christmas." *New York Tribune*, December 25, 1904, sec. 2, 2–3.

Nicholls, Jacqueline (@jacquelinenicholls). "detail of some work made for Maagal." *Instagram*, October 7, 2022, https://bit.ly/4eH8hmK.

Nirenberg, David. "The Two Faces of Sacred Violence." In *Communities of Violence: Persecution of Minorities in the Middle Ages*, 200–230. Princeton University Press, 1996.

Nissenbaum, Stephen. *The Battle for Christmas*. Alfred A. Knopf, 1996.

Nitzsch, Dr. "Über eine Reihe talmudischer und patristischer Täuschungen, welche sich an den mißverstandenen Spottnamen *Ben Pandera* geknüpft." *Theologische Studien und Kritiken* 13, no. 1 (1840): 115–20.

Norich, Anita. "Sholem Asch and the Christian Question." In *Sholem Asch Reconsidered*, Nanette Stahl ed., 251–65. Beinecke Rare Book and Manuscript Library, 2004.

Northern Exposure. Season 6, episode 3: "Shofar, So Good." Directed by James Hayman. Aired October 3, 1994, on CBS.

Nosseck, Max (dir.). *Der Vilner Shtot Khazn*. Elite Productions, 1940.

Nothaft, C. Philipp E. "The Origins of the Christmas Date: Some Recent Trends in Historical Research." *Church History* 81 (2012): 903–11.

Observer. "To the Editor of the American Israelite." *The American Israelite*, January 16, 1880, 3.

O.C., The. Season 1, episode 13: "The Best Chrismukkah Ever." Directed by Sanford Bookstaver. Aired December 3, 2003, on FOX.

Oguz, A. D. "B'layle ha'hu." *Der Morgen Zhurnal*, December 25, 1918, 4.

Oişteanu, Andrei. *Inventing the Jew: Antisemitic Stereotypes in Romanian and Other Central- East European Cultures*, trans. Mirela Adăscăliţei. University of Nebraska Press, 2009 [2001].

Opatoshu, Joseph. "A goy in goles." *Minikes Yontef Bleter* 27 (1922): 12–13.

———. "Der mishpet." *Literarishe Bleter* 72 (1925): 102–4.

———. "In der nakht fun 'nitl.'" *Der Tog*, December 28, 1925, 5.

———. "In der nakht fun nitul." *Der Tog*, December 24, 1935, 5.

———. *In poylishe velder*. M. N. Mayzl, 1921.

———. "Vekhter." *Der Tog*, January 3, 1931, 5.

Origen. *Contra Celsum*, trans. Henry Chadwick. Cambridge University Press, 1980 [c. 248].

Othloni, monachi S. Emerammi. *Opera omnia*. Garnier, 1884.

Otto, Julius Conrad. *Gali Razia occultorum detectio*. Sebastian Körber, 1605.

Palachi, Haim. *Seyfer yimtso Khayim*. Izmir: n.p., c. 1863.

Palatnik, Rosa. "Af dervayl." In *Kroshnik Rio*, 128–38. Monte Scopus, 1953.

———. "Gebrakht." In *Baym geroysh fun Atlantik*, 93–96. Monte Scopus, 1957.

———. "Nitl beymer." In *13 dertseylungen*, 138–43. Rosa Palatnik, 1961.

———. "Oysgeloshn s'yonkiper likht." In *Kroshnik Rio*, 194–98. Monte Scopus, 1953.

Palestine. "Notes on the Palestine Situation." *Palestine* 3, no. 1 (1946): 11–12.

Pall Mall Gazette. "Christmas Customs in Russia." *Public Opinion*, December 23, 1898, 824.

Partridge, Christopher. *The Re-Enchantment of the West*. T & T Clark, 2004.

Passy, Charles. "Christmas & Chopsticks, L'Chaim!" *Palm Beach Post*, December 25, 2004, 4A.

Patai, Raphael. *The Hebrew Goddess*. Wayne State University Press, 1990.

Patinkin, Mandy. "Der Alter Tzigayner." Track #15 on *Mamaloshen*. Nonesuch Records, 1998.

Penkower, Monty Noam. "The Kishinev Pogrom of 1903: A Turning Point in Jewish History." *Modern Judaism* 24, no. 3 (2004): 187–225.

Peretz, Isaac Leib. *Ertseylungen IV*. Farlag "Yidish," 1920.

———. "Oyb nisht nokh hekher!" *Der Yud*, January 11, 1900, 12–13.

Perles, Joseph. "Die Berner Handschrift des kleinen Aruch." In *Jubelschrift zum siebzigsten Geburtstage des Prof. Dr. H. Graetz*, 1–38. S. Schottlaender, 1887.

Perry, Joe. *Christmas in Germany: A Cultural History*. University of North Carolina Press, 2010.

Person, Katarzyna. "The 1940 'Easter Pogrom' in Warsaw from the Perspective of the Jewish Witnesses." In *The Jews, the Holocaust, and the Public: The Legacies of David Cesarani*, Larissa Allwork and Rachel Pistol ed., 145–60. Palgrave Macmillan, 2019.

Petri venerabilis. *Opera omnia*. J.-P. Migne, 1854.

Petrovsky-Shtern, Yohanan. *Jews in the Russian Army, 1827–1917: Drafted into Modernity*. Cambridge University Press, 2009.

Pfefferkorn, Johannes. *Handt Spiegel*. Schöffer, 1511.

Phillips, Coles. "The Spirit of Christmas in New York." *Life*, December 21, 1911, 1124.

Pietruszka, Symcha. *Yidishe folks-entsiklopedye II*. Eagle, 1943.

Pinski, David. "*Erev yonkiper.*" In *Ertseylungen II*, 256–66. Literarisher Ferlag, 1918 [1895].

Planter, A. "*Arunter di maskes.*" In *7ter November II*, 42–44. International Worker Order, 1930.

Plaut, Joshua Eli. *A Kosher Christmas: 'Tis the Season to be Jewish*. Rutgers University Press, 2012.

Ployne v'Koyen. "*Santa Klouz in yidishe kromen.*" *Der Morgen Zhurnal*, December 23, 1936, 6.

Polish Review, The. "Christmas in Poland." *The Polish Review* 1, no. 17, December 22, 1941, 3, 9.

Pomerancblum, Hershl. "*Azoy hot oysgezen Stashev.*" In *Seyfer Stashev*, Elkhonen Erlich ed., 245–59. Yotse Stashev b'Yisrael, 1962.

Prisha, *Orekh khayim*. Sefaria, https://bit.ly/3BSmi2c.

Provinzialnachrichten aus den kaiserlich königlichen Staaten I. Johann Thomas von Trattnern, 1783.

Raphaelson, Sampson. "The Day of Atonement." *Everybody's Magazine*, January 1922, 44–55.

Rappaport, Samuel. "Nittel." In *Jüdisches Lexikon IV*. Jüdischer Verlag, 1927.

Rawnitzki, Y. Kh. *Yudishe vitsn*. Moriah, 1922.

Rechtman, Abraham. *Yidishe etnografye un folklor*. YIVO, 1958.

Reisen, Avrom. "*Afn farher.*" In *Ale verk fun Avrom Reyzen: Nyu-Yorker noveln*, 44–49. B. Kletzkin, 1929.

Reporter, A. "*Irving Berlin hot ayngenumen Brodvey.*" *Morgn Frayhayt*, August 13, 1942, 5.

Resneck, John. "Let Others Share in Your Christmas Joy." *The Lutheran Companion* 28, no. 50 (1920): 799–800.

Rich, Louis. "Paying for Praying." *Forverts*, October 2, 1927, E1–2.

Ridenour, Al. *The Krampus and the Old, Dark Christmas: Roots and Rebirth of the Folkloric Devil*. Feral Hours, 2016.

Riser, Alfred. "Volksbrauch und Volksglauben aus dem Emmental." *Schweizerisches Archiv für Volkskunde* 24 (1922): 61–71.

Rivesman, M. "*A khanike-lid.*" In *Tekstn tsum lider-zamlbukh*, S. Kiselgof ed., no. 24. Gezelshaft far Idishe Folks-Musik in Peterburg, 1912.

Rivkind, Isaac. *Der kamf kegn azartshpiln bay yidn*. YIVO, 1946.

———. "*Nitl: A kapitl yidishe kultur-geshikhte.*" *Di Tsukunft* 34 (1929): 840–43.

Robertson, Alec. *Requiem: Music of Mourning and Consolation*. Frederick A. Praeger, 1967.

Rochholz, E. L. *Drei Gaugöttinnen: Walburg, Verena und Gertrud als deutsche Kirchenheilige*. F. Fleischer, 1870.

Rosenfeld, Jonah. *Eyner aleyn: Oytobiografisher roman*. Max N. Mayzl, 1940.

Rosenfeld, Morris. "*Der kristmes tri.*" *Yidishe Velt*, December 24, 1902, 4.

———. "*Erev kristmas.*" *Forverts*, December 14, 1910, 4.

———. "*Ha'neyres halole.*" In *Lieder-bukh I*, 34–36. Grover Brothers, 1897.

———. "*Kristmes.*" *Minikes Yontef Bleter*, December 1902, 40.

———. "*Vaynakhts-glokn.*" In *Shriftn fun Moris Rozenfeld II*, 247. A. M. Evalenko, 1908.

Rosenzweig, Franz. *Der Mensch und sein Werk: Gesammelte Schriften II*. Martinus Nijhoff, 1976.

Rosenzweig, Claudia. "When Jesus Spoke Yiddish: Some Remarks on a Yiddish Manuscript of the 'Toledot Yeshu' (MS. Günzburg 1730)." *PaRDeS: Zeitschrift der Vereinigung für Jüdische Studien* 21 (2015): 199–214.

Rosewarne, Lauren. *Analyzing Christmas in Film: Santa to the Supernatural*. Lexington Books, 2018.

Roskies, David G. *A Bridge of Longing: The Lost Art of Yiddish Storytelling*. Harvard University Press, 1996.

———. *The Jewish Search for a Usable Past*. Indiana University Press, 1999.

———. "The Shtetl as Imagined Community." In *The Shtetl: Image and Reality*, Gennady Estraikh ed., 4–22. Routledge, 2017.

Rotenberg, Moyshe. "*Unzere kinder-yorn.*" In *Seyfer Stashev*, Elkhonen Erlich ed., 286–94. Yotse Stashev b'Yisrael, 1962.

Roth, Cecil. "The Eastertide Stoning of the Jews and Its Liturgical Echoes." *Jewish Quarterly Review* 35, no. 4 (1945): 361–70.

———. "The Feast of Purim and the Origins of the Blood Accusation." *Speculum* 8, no. 4 (1933): 520–26.

Rubin, Moises. *Hantbukh far idishe geshikhte un khronologye II*. Cultura, 1932.

Rubin, Solomon. *Geschichte des Aberglaubens*, trans. Jakob Stern. E. Thiele, 1888 [1887].

Rumpf, Marianne. *Perchten: Populäre Glaubensgestalten zwischen Mythos und Katechese*. Königshausen & Neumann, 1991.

Rus, Rivke. *Der Dnyester roysht*. Farlag "I. L. Peretz," 1978.

Rutland, Suzanne D. "Reflections on 'Culture Mavens' from an Australian Jewish Perspective." In *Jews at Home: The Domestication of Identity*, Simon J. Bronner ed., 307–14. Littman Library of Jewish Civilization, 2010.

Rzepka, Susan. "It's beginning to look a lot like . . ." *Cleveland Jewish News*, December 21, 2000, 34.

Sable, Martin H. "The Day of Atonement in Charles Dickens' 'A Christmas Carol.'" *Tradition: A Journal of Orthodox Jewish Thought* 22, no. 3 (1986): 66–76.

Sacks, Trevor. "Lucky Packet." MA diss., University of Cape Town, 2012.

Sadan, Dov. "*Di blinde nakht un arum ir.*" *Yidish-velt* 36, no. 1 (1987): 2.

———. *Mi'mekhoz ha'yaldut*. Am Oved, 1981.

———. "*Marat Hole (gilgulo shel motiv).*" *Yeda Am* 9 (1952): 15–17.

Sambatyon, Moshe. *Khayey Sambation: Epos Adam Elyon*. Fan-Club Yehudi Olami "Eshkolon," 1945.

Sandberg-Mesner, Mila. *Light from the Shadows*. Polish-Jewish Heritage Foundation of Canada, 2005.

Saphire, Saul. "*Yene gliklikhe kinder-yoren: Khanike zikhroynes.*" *Der Morgen Zhurnal,* December 20, 1935, 4.

Saurette, Marc. "Making Space for Learning in the Miracle Stories of Peter the Venerable." In *Horizontal Learning in the Middle Ages,* Micol Long, Tjamke Snijders, and Steven Vanderputten ed., 111–40. Amsterdam University Press, 2019.

Schäfer, Peter. *Jesus in the Talmud.* Princeton University Press, 2007

———. "Toledot Yeshu as a Tool of Polemic." In *Toledot Yeshu: The Life Story of Jesus,* 3–18. Mohr Siebeck, 2014.

———. *Toledot Yeshu: The Life Story of Jesus.* Mohr Siebeck, 2014.

Schäfer, Peter, Michael Meerson, and Yaacov Deutsch (eds). *Toledot Yeshu ("The Life Story of Jesus") Revisited.* Mohr Siebeck, 2011.

Schainker, Ellie R. *Confessions of the Shtetl: Converts from Judaism in Imperial Russia, 1817–1906.* Stanford University Press, 2016.

Scharbach, Rebecca. "The Ghost in the Privy: On the Origins of Nittel Nacht and Modes of Cultural Exchange." *Jewish Studies Quarterly* 20, no. 4 (2013): 340–73.

Scharbach Wollenberg, Rebecca. *The Closed Book: How the Rabbis Taught the Jews (Not) to Read the Bible.* Princeton University Press, 2023.

Scharf, Stuart. "'Jewish style' doesn't mean a thing." *Boston Globe,* December 30, 1993, 10.

Schmitt, Jean-Claude. *Ghosts in the Middle Ages: The Living and the Dead in Medieval Society,* trans. Teresa Lavender Fagan. University of Chicago Press, 1998 [1994].

Schoenfeld, Joachim. *Shtetl Memoirs: Jewish Life in Galicia Under the Austro-Hungarian Empire and in the Reborn Poland 1898–1939.* Ktav, 1985.

Scholem, Gershom. *Von Berlin nach Jerusalem: Jugenderinnerungen.* Suhrkamp, 1977.

Schreig, Samuel. "From Everywhere." *The Sentinel,* January 5, 1967, 10.

Schudt, Johann Jakob. *Jüdische Merkwürdigkeiten.* Multzer, 1714.

Schuldes, Luis. *Die Teufelsszenen im deutschen geistlichen Drama des Mittelalters.* Alfred Kümmerle, 1974.

Schwab, Dietrich. *Detectum velum Mosaicum Judæorum nostri temporis.* Pontanus, 1615.

Scovell, Adam. *Folk Horror: Hours Dreadful and Things Strange.* Liverpool University Press, 2017.

See, Katharine Allyn. "The Christmas Story in American Literature." PhD diss., University of Louisville, 1943.

Seiden, Joseph (dir.). *Kol Nidre.* Cinema Service, 1939.

Seinfeld TV. "Make Festivus a National Holiday." *Change.org,* December 2, 2022, https://bit.ly/3Yn3aSP.

Selengut, Suzanne. "How to have yourself a very Yiddishe Christmas in NY." *The Times of Israel,* December 24, 2015, https://bit.ly/3DpuIvy.

Senn, Frank C. *Introduction to Christian Liturgy.* Fortress Press, 2012.

Senn, Harry. "Romanian Werewolves: Seasons, Ritual, Cycles." *Folklore* 93, no. 2 (1982): 206–15.

Sforim, Mendele Mocher. *Ale Verk IX*. Hebrew Publishing Company, 1920.

S. G. B. "Menorah or Christmas Tree?" *Canadian Jewish Chronicle*, December 27, 1929, 5.

Shandler, Jeffrey. *Adventures in Yiddishland: Postvernacular Language and Culture*. University of California Press, 2006.

———. *Jews, God, and Videotape: Religion and Media in America*. New York University Press, 2009.

———. *Shtetl: A Vernacular Intellectual History*. Rutgers University Press, 2014.

———. *Yiddish: Biography of a Language*. Oxford University Press, 2020.

Shapira, Zvi Elimelekh of Dinov. *Seyfer regel yeshoro*. Bnei Shloshim, 1998 [1858].

Shapiro, Adam B. "*Mazl-brokhe*." *YouTube*, December 18, 2022, https://bit.ly/44aCsNI.

Shapiro, Marc. "Torah Study on Christmas Eve." *Journal of Jewish Thought and Philosophy* 8, no. 2 (1999): 319–53.

Sharaby, Rachel. "*M'khag ha'khanuka v'ad festival 'ha'khag shel ha'khagim': Zehut kolektivit mishtana*." *Moed* 17 (2006): 137–64.

Sher, Olga with Margrit Rosenberg Stenge. "Olga's Story." *The Concordia University Chair in Canadian Jewish Studies and The Montreal Institute for Genocide and Human Rights Studies*, 2002, https://bit.ly/4b42SFl.

Sheyn, Yitzkhok. "*Humor fun amerikaner yidishn lebn*." *Forverts*, January 3, 1965, sec. 2, 7.

Shinan, Avigdor. *Oto ha'ish: Yehudim mesaprim al Yeshu*. Yedioth Ahronoth, 1999.

Shire, Emily. "Finding Love, or Just Another Makeout, at a Rowdy Jewish Singles Party." *Jewcy*, December 20, 2012, https://bit.ly/4h2CvlE.

———. "The Craziest Date Night for Single Jews, Where Mistletoe Is Ditched for Shots." *Daily Beast*, December 26, 2014, https://bit.ly/4h5WZKf.

Shmulewitz, I. "*Di yomim neroim amol un haynt*." *Forverts*, September 8, 1961, 6–5 [article concludes on page 5].

Shnayderman, Sh. L. *Ven di Vaysl hot geredt yidish*. Farlag "I. L. Peretz," 1970.

Shneour, Zalman. *Noyekh Pandre*. Nay Lebn, 1956.

Shneyman, L. "*Bilder un stsenes fun dem kristmes-yarid*." *Forverts*, December 10, 1956, 5.

Shore, Eliezer. *Baal Shem Tov: Ki Tiso*. *Sefaria*, https://bit.ly/4dLJAUE.

Shyovitz, David I. "'You Have Saved Me from the Judgment of Gehenna': The Origins of the Mourner's Kaddish in Medieval Ashkenaz." *AJS Review* 39, no. 1 (2015): 49–73.

Sidroni, I. M. "*Pirke zikhroynes*." In *Kehiles Sherpts*, Efraim Talmi ed., 282–322. Yotse Sherpts b'Yisrael, 1959.

Siegler, Moshe. *Tife vortslen: Fun Sasev biz Yerushelayim*. M. Siegler, 1981.

Simek, Rudolf. *Dictionary of Northern Mythology*, trans. Angela Hall. D. S. Brewer, 1993 [1984].

Simon, Ron. "Jews volunteer so hospital workers get holiday off." *News Journal*, December 25, 1989, 1.

Simon, Shloyme. "*Yidishe vortslen*." *Der Tog—Morgn Zhurnal*, November 15, 1953, 10.

Singer, Jenny. "Three Hours and Six Minutes at the MatzoBall, the Biggest Jewish Singles Event of the Year." *Forward*, January 4, 2018, https://bit.ly/4f6INit.

Slobin, Mark. *Global Soundtracks: Worlds of Film Music*. Wesleyan University Press, 2008.

Słomka, Jan. *Pamiętniki włościanina: Od pańszczyzny do dni dzisiejszych*. Towarzystwo Szkoły Ludowej, 1929 [1912].

Smith, John B. "Perchta the Belly-Slitter and Her Kin: A View of Some Traditional Threatening Figures, Threats and Punishments." *Folklore* 115, no. 2 (2004): 167–86.

Sofer, Moses. *Igros Sofrim*. Joseph Schlesinger, 1929 [c. 1800].

Sommer, Bettina. "The Pre-Christian Jól: Not a Cult of the Dead, but the Norse New Year Festival." In *Supernatural Encounters in Old Norse Literature and Tradition*, Daniel Sävborg and Karen Bek-Pedersen ed., 31–58. Brepols, 2018.

South Park. Season 1, episode 9: "Mr. Hankey, the Christmas Poo." Directed by Trey Parker and Matt Stone. Aired December 17, 1997, on Comedy Central.

Spatola, Morgan (@Morganspatola). "Gut Nittel Nacht, fellow Yids." *Twitter*, December 24, 2021, https://bit.ly/4flKNUf.

Spector, Meir. "*Vos ikh gedenk fun Stavishtsh*." In *Stavishtsh*, Aharon Weissman ed., 85–94. Stavisht Society, 1961.

Spector, Roslyn. "'Erev Christmas' is contrary to Jewish values." *Boston Globe*, January 2, 1994, 70.

Staetsky, L. Daniel. "Haredi Jews Around the World: Population Trends and Estimates." *Institute for Jewish Policy Research*, May 2022 report.

Stampfer, Shaul. "Settling Down in Eastern Europe." In *Jews and Germans in Eastern Europe: Shared and Comparative Histories*, Tobias Grill ed., 1–20. De Gruyter Oldenbourg, 2018.

Standiford, Les. *The Man Who Invented Christmas*. Crown, 2008.

Stanislawski, Michael. "A Preliminary Study of a Yiddish 'Life of Jesus' (*Toledot Yeshu*): JTS Ms. 2211." In *Toledot Yeshu ("The Life Story of Jesus") Revisited*, Peter Schäfer, Michael Meerson, and Yaacov Deutsch ed., 79–88. Mohr Siebeck, 2011.

Starkman, Moshe. "*Baym dernentern zikh tsu nitl*." *Forverts*, December 1, 1974, M3.

Steiman, Sidney. *Custom and Survival: A Study of the Life and Work of Rabbi Jacob Molin (Moelln)*. Bloch, 1963.

Stein, Abby. "'The Most Wonderful Night': A Christmas/Nittel Jewish Story." *The Second Transition*, December 24, 2017, https://bit.ly/3ptKPCn.

Steinberg, Judah. "*In der 'nitel-nakht*,'" trans. B. Epelboym. *Der Morgen Zhurnal*, April 30, 1943, 6.

Stern, Zehavit. "From Jester to Gesture: Eastern European Jewish Culture and the Reimagination of Folk Performance." PhD diss., UC Berkeley, 2011.

———. "The Idealized Mother and Her Discontents: Performing Maternity in Yiddish Film Melodrama." In *Choosing Yiddish: New Frontiers of Language and Culture*, Lara Rabinovitch ed., 163–78. Wayne State University Press, 2012.

Stoppard, Tom. *Leopoldstadt*. Faber & Faber, 2020.

Storey, John. "The Invention of the English Christmas." In *Culture and Power in Cultural Studies: The Politics of Signification*, 135–46. Edinburgh University Press, 2010.

Strawn, Brent A. "Moses' Shining or Horned Face?" *TheTorah.com*, 2021, https://bit.ly/3LVpMSN.

Stuchkoff, Nokhem. *Der oytser fun der yidisher shprakh*. YIVO, 1950.

Stutz, Jakob. "Nidelnacht." *Schweizer Volkskunde: Korrespondenzblatt der Schweizerischen Gesellschaft für Volkskunde* 1, no. 10 (1911): 73–74.

Suslin HaKohen, Alexander. *Seyfer ha'agudo*. Isaac ben Aaron Prostitz, 1571 [c. 1300].

Sutzkever, Abraham and Szmerke Kaczerginski (eds.). "Customs for Nitl, undated." *YIVO Archives*, RG 223.2, folder 165.1.

Svarch, Ariel. "'Don Jacobo en la Argentina' Battles the *Nacionalistas*: *Crítica*, the Funny Pages, and Jews as Liberal Discourse (1929–1932)." In *The New Jewish Argentina: Facets of Jewish Experiences in the Southern Cone*, Adriana Brodsky and Raanan Rein ed., 109–30. Brill, 2012.

Syfy, S. O. "Cafay." *B'nai B'rith Messenger*, December 24, 1971, 26.

Sylvetsky, Rochel. "Sylvester Night is not a holiday." *Israel National News*, December 31, 2017, https://bit.ly/3PKIYXh.

Ta-Shma, Israel. "*Yemey eydeyhem*." *Tarbiz* 47, no. 3–4 (1978): 197–215.

Tendlau, Abraham M. *Sprichwörter und Redensarten deutsch-jüdischer Vorzeit*. Heinrich Keller, 1860.

Thissen, Judith. "Something Special for the High Holidays." *Digital Yiddish Theatre Project*, September 24, 2017, https://bit.ly/46gpcrV.

Thompson, Danièle (dir.). *La Bûche*. Canal+, 1999.

Thornton, T. C. G. "The Crucifixion of Haman and the Scandal of the Cross." *Journal of Theological Studies* 37, no. 2 (1986), 419–26.

Tille, Alexander. *Die Geschichte der deutschen Weihnacht*. E. Keil, 1893.

——. *Yule and Christmas: Their Place in the Germanic Year*. David Nutt, 1899.

Timm, Erika and Gustav Adolf Beckmann. *Frau Holle, Frau Percht und verwandte Gestalten*. S. Hirzel, 2003.

Tsesler, Shmuel. *Feygl in der luftn*. R. Zaslovski, 1939.

——. *Fun gantsn hartsn*. S. Tsesler, 1946.

Tokarska-Bakir, Joanna. "'The Hanging of Judas'; or, Contemporary Jewish Topics," trans. Wiktoria Dorosz. In *Jews and Their Neighbours in Eastern Europe Since 1750*, Israel Bartal, Antony Polonsky, and Scott Ury ed., 381–400. Liverpool University Press, 2011.

Töyrylä, Hannu. *Abraham Bar Hiyya on Time, History, Exile and Redemption*. Brill, 2014.

Trachtenberg, Joshua. *Jewish Magic and Superstition: A Study in Folk Religion*. University of Pennsylvania Press, 2004 [1939].

——. *The Devil and the Jews: The Medieval Conception of the Jews and Its Relation to Modern Antisemitism*. Yale University Press, 1943.

Treyster, L. "*Der shuldiker*." *Der Nayer Moment*, December 23, 1955, 7.

Troy Sentinel, The. "Account of a Visit from St. Nicholas." *The Troy Sentinel*, December 23, 1823, 3.

Tsvien. "*Yidishe interesen.*" *Forverts*, January 10, 1948, 6.

Tuchman, Gaye and Harry G. Levine. "New York Jews and Chinese Food: The Social Construction of an Ethnic Pattern." *Journal of Contemporary Ethnography* 22, no. 3 (1993): 382–407.

Tuszewicki, Marek. *A Frog Under the Tongue: Jewish Folk Medicine in Eastern Europe.* Littman Library of Jewish Civilization, 2021.

TV21 Austria. "Blinde Nacht von Simon Kronberg." *YouTube*, December 23, 2019, https://bit.ly/46jg5al.

Tyrnau, Isaac. *Seyfer ha'minhogim.* Machon Yerushalayim, 1979 [c. 1400].

Tzion, Rav Mordechai. *Hilkhes nitl nakht.* Sifriyas Chava, 2021.

Ungar, Amiel. "*L'vade bitsua.*" *Nekuda* 211 (1998): 38–41.

Ungar, Menashe. "*A modner mineg um shabes ha'godl.*" *Der Tog—Morgn Zhurnal*, April 12, 1960, 8.

———. "*Der opshtam fun vort 'blinde nakht.*'" *Der Tog—Morgn Zhurnal*, March 20, 1958, 16.

———. "*Khanike minhogim bay yidn in farshidene lender.*" *Der Tog—Morgn Zhurnal*, December 22, 1946, 5.

———. "*Nokh mayses vegn litvishn gutn-yidn R' Yishay Zhukhovitser.*" *Der Tog—Morgn Zhurnal*, March 16, 1958, 16.

———. "*Vegn opshtam fun vort 'nitl.*'" *Der Tog—Morgn Zhurnal*, January 12, 1958, 10.

———. "*Yidn shraybn.*" *Der Tog—Morgn Zhurnal*, February 21, 1958, 18.

Unzer ekspres. "'Karbones' fun der nitl-nakht." *Unzer expres*, December 26, 1935, 9.

Veltz, Israel. *Shayles u'tshuves divrey yisroel: Kheylekh Yoyre Deye.* Tzvi Yehuda Wolner, 1980.

Vice, Sue. "Christmas Trees and Hanukkah Bushes: The 'Emancipation Contract' in the Contemporary British Television Dramas Hebburn and Friday Night Dinner." In *Hidden in Plain Sight: Jews and Jewishness in British Film*, Nathan Abrams ed., 227–51. Northwestern University Press, 2016.

Viera, Nelson H. "Outsiders and Insiders: Brazilian Jews and the Discourse of Alterity." In *The Jewish Diaspora in Latin America: New Studies on History and Literature*, David Sheinin and Lois Baer Barr ed., 101–16. Routledge, 2019.

Vigée, Claude. *Moisson de Canaan.* Flammarion, 1967.

Viswanath, Arun (@a_a_viswanath). "👍." *Twitter*, December 24, 2020, https://bit.ly/4eNrrav.

———. "1. Nidelnacht (alt. Nideln, Nidelte)." *Twitter*, December 25, 2020, https://bit.ly/3Y41Z9t.

———. "I'm not sure if it's the actual truth." *Twitter*, December 24, 2020, https://bit.ly/3U4cp83.

———. "These three factors together." *Twitter*, December 25, 2020, https://bit.ly/3U2N26j.

———. "*Vertshpiln un folks-etimologies.*" *Twitter*, December 24, 2020, https://bit.ly/4eFG5AI.

———. "Yeah that's what's odd." *Twitter*, December 24, 2020, https://bit.ly/3UcoN2L.

Vitalis, Orderic. *The Ecclesiastical History of Orderic Vitalis II*, trans. Thomas Forester. Henry G. Bohn, 1853 [c. 1100].

Voß, Rebekka. *Sons of Saviors: The Red Jews in Yiddish Culture*. University of Pennsylvania Press, 2023.

von Perger, Anton Ritter. *Deutsche Pflanzensagen*. August Schaber, 1864.

Wallas, Armin A. "Kibbuznik, Schuhmacher, Simon Kronberg in Palästina (1934–1947)." *Exil* 15 (1995): 36–68.

Ward Biederman, Patricia. "Jews Celebrate Dec. 25 with Bagels and Lox." *Los Angeles Times*, December 26, 1984, Valley Edition, 6, 8.

Waschnitius, Viktor. *Perth, Holda und verwandte Gestalten: Ein Beitrag zur deutschen Religionsgeschichte*. A. Hölder, 1913.

Weber, Max. *Wissenschaft als Beruf*. Duncker & Humblot, 1919.

Weill, Emmanuel. "Le Yidisch alsacien-lorrain, recueil de mots, locutions et dictons particuliers aux Israélites d'Alsace et de Lorraine (suite et fin)." *Revue des Études Juives* 72, no. 143 (1921): 65–88.

Weinfeld, Morton. "Antisemitism in Canada." In *The Ever-Dying People? Canada's Jews in Comparative Perspective*, Robert Brym and Randal F. Schnoor ed., 39–55. University of Toronto Press, 2023.

Weinreich, Max. *Geshikhte fun der yidisher shprakh: Bagrifn, faktn, metodn*. YIVO, 1973.

———. "Holekrash: A Jewish Rite of Passage." In *Folklore International: Essays in Traditional Literature, Belief, and Custom in Honor of Wayland Debs Hand*, D. K. Wilgus ed., 243–53. Folklore Associates, 1967.

Weinstein, Larry (dir.). *Dreaming of a Jewish Christmas*. CBC Television, 2018.

Weiser, Alex, "Are We in the Midst of a Yiddish Renaissance?" *YIVO Institute for Jewish Research* (lecture, June 1, 2022).

Weissman, Susan. *Final Judgement and the Dead in Medieval Jewish Thought*. Liverpool University Press, 2020.

Weissman Joselit, Jenna. "Holiday Cheer." *Pakn Treger*, no. 42 (2003): 8–13.

———. *The Wonders of America: Reinventing Jewish Culture, 1880–1950*. Henry Holt, 1994.

Welsford, Enid. *The Fool: His Social and Literary History*. Farrar & Rinehart, 1935.

Werner, Eric. *The Sacred Bridge*. Columbia University Press, 1963.

West Wing, The. Season 4, episode 11: "Holy Night." Directed by Thomas Schlamme. Aired December 11, 2002, on NBC.

Wexler, Paul. *The Ashkenazic Jews: A Slavo-Turkic People in Search of a Jewish Identity*. Slavica, 1993.

White, Newman Ivey (ed.). *The Frank C. Brown Collection of North Carolina Folklore II*. Duke University Press, 1964.

Wigoder, Geoffrey. "Chanukah and all the glitter of 'Father Christmas.'" *Australian Jewish Times*, January 9, 1975, 12.

Wilkansky, Meir. *B'Kheder*. A. Y. Shtibel, 1933.

Williams, Peter. *The Organ in Western Culture, 750–1250*. Cambridge University Press, 1993.

Wolfenstein, Martha. "Nittel Nacht." *Jewish Comment* 14, no. 10 (December 20, 1901): 1–3.

Wülfer, Johann. *Theriaca Judaica*. Andreas Knorzius, 1681.

Würfel, Andreas. *Historische Nachricht von der Judengemeinde in dem Hofmarkt Fürth Unterhalb Nürnberg*. Frankfurt and Prague: n.p., 1754.

Wuttke, Adolf. *Der deutsche Volksaberglaube der Gegenwart*. Wiegand & Grieben, 1869.

Yiddish New York. "Would You Like to Hear a Song?" Streamed on Zoom, December 25, 2021.

Yiddish Translator (@JewYid). "*A gut nitl.*" *Twitter*, December 24, 2020, https://bit.ly/4eZooKz.

———. "*Ikh meyn az s'iz a shtokh.*" *Twitter*, December 24, 2020, https://bit.ly/4f5oheP.

Yidishe Velt, Di. "*Kunst geshmak, un talant vet zikh fareynikn in Karnegi Hol.*" *Di Yidishe Velt*, December 26, 1902, 6.

YidLife Crisis. "The YidLife Crisis Guide to the Holiday Classics." *YouTube*, December 8, 2016, https://bit.ly/3OoK8wE.

Young, Hersh Leib. "*Der sholem-prints.*" In *Durkh likht un finsternish*, 368–69. Farlag "I. L. Peretz," 1967.

———. "*In blinder nakht.*" In *Af zunzink-shlyakh*, 185–87. Farlag "I. L. Peretz," 1976.

Young, Karl. *The Drama of the Medieval Church II*. Clarendon Press, 1933.

Yushzon, B. "*Fun unzer alten oytser.*" *Haynt*, December 28, 1934, 6.

Yuval, Israel Jacob. "Gedichte und Geschichte als Weltgericht." *Kalonymos* 8, no. 4 (2005): 1–6.

———. *Two Nations in Your Womb: Perceptions of Jews and Christians in Late Antiquity and the Middle Ages*, trans. Barbara Harshav and Jonathan Chipman. University of California Press, 2006 [2000].

———. "Was das Judentum dem Christentum verdankt." *Münchener Theologische Zeitschrift* 69, no. 2 (2018): 167–79.

Zahavy, Tzvee. "A Pragmatic Study of Kol Nidre: Law and Compassion." In *Pragmatic Studies in Judaism*, Andrew Schumann ed., 179–94. Gorgias Press, 2013.

Zayfert, Moyshe. "*Khane mit ire 7 zin.*" *Der Idisher Zhurnal*, December 16, 1904, 8.

Zeltzer, Chaim. "*Di blinde nakht.*" In *Zibn fun eyn shif: Balades un baladish*, 7–8. Yisroel Bukh, 1982.

Zemeckis, Robert (dir.). *The Polar Express*. Warner Bros. Pictures, 2004.

Zhitlowsky, Chaim. "*Di kristenthum-shayle far gebildete iden.*" *Dos Naye Lebn* 1, no. 11 (1909): 621–31.

Zinger, Eli. "*Di literatur bay der shisl.*" In *Zalmen Zilbertsvayg: Yoyvl-bukh*, 115–16. Yubiley-Komitet, 1941.

Zipperstein, Steven J. *Imagining Russian Jewry: Memory, History, Identity*. University of Washington Press, 1999.

Zolf, Falek. *Af fremder erd: Bletlekh fun a lebn*. Israelite Press, 1945.

Zweifel, Eliezer. *Likutey Tsvi*. A. Sh. Shadov, 1866.

INDEX

Advent, 19–20, 55, 112
Africa, South, 89, 95
Age of Enlightenment, 89
alcohol. *See* drinking, at Christmas
Aleichem, Sholem (author), 100, 127
Aleinu. See *"Oleynu"*
Ansky, S., 69, 74
antisemitism: devil trope, 36–37, 40, 42, 55–56, 68, 132, 136–37; filth trope, 36, 38, 67–68; greed trope, 110–12, 132; Jewface and, 77–78; in Jewish imagination, 87–89, 97–106, 156; Jewish literary depictions of, 90–91, 131–40, 143–45, 155–56
antisemitism, religious, 29–30, 36–40; exposés by Jewish apostate and, 10–11, 13, 16, 22–23, 31, 47, 57–63, 65, 83, 155; Jewish deicide canard and, 73, 96, 136. *See also* violence
apostate, Jewish: biological conception of, 9, 17, 84; exposés by, 10–11, 13, 16, 22–23, 31, 47, 57–63, 65, 83, 155
Argentina, 3, 141, 182n26
Asch, Sholem, 90–91, 135
Ashkenaz (region), 13, 22, 33, 40, 52, 54, 65–66; liturgy of, 112–13
assimilation, 2, 5, 82; in fiction, 124, 127–30, 133–34, 143–44, 155; opposition to, 86, 99, 102–3, 106, 147
Australia, 89, 95, 115, 119, 134, 149, 157, 182n26
Austria, 14, 20, 51, 53–57, 65; Vienna, 52, 93, 143, 155–56. *See also* Galicia

Barbu, Daniel, 25, 57
bar mitzvah, 40

Belarus, 75, 77, 79–80, 118. *See also* Litvak
Berchta, Frau. *See* Holle, Frau.
Berlin, Germany, 94
Berlin, Irving, 128–29. *See also* "White Christmas"
besmedresh (Jewish study hall), 71, 77–79, 98
Bialystok, Poland, 82, 93
birthday (*natalis*), 19, 44–46, 53, 63, 104. *See also* Nativity
bitl-toyre (not studying Torah/waste of time), 5, 76, 148
Blinde Nacht (*Nittel*) (Kronberg), 143–44, 156
blinde nakht (Blind Night), 71–73, 75–79, 84, 87, 103, 133, 143, 156
blood: in Christianity, 30, 73; as Christmas Eve pollutant, 73–74, 95, 101, 105; violently spilled, 87–88, 101, 103, 105–6, 132, 140
borkhu (call to prayer), 22, 33–34
Boston, Massachusetts, 44, 119, 152–53
braided bread. *See* challah
Brazil, 182n26; Rio de Janeiro, 139–40; São Paulo, 93–94
Brenz, Samuel Friedrich, 23, 58, 60–61
Broverman, Sam, 1, 147, 156, 162

California, 79, 157, 189n31
Callicantzari (vampiric creature), 13, 17, 21
Canada, 5, 119, 182n26; Montreal, 96, 121; Toronto, 1, 149, 152, 157–58, 162
cardplaying: in literature, 118, 132, 135, 143; in the Old World, 5–6, 23–24, 47, 62, 65, 75–77, 79–82; reevaluation in the New World, 92–95

ABOUT THE AUTHOR

Jordan Chad is a multidisciplinary researcher based in Toronto. He has published on various topics, ranging from neuroimaging physics and brain development to Jewish intellectual attainment and Yiddish popularizations of physics. He is affiliated with the Centre for Jewish Studies at the University of Toronto.